FASTING

A CENTRE FOR PENTECOSTAL THEOLOGY SHORT INTRODUCTION

FASTING

A CENTRE FOR PENTECOSTAL THEOLOGY
SHORT INTRODUCTION

Lee Roy Martin

CPT Press
Cleveland, Tennessee

FASTING
A Centre for Pentecostal Theology Short Introduction

Published by CPT Press
900 Walker ST NE
Cleveland, TN 37311
USA
email: cptpress@pentecostaltheology.org
website: www.cptpress.com

Library of Congress Control Number: 2014909962

ISBN-10: 1935931423
ISBN-13: 9781935931423

Copyright © 2014 CPT Press

All rights reserved. No part of this book may be reproduced or translated in any form, by print, photoprint, microfilm, microfiche, electronic database, internet database, or any other means without written permission from the publisher.

Citations of Scripture are translations of the author.

The material contained in this book is provided for informational purposes only. It is not intended to diagnose, provide medical advice, or take the place of medical advice and treatment from your personal physician. The author in no way claims to be a medical doctor. Readers are advised to consult qualified health professionals regarding fasting and/or treatment of their specific medical problems. Neither the publisher nor the author is responsible for any possible consequences from any person reading or following the information in this book. If readers are taking prescription medications, they should consult their physicians and not take themselves off medicines without the proper supervision of a physician.

Dedicated to
Stephen, Michael, and Kendra
My children
Who have brought immeasurable joy to my life

TABLE OF CONTENTS

Series Preface x

Preface.. xi

Chapter 1
Introduction to Fasting 1

Chapter 2
Fasting in the Old Testament... 9

Chapter 3
Fasting in the New Testament... 57

Chapter 4
Toward a Biblical Theology of Fasting 79

Chapter 5
Fasting in Christian History... 101

Chapter 6
Fasting in Early Pentecostalism 115

Chapter 7
Toward a Pentecostal Theology of Fasting 147

Chapter 8
Practical Guidelines for Fasting 165

Chapter 9
Conclusion 169

Bibliography... 171

Index of Biblical (and Other Ancient) References 180

Index of Authors 182

SERIES PREFACE

The Centre for Pentecostal Theology Short Introductions are monographs that offer a distinctively Pentecostal perspective on various topics that are of relevance to the movement. Based on current and sound research, these short books are designed to introduce the reader to the topic at hand while not overwhelming him or her with all the secondary literature on the subject. The goal is a straightforward introduction with helpful assessments by leading scholars in the tradition.

Preface

This project sneaked up on me unawares. I had practiced fasting and preached on fasting, but I had never planned to write a book on fasting. When invited to contribute to a multi-authored work on the spiritual disciplines, edited by Sang-Ehil Han and Jackie Johns; I agreed to write a 15-page chapter on fasting. Upon finishing my research for the chapter, I realized that I had produced about 45 pages. At that point, I entertained the possibility of expanding the material into a monograph, but I was not certain that another book on fasting was needed. After consideration and prayer (with fasting), four factors convinced me to write the book. First, my research had not turned up a systematic exploration of fasting in the biblical text. I was unable to find a book on fasting that included a discussion of every biblical passage related to fasting. Second, while several Pentecostal monographs on fasting are available at the popular level, I could not find a scholarly Pentecostal book-length study of fasting. Third, as far as I could determine, the role of fasting in Pentecostalism had not been studied extensively. Fourth, I discerned that God had put it in my heart to write this book – it was something that I felt called to do.

I would be the first to admit that the Pentecostal theology and practice of fasting deserves much more attention than I have been able to give it in this short introduction, but I have done my part to get the conversation going. I hope an industrious doctoral student will do a proper thesis on fasting in Pentecostalism.

As always, I am grateful for my wife Karen, who cheerfully endures my hours of research and writing. Many thanks as well to Larry Flickner, my graduate assistant. I also thank God for the Pentecostal Theological Seminary and the Society for Pentecostal Studies, two communities of scholars who recognize that academic study can be a ministry. Last but not least, I appreciate the valuable discussions with the researchers at the Centre for Pentecostal Theology: Chris Thomas (who also read the manuscript), Daniela Augustine, Stephen Mills, David Johnson, and Tony Richie.

Lee Roy Martin

1

INTRODUCTION TO FASTING

The disciplines of private and corporate prayer, living in the Scriptures, walking in fellowship, the Lord's Supper, fasting, all are ways of learning to attend to the Spirit in following Christ. – Steven Jack Land[1]

Describing an intense hunger for God, the psalmist wrote, 'As the deer pants for streams of water, so my soul pants for you, O God. My soul thirsts for God, for the living God …' (Ps. 42.1-2). Another psalm begins with these words: 'O God, you are my God, early will I seek you, my soul thirsts for you; my flesh longs for you, as in a dry and thirsty land where there is no water' (Ps. 63.1-2). It is that kind of spiritual hunger that moves people to fast. A passionate pursuit of God calls for fasting and prayer.[2] When we hunger and thirst for God, fasting opens the door to God's presence.

A. The Importance of Food

However, someone might ask, 'Isn't food a blessing from God?' Aren't we instructed to pray, 'Give us this day our daily bread?' Yes, food is one of God's greatest blessings, and in addition to providing nourishment to our bodies, eating fulfills a number of other important functions. Eating enhances many joyous occasions, such as weddings, parties, family reunions, and church gatherings. We take

---

[1] Steven Jack Land, *Pentecostal Spirituality: A Passion for the Kingdom* (Cleveland, TN: CPT Press, 2010), p. 176.
[2] Cf. John Piper, *A Hunger for God: Desiring God through Fasting and Prayer* (Wheaton, IL: Crossway Books, 1997), p. 13.

great pleasure in sharing a meal with family and friends. Coffee break or tea time is often the high point of our day. Eating together is an important part of family and community life, and it is a universal sign of hospitality.

In the Bible, food often carries theological implications. Plentiful food is a fundamental sign of God's blessing, and the annual feasts were celebrated with great enthusiasm and thanksgiving. When God decided to save Israel from their bondage in Egypt, he instructed them to eat a special meal called the Passover. Each family gathered around the table and consumed the Passover lamb, which represented their redemption. During the time that Israel was encamped at Mt. Sinai, Moses ascended part way up the mountain accompanied by Aaron, Aaron's sons, and seventy elders. There on the mountain, they saw God and ate and drank in God's presence (Exod. 24.9-11). Moses continued alone to the top of Sinai, where he fasted for forty days.

The Christian sacrament of the Lord's Supper consists of eating and drinking as a reminder that Christ our Passover lamb was slain for our sins. Food will also play a role in the future, for the kingdom of God is pictured in Isaiah 25 as a great feast prepared by God for all the nations; and in Revelation 19 the redeemed are invited to the marriage supper of the Lamb. At the Last Supper, Jesus declared to his disciples that he would not eat of the Passover or drink of the fruit of the vine until the kingdom of God comes (Lk. 22.16, 18). Therefore, Jesus himself is now abstaining from a certain kind of food and drink.

Although food is necessary for the health of the human body and although food is a blessing and the act of eating is a part of many of life's most valued and sacred moments, food can become an addiction that replaces healthy relationships, including our relationship with God. It was eating the forbidden fruit that caused Adam and Eve to be expelled from the Garden of Eden. God had provided an abundance of food for Adam and Eve, but they chose to eat from the one tree that was forbidden. Later, a bowl of lentils was enough to entice Esau to trade away his birthright. Esau did not value his birthright as much as he valued his physical comfort; therefore, his future was endangered (Gen. 25.27-34).

In order to make his people distinct from the other nations, Yahweh imposed upon them certain food restrictions. Some foods were considered 'unclean' and were, therefore, forbidden (Leviticus 11; Deuteronomy 14). Similarly, anyone who took the Nazirite vows was prohibited from consuming any product of the grapevine (Num. 6.1-21). That prohibition, along with the other Nazirite requirements, was a means of setting apart that person from the general population.[3]

More than once it was complaints about the quality of food that caused the Israelites to suffer plagues in the wilderness. They grumbled against God, saying, 'O that we had meat to eat! We remember the fish we ate freely in Egypt, the cucumbers, the melons, the leeks, the onions, and the garlic; but now our strength is dried up, and there is nothing at all to look at but this manna' (Num. 11.4-6). The complaints of the Israelites later became an occasion for teaching when Moses explained God's purpose in withholding certain foods from them:

> [God] humbled you by letting you hunger, then by feeding you with manna, with which neither you nor your ancestors were acquainted, in order to make you understand that one does not live by bread alone, but by every word that comes from the mouth of the LORD (Deut. 8.3).

Food is important, but only God has the power to give life and to sustain life.

Job learned that the life-giving power of the word of God is more valuable than any benefits that come from food, which is why he could say, 'I have esteemed the words of his mouth more than my necessary food' (Job 23.12). In the New Testament, we read that Jesus fasted forty days in the wilderness and was tempted by the devil. Although Jesus was hungry from fasting, he rejected the devil's suggestion that he turn stones into bread to satisfy his craving.

---

[3] On the surface, these Old Testament food restrictions appear similar to the Roman Catholic rules regarding abstinence, the Eastern Orthodox ascetic fasting, and the monastic practice of limiting the diet. However, Israel's dietary laws did not fulfill the same purpose as fasting; therefore, they will not be discussed here. See Kent D. Berghuis, *Christian Fasting: A Theological Approach* (Richardson, TX: Biblical Studies Press, 2007), p. 17, who explains, 'These dietary restrictions were ways of normativizing a sanctified lifestyle, whereas fasting is generally an unusual behavior, an action taken that is conspicuously out of the ordinary'. Similarly, according to Jewish tradition, the Nazirite dietary laws did not constitute fasting. See Emil G. Hirsch, 'Asceticism', in Isidore Singer and Cyrus Adler (eds.), *The Jewish encyclopedia* (12 vols.; New York: Ktav Pub. House, 1964), II, p. 166.

Jesus cited the text from Deut. 8.3, affirming that the power of bread is limited, and it is God who gives and sustains life. It is important that God's people learn to rely upon God rather than upon natural means (including food).

Fasting, therefore, teaches us to trust God for our strength, and in so doing, it feeds and sustains our spiritual appetite. But which comes first, fasting or spiritual hunger? That is, does fasting make us more hungry for God, or does our hunger for God cause us to fast? I would suggest that the relationship between fasting and spiritual desire is a reciprocal one.[4] That is, spiritual desires are enhanced by fasting, and fasting is an expression of spiritual passion. As with other spiritual disciplines, the divine-human synergy that fasting generates is something of a mystery.

The practice of fasting has been an important component of Pentecostal spirituality from the beginning of the movement, yet this short introduction is the first scholarly book on fasting written by a Pentecostal. The purpose of this work is to examine fasting from the perspective of Pentecostal theology and practice and to suggest ways that fasting might function in contemporary Pentecostalism.[5] Pentecostal scholars have produced only a minimal liturgical theology and no stated theology of fasting, partly because Pentecostalism is not a monolithic movement and, therefore, resists universal theological conformity. Furthermore, Pentecostalism has been unduly influenced by the modern separation of theology from spirituality, a separation that has been challenged recently by many Pentecostal theologians.[6] However, while Pentecostalism may lack a formal, unified liturgical theology,[7] C.E.W. Green, argues that Pentecostals practice a lived sacramental spirituality.[8]

---

[4] Contra Piper, *A Hunger for God: Desiring God through Fasting and Prayer*, p. 90, who states that fasting 'expresses' but does not 'create' hunger for God.

[5] This work is only a brief introduction to fasting; therefore, I invite others to join in the discussion and bring deeper insights to the topic.

[6] Their numbers are now too many to list here, but the watershed was Land, *Pentecostal Spirituality*.

[7] But see, for example, Pentecostal theologians Daniela C. Augustine, *Pentecost, Hospitality, and Transfiguration: Toward a Spirit-Inspired Vision of Social Transformation* (Cleveland, TN: CPT Press, 2012); and S. Chan, *Liturgical Theology: The Church as Worshiping Community* (Downers Grove, IL: IVP Academic, 2006), who, among others, are making significant progress in this area.

[8] C.E.W. Green, *Toward a Pentecostal Theology of the Lord's Supper: Foretasting the Kingdom* (Cleveland, TN: CPT Press, 2012). See especially pp. 177-81. Cf. also

The design of a Pentecostal approach to fasting includes three primary components. First, inasmuch as Pentecostalism affirms the priority and authority of Scripture as our rule for faith and practice, the theological construction begins with the biblical text. Surprisingly, this is the first book of any kind to examine every biblical text that relates to fasting. Second, because Pentecostal theology is also *Christian* theology, the next task is to survey the place of fasting within Christian history. Special attention is given to John Wesley, the spiritual 'grandfather' of Pentecostalism.[9] The section on Wesley is one of the most detailed studies of Wesley's views on fasting. Third, because the ethos and core theology of Pentecostalism was birthed in the hearts of its founders, the role of fasting in the first ten years of the Pentecostal movement is explored by means of early periodicals. The chapter on the early literature is the most complete study on fasting in early Pentecostalism published to date.

B. Fasting Defined

Before proceeding further, we should define what we mean by the term 'fasting'. The biblical words for fasting (צום in Hebrew and νηστεύω in Greek) mean 'to abstain from food';[10] and according to the *Oxford English Dictionary*, to fast is 'To abstain from food, or to restrict oneself to a meagre diet, either as a religious observance or as a ceremonial expression of grief'.[11] Fasting is not a uniquely Jew-

---

D. Tomberlin, *Pentecostal Sacraments: Encountering God at the Altar* (Cleveland, TN: CPLC, Pentecostal Theological Seminary, 2010).

[9] Walter J. Hollenweger, 'After Twenty Years' Research on Pentecostalism', *Theology* 87 (November, 1984), p. 404.

[10] David J.A. Clines (ed.), *The Concise Dictionary of Classical Hebrew* (Sheffield, UK: Sheffield Phoenix Press, 2009), p. 377; Walter Bauer, *A Greek-English Lexicon of the New Testament, and Other Early Christian Literature* (trans. and ed. W.F. Arndt and F.W. Gingrich; Chicago: University of Chicago Press, 1957), p. 540.

[11] 'fast, v. 2'. *Oxford English Dictionary* Online. March 2014. Oxford University Press. http://0-www.oed.com.library.acaweb.org/view/Entry/68422?rskey=uk5kAG&result=7. The contemporary move to define fasting as any kind of abstinence, including 'news media, entertainment, information, shopping, email and the Internet' is based upon the view that fasting is essentially a way to free oneself from habits and 'make room for God'. See Lynne M. Baab, *Fasting: Spiritual Freedom Beyond Our Appetites* (Downers Grove, IL: IVP Books, 2006), pp. 10, 12, 16, 27, 28. Fasting, however, is much more than a change of habit; and part of its significance lies in its connection to the physical body and the transformation of normal human appetites.

ish or Christian practice. It is common in many religions and among many cultures. John Wesley observes that anyone 'who is under deep affliction, overwhelmed with sorrow for sin, and a strong apprehension of the wrath of God' would loose their appetite and forget to eat.[12] Scripture indicates that fasting is a natural bodily response to an intense affective experience, such as the experience of fear, danger, grief, suffering, humility, or awe. We do not fast 'to punish ourselves'.[13] The function of fasting as a spiritual discipline is to produce humility and single-mindedness in the person fasting, which will result in added effectiveness in the spiritual pursuits.

Outside of the religious realm, some people advocate fasting for its health benefits and for losing weight. Others have practiced fasting as a means of political protest or as a way to attract media attention to a grievance or to an important issue. However, this study looks at fasting only as a biblically based spiritual activity; therefore, we will not concern ourselves with other kinds of fasting.

Unless otherwise stated, fasting usually lasts from morning to evening. That is, a person who fasts will eat nothing but their evening meal. However, in the Bible and throughout history, fasting has been practiced in many ways and for various lengths of time. For the sake of simplicity, we might consider three categories of fasting.[14]

1. The Total Fast

The total fast, or absolute fast, is complete abstinence from both food and drink. Biblical examples of the total fast include the Day of Atonement, which lasts from one evening to the next (Lev. 23.32), and the Israelites' three-day fast for Esther in anticipation of her plea to the king to spare their lives (Est. 4.16). After his vision of Jesus, Saul of Tarsus abstained from both food and water for three days (Acts 9.9), and Moses neither ate nor drank for forty days while he was on the mountain with God. Because the human body cannot survive more than seven days or so without water, we assume that Moses was sustained miraculously in the presence of

---

[12] John Wesley, 'Upon Our Lord's Sermon on the Mount: Discourse Seven', in *Sermons on Several Occasions* (2 vols.; London: Caxton Press, by Henry Fisher, 9th edn, 1829), I, p. 308.

[13] Baab, *Fasting*, p. 15.

[14] Cf. Jentezen Franklin, *Fasting* (Lake Mary, FL: Charisma House, 2008), pp. 31-42.

God. The Eastern Orthodox church asks its members to fast all food and drink prior to receiving the Lord's Supper. A total fast of more than one day is not recommended because of the possible risks to health and safety.

2. The Normal Fast

The normal fast requires complete abstinence from food but allows the drinking of water. Most of the fasts in the Bible were normal fasts. In Judg. 20.26, the Israelites fasted from morning to evening as they sought divine guidance. On a later occasion, Samuel gathered the people together for repentance, and they fasted on that day (1 Sam. 7.6). At the beginning of his ministry, Jesus was led by the Spirit into the wilderness, where he fasted and prayed for forty days. During that time he 'ate nothing', and at the end of his fast 'he was hungry' (Lk. 4.2). The Scripture does not indicate that Jesus abstained from water. The Orthodox Church practices a normal fast during the first week of Lent, eating only two meals from Monday through Friday.[15] Roman Catholics are asked to fast from all food (drinking only water) for at least one hour before taking the Lord's Supper.[16]

3. Abstinence (or the Partial Fast).

Abstinence requires the avoidance of certain kinds of food, especially those that are most enjoyable, such as desserts and meats. For Roman Catholics, abstinence means avoiding meat and meat products. Abstinence in the Eastern Orthodox Church is called 'ascetic fasting'[17] and avoids the consumption of any meat product, fish, eggs, dairy, olive oil, and alcohol. In popular literature, abstinence is called the partial fast or the Daniel fast because it is based upon Daniel's experience of limiting his diet for spiritual reasons.[18] On one occasion, Daniel engaged in a normal fast for the purpose of seeking God by 'prayer and supplications, with fasting' (Dan. 9.3).

---

[15] The Orthodox calendar for fasting is quite extensive. A basic guide can be found online: http://www.abbamoses.com/fasting.html.

[16] Cf. this online guide to fasting for Roman Catholics: http://www.traditio.com/cal.htm.

[17] The word 'ascetic' comes from the Greek ἄσκησις, which means 'practice' and is used literally in reference to athletic training. See Bauer, *A Greek-English Lexicon*, p. 116. Asceticism is alien to the Hebraic view of spirituality. See Hirsch, 'Asceticism', p. 165.

[18] G. Jeffrey MacDonald, 'Fasting Like Daniel Gains a Following During Lenten Season', *Christian Century* 130.6 (2013), pp. 18-19.

8   *Fasting*

In Daniel 10, however, he abstains only from 'tasty food', 'meat', and 'wine' (Dan. 10.3). We are not told why he did not fast from all food. Perhaps he had grown weak in his old age and was unable to function without nourishment, or he may have suffered from diabetes or another chronic condition that prevented him from practicing a normal fast. It should be noted that neither the word 'fast' nor its synonym ('to afflict oneself') is found in Daniel 10; therefore, Daniel's practice should properly be called abstinence rather than fasting. Daniel states that he was 'mourning' for twenty-one days (Dan. 10.2), but he does not give the reason for his mourning. Abstinence has a long history in Christian history and is beneficial especially for those persons who are physically unable to go without food for any extended period of time.[19]

---

[19] See especially Baab, *Fasting*, pp. 21-33, 105-18, who offers helpful advice to women, particularly women who have suffered from eating disorders.

2

FASTING IN THE OLD TESTAMENT

Always when we voluntarily go without food, it's because something else is more important to us. – Thomas Ryan[1]

As a first step in developing a Pentecostal theology of fasting, we will examine fasting as it is practiced in the Bible. This study will include every biblical passage that addresses the topic of fasting. The passages will be considered in their canonical order, beginning with Genesis and moving forward book by book. In the Old Testament, we will follow the order of the Hebrew canon, which is organized in three parts: the Torah (תּוֹרה), the Prophets (נביאים), and the Writings (כתובים).

A. Fasting in the Torah

1. Moses on Mt. Sinai – Exodus 34.28-29

After Israel came out of Egypt, the Lord led them to Mt. Sinai. They encamped near the mountain, which was covered with clouds, fire, and smoke. From the midst of the fire, the Lord spoke the stipulations of his covenant, and the people were terrified at the sound of God's voice. Because of their fear, they asked Moses to speak to God alone, and Moses went up the mountain into the presence of God (Exod. 25.15-18). There on the mountain, Moses received from God instructions concerning the building and the

---

[1] Thomas Ryan, *The Sacred Art of Fasting: Preparing to Practice* (Preparing to Practice; Woodstock, VT: SkyLight Paths Pub., 2005), p. 63.

services of the tabernacle. He also received the two stone tables of the testimony, written by the finger of God.

Coming down from the mountain, he discovered that the Israelites had built a golden calf. In his anger, he shattered the stone tables, and he destroyed the golden calf. Furthermore, about 3,000 Israelites were executed on account of their idolatrous rebellion and the Lord sent a plague among the people.

Moses immediately returned to the mountain where he met with God once again (Exod. 34.2). In God's presence, Moses fasted:

> And he was there with the LORD forty days and forty nights; he neither ate bread nor drank water. And he wrote upon the tables the words of the covenant, the ten commandments. Then Moses came down from Mount Sinai, with the two tables of the testimony in his hand as he came down from the mountain. And Moses did not know that the skin of his face shone because he had been talking with God (Exod. 34.28-29).

For forty days and nights, Moses practiced a total fast – he neither ate nor drank. In light of the fact that the human body cannot survive more than about seven days without water, we must conclude that Moses was sustained by God in a miraculous fashion. Evidently, the presence of God was so powerful, that Moses was nourished by the divine energy. The fact that his face glowed with light when he came down from the mountain was evidence that Moses' body was to some extent transformed by the experience. The fasting of Moses teaches us that although the consumption of food and water is the normal requirement for human existence, the power and presence of God are sufficient to overcome that normal requirement.

It has been argued that Moses fasted in order to make himself receptive to divine revelation, but there is no evidence in the biblical text that Moses fasted with that purpose in mind or that fasting was a prerequisite to his divine encounter.[2] More likely, Moses fasted because the divine presence overwhelmed his desire for food. Therefore, Moses' story demonstrates that profound spiritual experiences can be more captivating than the allure of physical appetites. There are times when food becomes unimportant in comparison to

---

[2] Cf. Scot McKnight, *Fasting* (The Ancient Practices Series; Nashville, TN: Thomas Nelson, 2009), p. 112.

the attraction of the divine presence, when God's glory overpowers every other sight, sound, and sensation.

2. Day of Atonement – Leviticus 16.29-31; 23.32; and Numbers 29.7

The only fast required by the Mosaic Law was the yearly fast on the Day of Atonement (*Yom Kippur*). After the Babylonian exile four other annual fasts were held in memory of the national calamities that had passed (Zechariah 7–8). While the normal length of a biblical fast was morning to evening, and the normal practice was to abstain from all food but to drink water, the fast on the Day of Atonement lasted from evening to evening (Lev. 23.32)[3] and neither food nor drink was consumed.

While the Israelites were encamped at Mt. Sinai, the Lord gave them all the details of his covenant, including the Decalogue, the instructions for building the tabernacle, the requirements for all of the sacrifices, the guidelines for the priestly ministry, and the commandments regarding all of the holy days in the week, month, and year.

Although Leviticus is made up mostly of instructions for worship, the book also includes two narratives (Lev. 10.1-29; 24.10-23). In the first narrative, Aaron's sons Nadab and Abihu enter the tabernacle without authorization and they are struck dead by the hand of God. In the wake of that awful event, the Lord explains to Moses, 'Tell Aaron your brother not to come into the Holy of Holies just any time … lest he die' (Lev. 16.2). The Lord goes on to say that the only day in which the high priest can enter the Holy of Holies is the Day of Atonement. On that day, the high priest would offer sacrifices for his own sins and for the sins of all the people of Israel. On that day alone he would enter the Holy of Holies. The high priest would offer sacrifices that included a bull, a goat, and two rams. The blood of the bull would be sprinkled upon the mercy seat inside the Holy of Holies. The priest would lay his hands

---

[3] 'Evening to evening' suggests sundown to sundown, but later Jewish tradition specifies that the fast is to begin at sundown of one day and end at darkness of the following day, which would be about 25 hours rather than 24. Darkness officially begins when three stars are visible. Outside of the Day of Atonement, the custom was to begin fasting in the morning and fast until the evening (basically 12 hours). See Abraham P. Bloch, *The Biblical and Historical Background of the Jewish Holy Days* (New York: Ktav Pub. House, 1978), pp. 27-38.

upon the head of a goat (called the scapegoat), transferring all of Israel's guilt onto the goat, which would then be sent away into the wilderness, bearing Israel's sin away from the camp. As a part of this ceremony of repentance, the Israelites were to fast all food and drink for a night and a day as a way of 'afflicting themselves':

> And it shall be a statute to you for ever that in the seventh month, on the tenth day of the month, you shall afflict yourselves, and shall do no work, either the native or the alien who sojourns among you; for on this day shall atonement be made for you, to cleanse you; from all your sins you shall be clean before the Lord. It is a sabbath of solemn rest to you, and you shall afflict yourselves; it is a statute for ever ... that atonement may be made for the people of Israel once in the year because of all their sins (Lev. 16.29-34).

The Day of Atonement is mentioned later in a different context, when the Lord gives Moses a complete list of the 'appointed festivals':

> On the tenth day of the seventh month is the day of atonement; it shall be for you a time of holy convocation, and you shall afflict yourselves and present an offering by fire to the LORD. And you shall do no work on this same day; for it is a day of atonement, to make atonement for you before the LORD your God. For whoever is not afflicted on this day shall be cut off from his people. And whoever does any work on this day, that person I will destroy from among his people ... It shall be to you a sabbath of solemn rest, and you shall afflict yourselves; on the ninth day of the month beginning at evening, from evening to evening you shall keep your sabbath (Lev. 23.27-32).

This much briefer instruction regarding the Day of Atonement does not include any of the information regarding the sacrifices or the work of the priest. It emphasizes only three things about the Day of Atonement: 1. It is a day of atonement for sin. 2. It is a day of rest from all labor. 3. It is a day of total fasting as a sign of 'affliction'.

The Day of Atonement is described a third time in still another context. The Israelites had remained at Mt. Sinai for a little over a year, when the Lord led them to the threshold of the promised land. The Lord instructed them to enter Canaan and claim the land that he had given to them; but, out of fear, they refused to obey God's directive. The Lord declared, therefore, that all of the adults (except for Joshua and Caleb) would wander in the wilderness until they died (Numbers 13-14). After forty years of wandering, the Israelites came once again to the edge of Canaan. The old generation had died, and a new generation was poised to receive the fulfillment of God's promises. This new generation had not been present at Mt. Sinai; therefore, Moses chooses to reiterate everything that happened there and restate the commands that God had given. Within this context, Moses summarizes the requirements concerning all of the holy days, including the Day of Atonement:

> On the tenth day of the seventh month you shall have a holy convocation, and afflict yourselves; you shall do no work, but you shall offer a burnt offering to the LORD, a pleasing odor: one young bull, one ram, seven male lambs a year old ... also one male goat for a sin offering, besides the sin offering of atonement, and the continual burnt offering and its grain offering, and their drink offerings (Num. 29.7-11).

All three of the above texts describe the Day of Atonement as an annual day of repentance for the Israelites, and fasting from both food and water was one of the day's essential requirements. In regard to fasting, these passages use the terminology 'afflict yourselves', which emphasizes the humbling of oneself that is necessary for true repentance. The Lord says, 'Those who will not afflict themselves on this same day shall be put to death' (Lev. 23.29). Everyone was required to fast on this day from evening to evening (24 hours) or be subject to a death sentence.

The Hebrew term 'to afflict oneself' (ענה נפש) means to bring pain or suffering upon oneself as an act of humility.[4] Thus, the fundamental concept of fasting here is to afflict oneself. We read in Hebrews 12 that God disciplines those whom he loves. However, fasting is a self-imposed discipline in which we cause our body to enter into suffering as an expression of humility.[5] 'Fasting helps en-

---

[4] See Josiah Derby, 'Fasting and Atonement', *Jewish Bible Quarterly* 23.4 (1995), pp. 238-41.

[5] Cf. Arthur Wallis, *God's Chosen Fast* (Ft. Washington, PA: Christian Literature Crusade, 1968), pp. 82-87.

gender a sense of loss and of vulnerability'.[6] Other biblical references to fasting as self-affliction include Ps. 69.10, 'I afflicted myself with fasting', and Ezra 8.21, 'Then I proclaimed a fast there, at the river Ahava, that we might afflict ourselves before our God' (See also Isa. 58.3, 5).

Although the Day of Atonement was a day devoted to repentance, fasting itself did not provide forgiveness of sins.[7] Forgiveness was secured by the offering of sacrifices, the release of the scapegoat, and by the genuine repentance of the people. Fasting accompanied their repentance out of recognition of the sacredness of the holy day and as a demonstration of their humility and their deep sorrow for sin.

3. A Woman's Vow to Fast – Numbers 30.13-15

As the Israelites were preparing to enter the land of Canaan, Moses gave instructions regarding various elements of the covenant. The generation who had been present at Mt. Sinai had died, and a new generation had grown up during the forty years of wilderness wandering. This new generation needed to hear the stipulations of their covenant with Yahweh.

Numbers 30 deals with the regulations regarding the making of vows. Moses states that while men must take full responsibility for the fulfillment of their vows, women may be overruled by their fathers or their husbands. If an unmarried young woman makes a vow, her father may annul it, and she is freed from the obligation. Similarly, if a married woman makes a vow, her husband may annul it and she also is freed from its obligation. This regulation extends to any vow regarding fasting:

> Regarding every vow and every binding oath to afflict herself, her husband may confirm it or her husband may annul it. But if her husband indeed says nothing to her from day to day, then he confirms all her vows or all her obligations which are on her; he has confirmed them, because he said nothing to her on the day he heard them. But if he indeed annuls them after he has heard them, then he shall bear her guilt (Num. 30.13-15).

---

[6] Ryan, *The Sacred Art of Fasting*, p. 27.

[7] See David Lambert, 'Fasting as a Penitential Rite: A Biblical Phenomenon?', *Harvard Theological Review* 96.4 (2003), pp. 477-512.

As was explained earlier, the phrase 'afflict herself' refers to fasting. The reason for this law is not stated, but the authority of the father or husband to revoke a woman's vow illustrates the ancient role of men as protectors of children and women. We learn from this regulation that individual, voluntary fasting must have been rather common. Otherwise, there would have been no need for its regulation.

4. Not by Bread Alone – Deuteronomy 8.3

The book of Deuteronomy contains the last three speeches of Moses, in which he reflects upon the Lord's dealings with Israelites as they journeyed from Egypt to the land of Canaan. Moses extracts an important lesson from the events of the wilderness wandering:

> [God] humbled you by letting you hunger, then by feeding you with manna, with which neither you nor your ancestors were acquainted, in order to make you understand that one does not live by bread alone, but by every word that comes from the mouth of the Lord (Deut. 8.3).

Although this text does not specifically mention fasting, the reference to the Israelites 'hunger' alludes to the times when both food and water were scarce. The larger context of Deut. 8.3 indicates that Israel's hunger in the wilderness was a time of testing, orchestrated by God so that he might discipline them as a man disciplines his son (8.5). Through this discipline, the Lord would learn what was in their hearts; he would discover whether they would be faithful to him or not (8.2). He assured them that he was bringing them to a good land where they would 'eat food without scarcity' and they would 'lack nothing' (8.9). They should be very careful, however, after they have 'eaten and are satisfied', to praise the Lord for 'the good land' that he has given them (8.10). They were warned of the dangers of forgetting that everything they have comes from God. God spoke and water flowed from the rock. God spoke and manna rained down from heaven. Therefore, even the bread itself was created by God's word. It was God who gave them the power to prosper (8.18). Everything they had needed for survival had been given to them by the word of God. However, if they should ever begin to trust in themselves or turn to other gods, they would 'surely perish' (8.19).

Like the Israelites, we are tempted to believe that food is our source of life and strength and that we obtained it by our own ingenuity.[8] Fasting humbles us and tests our commitment to the word of life. Fasting reveals what is in our hearts. Fasting reminds us to praise God for the 'good land' that he has given us. Fasting helps us to 'notice the false, non-life-giving things' on which we depend.[9] Through fasting we learn that it is the spiritual, not the physical, that sustains us.

5. Moses Recalls Mt. Sinai – Deuteronomy 9.9, 18

As Moses tells the story of Israel's salvation from Egyptian bondage and subsequent encounter with God at Mt. Sinai, he recalls his sacred time on the mountain in the presence of God:

> When I went up the mountain to receive the tables of stone, the tables of the covenant which the LORD made with you, I remained on the mountain forty days and forty nights. I neither ate bread nor drank water. The LORD gave me the two tables of stone written with the finger of God; and on them were all the words which the LORD had spoken with you on the mountain out of the midst of the fire on the day of the assembly. And at the end of forty days and forty nights the LORD gave me the two tables of stone, the tables of the covenant (Deut. 9.9-11).

In his retelling of the event, Moses points out that he had fasted during his first visit to the mountain, a part of the story that is omitted in the Exodus account. The Exodus version states only that Moses was 'on the mountain forty days and forty nights' (Exod. 24.18). At the end of his first stay on the mountain, God gave him the two tables of the covenant, which Moses broke when he saw the golden calf that the Israelites had made. The Lord called upon Moses to return to the mountain, where the Lord rewrote the commandments upon two tables of stone that Moses had cut out. We learn in Exod. 34.28 that Moses remained on the mountain for a second period of forty days and nights, during which he fasted. In Deuteronomy, however, Moses reveals that he had fasted during

---

[8] Cf. Mark Buchanan, 'Go Fast and Live: Hunger as Spiritual Discipline', *Christian Century* 118.7 (2001), p. 16.

[9] Baab, *Fasting*, p. 15.

both of his stays upon the mountain. In Deuteronomy 9, Moses restates the story of his second visit to Mt. Sinai:

> Then I lay prostrate before the LORD as before, forty days and forty nights; I neither ate bread nor drank water, because of all the sin which you had committed, in doing what was evil in the sight of the LORD, to provoke him to anger. For I was afraid of the anger and hot displeasure which the LORD bore against you, so that he was ready to destroy you. And the LORD listened to me that time also (Deut. 9.18-19).

Moses' retelling of his second divine encounter on Mt. Sinai includes a comment not found in the Exodus account. That is, he supplies a reason for his fasting. The Exodus story does not supply a reason or purpose for Moses' fasting; but, according to Deut. 9.18-19, he fasted 'because of' Israel's sin. Moses believed that their idolatry, as manifested in the golden calf episode, had angered God to the point that God would 'destroy' the Israelites. Therefore, Moses fasted as a means of intercession for the Israelites. He pleaded with God that God would have mercy upon the sinful people, and God heard Moses' prayer. For Moses, fasting functioned as a sign of mourning and repentance over the sins of his people, much in the same way that fasting functioned for Israel on the Day of Atonement. Scot McKnight reflects on Moses' reaction to Israel's sin:

> How do we respond when we discover the fresh, fatal sins of others? This story about Moses' body pleading speaks against our tendency to publicize our complaints about others. We have become a culture of cultural critics and a church of church critics. Perhaps more of us need to be quick to convert our concern about the moral failures of others into body pleading for them instead of public words against them.[10]

B. Fasting in the Former Prophets

1. Israel Seeks Divine Direction – Judges 20.26

A Levite and his secondary wife had stopped in the city of Gibeah to spend the night, and a group of had raped and murdered the

---

[10] McKnight, *Fasting*, p. 42.

helpless woman. The Levite called together the leaders of Israel and asked them to pass judgment on the offending men from Gibeah. The Israelites agreed that none of them would rest until the evil had been punished; therefore, they appealed to the tribe of Benjamin to hand over the offenders for punishment. When the Benjaminites refused to cooperate, the other tribes declared war upon Gibeah and Benjamin. A battle ensued, but the Benjaminites soundly defeated the other Israelites. They went to battle a second time, and again Benjamin was victorious. At that point, the defeated tribes gathered together to seek the face of God by prayer and fasting.

> Then all the Israelites, the whole army, went up and came to Bethel and wept; thus they remained there before the LORD and fasted that day until evening ... And the sons of Israel inquired of the LORD ... saying, 'Shall I yet again go out to battle against the sons of my brother Benjamin, or shall I cease?' And the LORD said, 'Go up, for tomorrow I will deliver them into your hand' (Judg. 20.26-28).

The urgency of the situation was clear – the Israelites had been defeated twice, though they believed their cause to be just. From the time of the first battle until now, the intensity of their prayers would naturally increase. After they lost the first battle, they would have been troubled; but after losing the second battle, they would have been utterly distressed. Therefore, they joined together in a corporate fast, which lasted from morning to evening (12 hours). In this case, fasting is both a sign of mourning over the state of affairs and a manifestation of urgency in prayer during a time of crisis.[11] After they wept and fasted and pleaded for guidance, the Lord answered them. Not only did the Lord give them specific direction, but he also gave them a word of hope. The Lord directed them to enter the fray once again; and this time they would win the victory. Therefore, they went to battle a third time, and they defeated the Benjaminites, whose survivors numbered only 600.

2. Hannah Prays for a Son – 1 Samuel 1.7

Hannah was Elkanah's first wife, but because she was unable to bear children, he married a second wife, Peninah, who soon gave

---

[11] Cf. Wallis, *God's Chosen Fast*, p. 52.

birth to children. Peninah made it a habit to ridicule and provoke Hannah on account of her childlessness.

Every year, Hannah's family would go up to the house of God in Shiloh to offer a sacrifice. On one of those visits, Peninah acted so cruelly toward Hannah that a crisis developed, and Hannah 'wept and would not eat' (1 Sam. 1.7). Elkanah her husband asked, 'Why don't you eat? Why is your heart sad? Am I not better to you than ten sons?' He did not understand the extent of Hannah's sorrow or the difficulty of her situation. 'One cannot very well weep and eat at the same time'.[12]

After the family had eaten, Hannah rose up and presented herself at the tabernacle of the Lord. She was deeply distressed, and she wept before the Lord and made a vow. She said, 'If you will look on my affliction … and give me a son, then I will give him to the LORD all the days of his life' (1 Sam. 1.11). Hannah viewed her inability to bear children as an 'affliction'. In this case, her self-imposed affliction (fasting) was an outward sign of her inward pain and her physical affliction. Hannah came to a place where she needed to get in touch with God. Compared to the constant pain that Hannah endured, food became unimportant to her. She had suffered all that she could bear, so she prayed, fasted, and wept. 'Hannah might become an example of a sacred desire being expressed by … pleading with God through fasting'.[13] Because of her insistence, which was authenticated by fasting, the Lord remembered her, and she soon gave birth to a son, Samuel.

Whenever our barrenness and the enemy's taunting become unbearable, fasting will help us to communicate our pain to God in prayer. It is not insignificant that Samuel, born in response to fasting and prayer, became a leader who was known for his effective practice of prayer.

3. Returning to the LORD – 1 Samuel 7.6

Samuel's miraculous birth was followed by his extraordinary call narrative and his acceptance in Israel as a judge and a prophet. One of the earliest and most important events in Samuel's career happened after the Philistines had defeated Israel and had taken the Ark of the Covenant. Even though the Philistines returned the Ark,

---

[12] Lambert, 'Fasting as a Penitential Rite: A Biblical Phenomenon?', p. 484.
[13] McKnight, *Fasting*, p. 47.

it had not been brought back to the tabernacle, and the Philistines continued to rule over the Israelites. When Samuel saw that the Israelites desired to follow the Lord once again (1 Sam. 7.1), he called them together to Mizpah where he challenged them to confess their sins and discard their idols:

> If you would return to the LORD with all your heart, then put away the foreign gods and the Ashtaroth from among you, and direct your heart to the LORD, and serve him only, and he will deliver you out of the hand of the Philistines. So Israel put away the Baals and the Ashtaroth, and they served only the LORD. Then Samuel said, 'Gather all Israel at Mizpah, and I will pray to the LORD for you'. So they gathered at Mizpah, and drew water and poured it out before the LORD, and fasted on that day, and they said, 'We have sinned against the LORD' (1 Sam. 7.3-6).

Israel's fasting was evidence of their sincerity in turning to the Lord, but fasting in itself did not constitute their repentance. Their repentance is described in four statements: (1) they must 'return' (Hebrew שׁוּב) to the Lord; (2) they disposed of their idols; (3) 'they served only the LORD'; and (4) they confessed, 'we have sinned'. The Hebrew 'return' (שׁוּב) is often used in the Old Testament to designate genuine repentance,[14] and their outward actions of discarding their idols and serving only God reveal the sincerity of their confession. Their fasting (along with the pouring out of water) was an outward visible sign of their inward sorrow over their sins.

4. An Unwise Fast – 1 Samuel 14.24

Saul was Israel's first king, and his reign was marked by extreme fluctuations. He began well, but he soon faltered through disobedience to God. The Spirit of the Lord departed from him; and, consequently, he proceeded to act erratically. His demand for fasting during a battle is an example of his instability.

During Saul's rule, the Philistines continued to assault the Israelites (1 Sam. 13.17). On one occasion, Saul's son Jonathan initiated a battle against the Philistines, and they were routed by the Israelites (1 Sam. 14.23). The Israelite soldiers, however, grew weary because

---

[14] The LXX translates שׁוּב with the Greek verb ἐπιστρέφω, which is often used in the NT to indicate conversion (Acts 3.19; 9.35; 11.21; 14.15; 15.19; 26.18, 20; 28.27; 2 Cor. 3.16; 1 Thess. 1.9; Jas 5.19, 20; 1 Pet. 2.25).

in his determination to defeat the Philistines, Saul had instituted a fast. We read, 'And the men of Israel were distressed that day; for Saul had laid an oath on the people, saying, 'Cursed be the man who eats food until it is evening and I am avenged on my enemies. So none of the people tasted food' (1 Sam. 14.24). Jonathan had not heard about his father's order; therefore, when the opportunity came for Jonathan to eat, he did so without reservation (1 Sam. 14.27). The soldiers informed Jonathan of the fast, and Jonathan replied,

> My father has troubled the land; see how my eyes have become bright, because I tasted a little of this honey. How much better if the people had eaten freely today of the spoil of their enemies which they found; for now the slaughter among the Philistines has not been great (1 Sam. 14.29-30).

Saul had commanded his soldiers to fast, thinking that God would honor their self-denial. However, he failed to understand that fasting is not a magical device that can be used to guarantee a certain result. He also failed to realize that the soldiers would need as much energy as could be mustered if they were to defeat the enemy. Normally, fasting was observed in conjunction with resting. The Day of Atonement, for example, was a 'sabbath of solemn rest' (Lev. 16.31). Although fasting is an important aid to prayer and a helpful method for dealing with crisis, there are times when fasting is counterproductive.

5. Grieving for a Friend – 1 Samuel 20.34

Because of Saul's disobedience, the Lord removed him from the throne and appointed David in his stead. Saul, however, unaware of David's anointing, continued to reign for a time, and David served in Saul's court as musician. After David defeated Goliath, Saul became extremely jealous of David and tried several times to kill him. Saul informed Jonathan that David was to be executed, but Jonathan objected to his father's plan. Jonathan loved David as a brother, and he also knew that David had done no wrong. Therefore, when Saul insisted on killing David, 'Jonathan rose from the table in fierce anger and ate no food the second day of the month, for he was grieved for David, because his father had disgraced him' (1 Sam. 20.34). Jonathan then assisted David to escape from Saul's grasp.

Jonathan's fast was provoked by two related motivations. First, 'he was grieved for David'.[15] Second, 'his father had disgraced him'. His grief for his close friend David and his own feelings of disgrace caused Jonathan to be so emotionally upset that he could not eat.

6. Terrified of the Enemy – 1 Samuel 28.20

As the reign of Saul was coming to a close, the Philistines gathered their army for another attack against Israel. When Saul saw the size of the Philistine army, 'he was afraid, and his heart trembled greatly' (1 Sam. 28.5). He called upon the Lord, asking for direction, but the Lord did not answer him. Therefore, he sought out the medium at Endor and asked her to bring up the spirit of Samuel. Surprisingly, Samuel appeared. He announced to Saul that the battle would be lost and that both Saul and Jonathan would be killed. At that point, 'Saul fell at once full length upon the ground, filled with fear because of the words of Samuel; and there was no strength in him, because he had eaten nothing all day and all night' (1 Sam. 28.20).

The reason for Saul's fasting is not stated in the text, but may have something to do with his emotional state. On the one hand, he was terrified of the Philistine army, and just as he fasted at the time of the earlier battle, perhaps he fasted in this case for the same reason: to induce God to give Saul the victory. On the other hand, Saul may have been so disturbed that he lost his appetite and had no desire for food.[16] In either case, when he fainted, the medium convinced him to eat something so that he might regain his strength.[17]

7. Mourning Saul's Death – 1 Samuel 31.13

The word of Samuel came to pass, and Saul and his three sons were killed in battle. The Philistines cut off Saul's head, and carried him to Bethshan:

> They put his armor in the temple of Ashtaroth; and they fastened his body to the wall of Bethshan. But when the inhabitants of Jabesh-gilead heard what the Philistines had done to

---

[15] Cf. McKnight, *Fasting*, pp. 53-54.
[16] Cf. Wesley, 'Upon Our Lord's Sermon on the Mount: Discourse Seven', I, p. 308.
[17] I chose to omit the story of the Egyptian who 'had not eaten bread or drunk water for three days and three nights' (1 Sam. 30.12), because his fasting was not intentional. He had fallen ill, and his people had abandoned him in the wilderness without food or drink.

Saul, all the valiant men arose, and went all night, and took the body of Saul and the bodies of his sons from the wall of Bethshan; and they came to Jabesh and burnt them there. And they took their bones and buried them under the tamarisk tree in Jabesh, and fasted seven days (1 Sam 31.10-13).

It was customary among the Jews to fast as a sign of mourning for the dead.[18] One example of that practice is found here, when King Saul and his sons are killed in battle. The Philistines cut off Saul's his head and fastened his body to a wall, but the men of Jabesh-gilead came and rescued the bodies of Saul and his sons. They brought them to Jabesh, burned them (to prevent any further humiliation) and buried their bones under a tree at Jabesh. Then the men from the tribe of Manasseh fasted seven days because of Saul's tragic death.

Even though Saul's reputation had declined in his latter days, the people of Jabesh-gilead continued to be thankful for what Saul had done for them. Early in his reign, he had saved the people of Jabesh-gilead from the Ammonites (1 Sam. 11.1). Therefore, they disposed of Saul's remains in a manner that was honorable, and they fasted for seven days as a symbol of their grief and mourning over their slain king.

8. David Mourns Saul – 2 Samuel 1.12

News of the death of Saul and Jonathan soon reached the ears of David, who had returned to Ziklag after his defeat of the Amalekite raiders. David responded to the news with much grief:

> Then David took hold of his clothes, and rent them; and so did all the men who were with him. And they mourned and wept and fasted until evening, for Saul and for Jonathan his son, and for the people of the LORD, and for the house of Israel; because they were fallen by the sword (2 Sam. 1.11).

David was a challenger to Saul's throne and an object of Saul's hatred; therefore, we might expect him to rejoice over the death of his adversary. However, David held the office of king in great respect, and he mourned greatly over the death of Saul, 'the LORD's anointed' and over Jonathan, David's close friend. In honor of the

---

[18] Baab, *Fasting*, p. 69.

slain king, David and his men fasted from morning until evening. Along with their fasting, they exhibited other signs of mourning: they tore their clothing, and they wept. The text gives no indication that David's grief was artificial or insincere. Therefore, his fasting resulted naturally from the intense shock of hearing about Saul's death. When grief is overwhelming, the appetite is diminished.

9. David Mourns Abner – 2 Samuel 3.35

After Saul's death, his descendants and allies fought a long war against David and his allies (2 Sam. 3.1). Abner had been a friend of Saul, but he chose to come over to David's side; and he and David entered into a covenant. Abner, however, in an earlier battle, had killed the brother of David's general, Joab. Therefore, without David's knowledge, Joab murdered Abner out of revenge. David attended the funeral:

> Then David said to Joab and to all the people who were with him, 'Tear your clothes, and put on sackcloth, and mourn before Abner'. And King David followed the bier. They buried Abner at Hebron; and the king lifted up his voice and wept at the grave of Abner; and all the people wept. And the king lamented for Abner ... Then all the people came to persuade David to eat bread while it was yet day; but David swore, saying, 'God do so to me and more also, if I taste bread or anything else till the sun goes down' (2 Sam. 3.31-36).

David had made a covenant with Abner; but Joab, a servant of David, had violated that covenant by murdering Abner. David did not mourn because Abner had been a friend or supporter of David's monarchy but because Abner had been dishonored by Joab. On this occasion, David's mourning and fasting was a matter of honor and duty rather than affection.

10. Fasting for Healing – 2 Samuel 12.16-23

After David had consolidated his kingdom and defeated his enemies, he had the leisure to remain in the palace. One day, while walking on the roof of his house, he caught a glimpse of a beautiful woman. Her name was Bathsheba; and, even though she was married, David ordered her to appear before him. He committed adultery with Bathsheba, and she became pregnant and gave birth to son.

When he was confronted by Nathan the prophet, David repented and was forgiven (2 Sam. 12.13), but his sin had given 'occasion to the enemies of the LORD to blaspheme' (12.14). Therefore, in order to impress upon David the gravity of his sin and to demonstrate to the people that even the king was not immune to divine judgment, God declared that the child would die. When the baby grew sick, 'David prayed to God for the child, and he fasted, and he went in and lay all night upon the ground' (12.16). David's elders came and tried to get him to eat, but he refused. David fasted and prayed for seven days, pleading with God for the life of the child.[19] Even though David prayed and fasted earnestly, the child died. After the child died David broke with tradition:

> David arose from the ground, washed, anointed himself, and changed his clothes; and he went into the house of the LORD and worshiped. Then he went to his own house, and when he asked, they set food before him and he ate. Then his servants said to him, 'What is this thing that you have done? While the child was alive, you fasted and wept; but when the child died, you arose and ate food'. He replied, 'While the child was alive, I fasted and wept; for I said, Who knows, the LORD may be gracious to me, that the child may live. But now he has died; why should I fast? Can I bring him back again? I will go to him, but he will not return to me' (2 Sam. 12.20-23).

We might find at least three lessons here regarding fasting. First, it is evident from this passage that David considered fasting to be an important companion to his prayers for the healing of his child.[20] He believed that fasting would verify his repentance, his humility, his sincerity, his pain, and his urgency. When presented with a crisis, David fasted. Second, it is also clear from the response of David's servants that fasting was expected as an expression of mourning for the dead, and that David went counter to that custom. Third, in light of the fact that the child died, we may discern that fasting has no automatic magical power that causes God to do

---

[19] David's fast is not penitential, as some have argued; he is fasting for the healing of the child. Cf. Lambert, 'Fasting as a Penitential Rite: A Biblical Phenomenon?', p. 485.

[20] Cf. Walter F. Fischer, 'Fasting and Bodily Preparation: A Fine Outward Training', *Concordia Theological Monthly* 30.12 (1959), p. 888.

our bidding. Fasting does not guarantee that God will do what we ask.

11. The Unnamed Prophet – 1 Kings 13.8-22

King Solomon married many foreign wives, and he allowed his heart to be turned away from the exclusive worship of Yahweh and toward the worship of foreign gods (1 Kgs 11.1-8). For this reason, the Lord was angry with Solomon; and when he died, the Lord divided the kingdom of Israel (1 Kgs 11.9-13). The Lord gave ten tribes to Jeroboam, but for the sake of David, the Lord allowed Solomon's son Rehoboam to retain the tribe of Judah. The Lord promised that if Jeroboam would be faithful and obedient, the Lord would establish Jeroboam's dynasty (1 Kgs 11.37-38). Jeroboam, however, did not believe that faithfulness to Yahweh was the way to establish his kingdom. Instead, he made two golden calves and placed them as gods in Bethel and Dan. The Lord, therefore, sent a prophet from Judah to bring a message of rebuke to Jeroboam. After their encounter, Jeroboam invited the prophet to dinner, but the prophet replied that it he was not allowed to eat in Bethel:

> And the man of God said to the king, 'If you give me half your house, I will not go in with you. And I will not eat bread or drink water in this place; for so was it commanded me by the word of the LORD, saying, "You shall neither eat bread, nor drink water, nor return by the way that you came"' (1 Kgs 13.8-9).

On his journey back to Judah, the man encountered an older prophet who lied to him, telling him that the Lord had reversed his order and that the young man should come and eat with the old prophet. The young prophet was deceived; and after he ate, the Lord sent a lion to kill him for his disobedience.

The biblical text does not specify why the prophet was forbidden to eat on his way to and from Bethel. However, given the way that biblical meals function as means of hospitality and bridges of friendship, we might deduce that the prohibition regarding eating was the Lord's way of stressing the conflict between Jeroboam and the Lord. Perhaps Jeroboam's introduction of idolatry meant that his kingdom was not to be considered as friendly territory for the Lord or the Lord's prophet. Therefore, fasting in the context of an offer of hospitality might be a confirmation of existing strife and an assertion of resistance to compromise.

12. Elijah's Journey to Horeb – 1 Kings 19.8

The prophet Elijah confronted the prophets of Baal on Mt. Carmel and then had them executed (1 Kgs 18.40). Consequently, Queen Jezebel, who sponsored Baalism and its prophets, threatened to kill Elijah. Feeling alone and helpless, Elijah fled to the wilderness of Beersheba, where he sat down under a juniper tree and prayed to die. He fell asleep under the tree, but he was awakened by the angel of the Lord, who had prepared food and drink. Elijah ate and drank and fell asleep again.

> And the angel of the LORD came again a second time and touched him and said, 'Arise, eat, because the journey is too great for you'. He got up, and ate and drank; then he went in the strength of that food forty days and forty nights to Horeb the mount of God (1 Kgs 19.7-8).

'The time of fasting between the juniper tree and Horeb was God's time of preparing Elijah to hear from Him'.[21] When Elijah reached Mt. Horeb, the Lord instructed him go up on the mountain and stand before the Lord. The Lord passed by in wind, earthquake, and fire; then Elijah heard the voice of the Lord. 'Fasting and the presence of God go together'.[22] The Lord instructed Elijah to return and anoint Elisha as his successor.

The experience of Elijah appears to be a reenactment of Moses' encounter with God on Mt. Sinai many years earlier.[23] Like Moses, Elijah fasted for forty days and forty nights. Like Moses, Elijah encountered a theophany on the mountain. Like Moses, Elijah received guidance from the voice of God. Later on, like Moses, Elijah was taken from the earth by God himself. As in the case of Moses, Elijah's fasting was apparently a sign of God's miraculous, sustaining power. Like Moses, Elijah did not live by bread alone, but by the word of God.

13. From Selfishness to Sincerity – 1 Kings 21.1-29

Naboth had a vineyard beside King Ahab's palace in Jezreel, and Ahab offered to buy it. However, Naboth was unwilling to sell the

---

[21] Marilyn Hickey, *The Power of Prayer and Fasting* (New York: Warner Faith, 1st edn, 2006), p. 231.
[22] McKnight, *Fasting*, p. 117.
[23] The names Sinai and Horeb refer to the same mountain.

property because it had been handed down to him from his ancestors. King Ahab was not pleased:

> And Ahab went into his house vexed and sullen because of what Naboth the Jezreelite had said to him; for he had said, 'I will not give you the inheritance of my fathers'. And he lay down on his bed, and turned away his face, and would eat no food. But Jezebel his wife came to him and said to him, 'Why is your spirit is so sullen that you are not eating food?' (1 Kgs 21.4-5).

When Ahab explained the situation, Jezebel replied, 'Do you now reign over Israel? Arise, eat bread, and let your heart be joyful; I will give you the vineyard of Naboth the Jezreelite' (1 Kgs 21.7). Jezebel gave orders (in the name of Ahab) to proclaim a fast, and when the people had gathered together, Naboth would be falsely accused of cursing God and the King. They would then take Naboth and stone him to death. Jezebel's henchmen did just as she had ordered, and Ahab claimed Naboth's vineyard. Because of Ahab's sin, the Lord sent Elijah to meet him and to inform him of God's displeasure. The word of the Lord to Ahab was, 'Behold, I will bring evil upon you, and will utterly sweep you away ... because ... you have provoked me to anger and have caused Israel to sin' (1 Kgs 21.21-22).

When Elijah delivered the message of doom, Ahab apparently took it very seriously:

> And it came about when Ahab heard these words, that he tore his clothes and put on sackcloth and fasted, and he lay in sackcloth and went about despondently. Then the word of the Lord came to Elijah the Tishbite, saying, 'Do you see how Ahab has humbled himself before me? Because he has humbled himself before me, I will not bring the evil in his days, but I will bring the evil upon his house in his son's days' (1 Kgs 21.27-29).

This passage includes three examples of fasting. In the first case, Ahab fasted because he was emotionally distraught. We might even say he was pouting, and his fasting was a manifestation of his selfish desires. In the second instance, the fasting was a ruse, intended to lend an air of solemnity and seriousness to the ostensible trial of Naboth. Although Naboth's trial was staged, the calling of a fast gave the appearance that the trial was a genuine attempt to address a serious wrongdoing. The fast, however, was a farce; and the wrongdoing was the trial itself. The third instance of fasting was a heartfelt act of humility, in which Ahab submitted himself to God. David Lambert comments that through fasting Ahab assumes 'the persona of a defeated, or thoroughly afflicted, supplicant. In much the same way, a defeated king is forced to prostrate himself and acknowledge the superiority of the victor.'[24] The text does not reveal the content of Ahab's prayers – we are not even told that he prayed – but apparently the Lord was convinced of Ahab's sincerity, and the Lord postponed the day of judgment for Ahab.[25] In response to this narrative, John Wesley exclaims, 'How powerful a means [fasting] is to avert the wrath of God'.[26] This very intriguing passage suggests that fasting is subject to abuse, but even an abuser of fasting can be capable of a legitimate and beneficial observance of the discipline.

C. Fasting in the Latter Prophets

1. The LORD's Chosen Fast – Isaiah 58.3-14

Fasting, like all religious practices, can become an empty ritual, performed out of habit or duty. A legalistic attitude toward religious rites, in which the rules surrounding a practice receive more attention than the theological functions of the practice, can erode the spiritual benefits to the point that deep reform is needed. The Old Testament prophets accused the Israelites of reaching that point. In the time of Isaiah, for example, the Lord considered Israel's sacrifices to be 'worthless' and their incense 'an abomination'. The religious rituals and holy days had become tiresome to the Lord, and he threatened to hear Israel's prayers no longer (Isa. 1.10-17). In Isaiah 58, the practice of fasting was singled out for more detailed attention, and if we are to prevent our fasting from degenerating into a valueless ritual, we must pay close attention to Isaiah's guidelines for fasting that is pleasing to God.

The Lord commands Isaiah, 'declare to my people their transgression and to the house of Jacob their sins' (Isa. 58.1). Given such an unqualified imperative, we would expect a catalog of sins to

---

[24] Lambert, 'Fasting as a Penitential Rite: A Biblical Phenomenon?', p. 492.
[25] According to Wallis, *God's Chosen Fast*, pp. 55-59, this biblical narrative shows the power of fasting to change God's mind.
[26] Wesley, 'Upon Our Lord's Sermon on the Mount: Discourse Seven', p. 310.

follow, but instead, the prophets words describe what seems to be exemplary behavior. The Lord says:

> Yet they seek me day by day
>   and delight to know my ways,
>   Like a nation that has done righteousness
>   And has not forsaken the ordinance of their God.
>   They ask me for just decisions,
>   They delight in the nearness of God (Isa. 58.2).

It appears that they had sought after God and had adhered closely to the rules, the ordinances of God. They had even practiced the difficult discipline of fasting. However, something was wrong; their fasting had gone unrewarded! Therefore, they complain to God: 'We have fasted, so why have you not seen us? We have afflicted ourselves, so why have you not paid attention to us?' (v. 3).

In his reply, God identifies the source of their dysfunction:

> Look, on the day of your fast, you do as you please,
>   And you exploit all your workers.
>   Your fasting ends in quarreling and strife,
>   And in striking each other with wicked fists.
>   You cannot fast like you are doing now
>   And expect to be heard on high! (Isa. 58.3-4).

Fasting should be a way to make prayer more effective, to cause one's voice to be 'heard on high', and to make God take notice. God, however, could not take notice of their fasting because noise of their wickedness was much louder than that of their fasting. The psalmist wrote, 'The eyes of the LORD are toward the righteous, and his ears are open to their cry; [but] the face of the LORD is against evildoers' (Ps. 34.15-16). Rather than humbling themselves and pursuing God's desires, they were pursuing their own selfish desires. Rather than afflicting themselves as an outward sign of inward mourning, they fought among themselves and oppressed the weak.

Apparently, the Israelites had followed the proper liturgy in their fasting – afflicting themselves, bowing down, lying in sackcloth and ashes – but the Lord asks, 'Is this the kind of fast that pleases me?'

(Isa. 58.5).[27] He does not wait for a response but supplies his own answer to the question:

> Is this not the fast that I have chosen,
> To loosen the bonds of wickedness,
> To undo the bands of the yoke,
> And to let the oppressed go free,
> And break every yoke?
>
> Is it not to divide your bread with the hungry,
> And bring the homeless poor into the house;
> When you see the naked, to cover him …
> (Isa. 58.6-7).

The fast that pleases God will cause those in power to release their wicked and oppressive grip on the weak. The fast that pleases God will include radical hospitality: those who prosper will share with the hungry, provide shelter for the homeless, and give clothing to the naked.[28] Fasting pleases God only when it is accompanied by the practice of justice and righteousness.[29] 'Selfishness, oppression, and contentiousness contradict justice, righteousness, and peace'.[30] It is not surprising that Jesus would approach religious practices in a similar spirit. Instructing those who bring sacrifices to the temple, Jesus says, 'if you are offering your gift at the altar, and there remember that your brother has something against you, then leave your gift there before the altar and go; first be reconciled to your brother, and then come and offer your gift' (Mt. 5.23-24).

Isaiah reminds the Israelites that many of their people are genuinely afflicted (v. 10), and in need of help. However, those who are fasting are not concerned about their neighbors but are concerned only about themselves. They are fasting to promote themselves and to meet their own needs. In fact, while they are fasting, they are taking advantage of others; they are paying no attention to the needs

---

[27] 'The passage never actually attacks the sincerity of Israel's fasting' (Lambert, 'Fasting as a Penitential Rite: A Biblical Phenomenon?', p. 501).

[28] Cf. Charles M. Murphy, *The Spirituality of Fasting: Rediscovering a Christian Practice* (Notre Dame, IN: Ave Maria Press, 2010), pp. 68-73; Baab, *Fasting*, p. 43-44.

[29] Cf. John Wesley, *The Journal of the Rev. John Wesley* (8 vols.; London: Robert Culley, Charles H. Kelly, 1909-1916), III, pp. 116-17; and Wesley, 'Upon Our Lord's Sermon on the Mount: Discourse Seven', p. 318.

[30] McKnight, *Fasting*, p. 103.

of those around them. Therefore, God declares, 'I do not respond to that kind of fasting'.

Isaiah insists that the motives for fasting are important.[31] Without proper motives, fasting is a meaningless ritual. The behavior of the person fasting is more important than the fast itself. Fasting is not an end in itself, and it does not earn God's favor or guarantee God's blessing. Fasting does not excuse unrighteous behavior, and it does not replace other ethical demands. It is not equivalent to obedience, and it is not a substitute for acting righteously, justly, and lovingly toward one's neighbor.

2. The Unfaithful – Jeremiah 14.10-12

In the days of the prophet Jeremiah, the land of Israel suffered a great drought. The water cisterns were empty; the ground was cracked; the crops were drying up; and even the livestock was dying. Therefore, the people mourned and cried out to the Lord for help, but the Lord reminded them of their sins:

> Thus says the LORD to this people, 'Even so they have loved to wander; they have not kept their feet in check'. Therefore the LORD does not accept them; now he will remember their iniquity and call their sins to account. So the LORD said to me, 'Do not pray for the welfare of this people. When they fast, I will not listen to their cry; and when they offer burnt offering and grain offering, I will not accept them. Rather I will make an end of them by the sword, famine, and pestilence' (Jer. 14.10-12).

Jeremiah's prophecy resembles Isaiah 58 in many ways. The people were calling upon the Lord, but he was unwilling to hear their prayers. Idolatry was rampant, and God had threatened judgment. However, while Isaiah emphasized Israel's sins of injustice and selfishness (failure to love one's neighbor), Jeremiah stressed Israel's sin of idolatry (failure to love God). Therefore, Jeremiah says of the Israelites, 'they have loved to wander' (v. 10). Without a complete return to God, fasting would do them no good.[32] They could fast, they could pray, they could offer sacrifices, but they still have their idols. They must give up those idols before the Lord would honor their fasting and prayer. John Wesley summarizes Israel's condition:

---

[31] Cf. Hickey, *The Power of Prayer and Fasting*, p. 100.
[32] Lambert, 'Fasting as a Penitential Rite: A Biblical Phenomenon?', p. 499.

'God continually declared to those formal worshippers, that their outside religion was but vain'.³³

3. Fasting but not Repenting – Jeremiah 36.6-9

Israel's idolatry in the days of Jeremiah led not only to a drought in the land but also to threats from the Babylonians. Because of the imminent danger of Babylonian invasion, the people of Israel proclaimed a fast in the ninth month; and Jeremiah recognized that the fast day would be a fitting opportunity for his prophecy to be heard. However, Jeremiah was prevented from entering the house of God, so he sent his scribe Baruch to deliver the message:

> Go and read ... the words of the LORD to the people in the LORD's house on a fast day ... Perhaps their supplication will come before the LORD, and everyone will turn from his evil way, for great is the anger and the wrath that the LORD has pronounced against this people ... Now it came about ... that all the people in Jerusalem and all the people who came from the cities of Judah to Jerusalem proclaimed a fast before the LORD. Then Baruch read from the book the words of Jeremiah in the house of the LORD (Jer. 36.6-10).

This particular fast day was not the Day of Atonement (which came in the seventh month); instead, it was a fast that was called in response to impending Babylonian crisis. The fast presented Jeremiah with at least two good reasons for presenting his message. First, the crowds at the temple would be much larger than usual. People came in from all over Judah to join together in prayer and fasting. Second, inasmuch as the Jews recognized fasting as an aid to repentance, the hearers might be more inclined on a fast day to listen and receive Jeremiah's call to repentance.

While we learn from this text that the Jews practiced national fasting in times of crises, we are disappointed to learn that they refused to accept Jeremiah's message. When Jeremiah's scroll reached king Jehoiakim, he cut it into pieces and burned it in his firepot. Given Jehoiakim's actions, I would suggest that although fasting is a

---

³³ John Wesley, *The Works of the Rev. John Wesley* (14 vols.; London: Wesleyan-Methodist Book-Room, 1872), VIII, p. 142.

helpful accompaniment to repentance, it does not always generate it.[34]

4. Proclaim a Fast! – Joel 1-2

The prophet Joel describes a time of great loss and devastation, which he attributes to God's judgment. Therefore, he summons the people of Israel to repent in hope that God will forgive and restore favor to Israel. In light of Israel's distress, Joel calls for a fast. He says, 'Lament, O priests; wail, O ministers of the altar! ... Consecrate a fast; proclaim a solemn assembly. Gather the elders and all the inhabitants of the land to the house of the LORD your God and cry out to the LORD' (Joel 1.13-14). He continues with a more explicit demand for repentance, which he states in terms of 'returning' (שׁוּב) to the Lord:

> Yet even now, declares the LORD, 'Return to me with all your heart, and with fasting, weeping, and mourning; and rend your heart and not your garments'. Now return to the LORD your God, for he is gracious and compassionate, slow to anger, abounding in lovingkindness, and relenting of evil. Who knows whether he will turn (שׁוּב) and relent, and leave a blessing behind him ...? Blow a trumpet in Zion; consecrate a fast; proclaim a solemn assembly; gather the people ... Let the priests, the LORD's ministers, weep between the porch and the altar, and let them say, 'Spare your people, O LORD ...' Then the LORD will be zealous for his land, and will have pity on his people (Joel 2.12-18).

Here, Joel includes fasting as one of the aids to repentance, along with weeping, mourning, and prayers for divine mercy. Fasting, however, does not accomplish anything apart from their returning (שׁוּב) to the Lord and their prayers for grace. Like weeping, fasting is a sign of grief's gravity and sorrow's sincerity. For Israel, it is

---

[34] We will not be looking at Ezek. 24.16-17, which relates to the death of Ezekiel's wife. Although at first glance the words, 'do not eat the bread of men', might seem to suggest fasting, the wording and the context indicate otherwise. Ezekiel is told that he must not demonstrate any outward sign of mourning; and, since fasting is a part of mourning, it would be forbidden. The 'bread of men' refers to food that is brought to a mourner by friends and neighbors. Ezekiel, therefore, must eat normally, as if the death of his wife had not occurred.

an outward expression of the inward pain that is caused by their sin and their unfaithfulness to God.

As a means of spiritual renewal, fasting can open the door to a variety of divine blessings. In the book of Joel, the culmination of God's beneficent response to fasting is his gift of the Holy Spirit.[35] The LORD says, 'and it will happen after this that I will pour out my Spirit upon everyone' (Joel 2.28).[36] The words, 'after this', refer to all that had occurred earlier in the book, which includes Israel's fasting and repentance. Therefore, as Larry McQueen observes, 'The promise of the pouring out of Yahweh's spirit comes as a response to the people's lamentation and repentance'.[37] In light of Joel, the Pentecostal practice of fasting in preparation for Spirit baptism is not surprising.[38]

5. Judgment Averted – Jonah 3.5

On account of the great wickedness of the Assyrian city of Ninevah, God sent Jonah to proclaim judgment against it: 'Yet forty days and Ninevah will be overturned' (Jon. 3.4). Quite unexpectedly, the people of Ninevah believed Jonah's preaching; and, consequently, they repented of their evil and sought to change God's verdict against them.

> So the people of Nineveh believed in God; and they called a fast ... When the word reached the king of Nineveh, he arose from his throne, laid aside his robe from him, covered himself with sackcloth, and sat on the ashes. And he issued a proclamation ... 'Do not let man, beast, herd, or flock taste a thing. Do not let them eat or drink water. But both man and beast must be covered with sackcloth; and let men call on God earnestly that each

---

[35] See Raymond B. Dillard, 'Joel', in T.E. McComiskey (ed.) *The Minor Prophets: An Exegetical and Expository Commentary – Volume 1: Hosea, Joel, and Amos* (Grand Rapids, MI: Baker, 1992), pp. 239-314 (p. 294). Cf. Franklin, *Fasting*, pp. 47-48.

[36] Versification of the Old Testament texts follows the English version.

[37] Larry R. McQueen, *Joel and the Spirit: The Cry of a Prophetic Hermeneutic* (Cleveland, TN: CPT Press, 2009), p. 31. Cf. the use of Joel by early Pentecostal minister A.H. Post, *Apostolic Faith* 1.5 (Jan. 1907), p. 4. The connection between fasting and the Spirit's outpouring is also noted by Wesley, 'Upon Our Lord's Sermon on the Mount: Discourse Seven', pp. 312-13.

[38] It should be noted that the LXX, which is cited in Acts 2, uses the words, 'in the last days' instead of 'after this'; a point which relates to the Pentecostal movement's view of itself as a last days restoration movement that is heir to the eschatological promise of Joel.

may turn (שׁוּב) from his wicked way and from the violence which is in his hands. Who knows, God may turn and relent, and withdraw his burning anger so that we shall not perish?' When God saw their deeds, that they turned from their wicked way, then God relented concerning the calamity which he had declared he would bring upon them (Jon. 3.5-10).

When all of the people in Ninevah fasted and repented, God changed his mind. The outward sign of fasting was imposed even upon all the animals. The people, however, in addition to their fasting, 'believed in God', called on God, and 'repented' (שׁוּב) of their wickedness and violence. Therefore, God's mercy was evoked, and Ninevah was spared. Here as in the earlier texts, fasting does not accomplish repentance, rather it accompanies repentance as an outward expression of sorrow and grief over sin.

6. Memorial Fasting – Zechariah 7-8

Zechariah is an important text because it provides insight into the fasting practices of post-exilic Judaism. By the time of Zechariah, the Jews had established four other fast days in addition to the Day of Atonement, which was the one fast required by the Law of Moses. These four new fasts were days of mourning over the calamities that led up to the exile.

Zechariah reports that the people of Bethel sent representatives to speak to the priests and to the prophets and to receive direction from the Lord regarding the new fast days. They asked if they should continue to observe the four new fasts:

> Should I weep and fast in the fifth month, as I have done for so many years? Then the word of the LORD of hosts came to me; 'Say to all the people of the land and the priests, "When you fasted and lamented in the fifth month and in the seventh, for these seventy years, did you truly fast for me – for me?"' (Zech. 7.2-6).

The tenth day of the fifth month was a fast day because it was the anniversary of the destruction of the temple (Jer. 52.12-14). On the third day of the seventh month they observed a fast for the murder of the Judean governor Gedaliah, and the dispersion of the remnant of the people which were with him (see Jer. 41.1, and 2 Kgs 25.25). Now that the Jews had returned to Judah, and they were in the process of rebuilding the temple, they asked, 'Should the fast be continued, now that the temple is being rebuilt?'

When the men of Bethel questioned the validity of their fasts, the Lord did not answer as expected. Instead of telling them whether or not they should continue the fasts, the Lord questioned their motives. They had practiced these annual fasts for seventy years, but had they fasted for God's glory? Quite emphatically, the Lord asks, 'did you truly fast for me – for me?'[39]

The Lord goes on to say, 'And when you eat and drink, do you not eat and drink for yourselves?' (Zech. 7.6). That is, it does not seem to matter whether they are eating or fasting, their motives have been selfish. Their fasts were an expression of their self-pity, but not directed to God as a real and genuine prayer.

At this point, the Lord reminds them of his pre-exilic warnings through the earlier prophets (which would include Hosea, Amos, Isaiah, Micah, and Jeremiah). The prophets had said to Israel, 'Render honest judgments, show kindness and mercy each to his brother. Do not oppress the widow, the fatherless, the immigrant, or the poor; and let none of you devise evil against his brother in your heart' (Zech. 7.9-10). Israel, however, had disregarded the Spirit's warnings; therefore, the Lord sent the people into exile, scattering them among the nations and making Judah a desolation (7.13-14). Just because God had been gracious enough to restore Israel to the land of Judah, it did not mean that his demands for righteousness were invalid. The pre-exilic covenantal requirements continued to be just as important in post-exilic life. Therefore, the love of one's neighbor as expressed in generosity, justice, and kindness was more important than fasting.[40] If the Jews fasted but did not repent of their ways and did not obey God's commands, their fasting would be ineffectual.

After rebuking the Judahites for their impure motives in fasting, the Lord returns to their original question, 'Should we fast?' His answer is prefixed by a lengthy description of God's faithfulness and stubborn commitment to Israel's well-being (8.1-18), in which he declares 'great jealousy' for his people (v. 2). He promises to 'return to Zion' and 'dwell in the midst of Jerusalem' (v. 3). The land

---

[39] The Hebrew text reads, הצום צמתני אני. Cf. Wallis, *God's Chosen Fast*, pp. 39-43.

[40] Cf. Ryan, *The Sacred Art of Fasting*, pp. 133-40.

will prosper, and the exiles will come home and dwell in peace, safety, and plenty. The temple will be rebuilt, and all enemies will be punished. The Lord 'will do good to Jerusalem and to the house of Judah' (Zech. 8.15).

Finally, the Lord speaks to the question about fasting: 'Thus saith the Lord of hosts; The fast of the fourth month, and the fast of the fifth, and the fast of the seventh, and the fast of the tenth, shall become joy and gladness and cheerful feasts for the house of Judah' (8.19). The answer, therefore, is 'No, you should not fast on these days any longer. Your fast days shall become feast days'.

The fast of the tenth month was a fast day commemorating the beginning of Nebuchadnezzar's siege of Jerusalem, and the fast of the fourth month commemorated his breaking down of the walls of Jerusalem and his taking of the city. However, in light of the Lord's promise to rebuild the temple and to restore Judah, these fast days that commemorate the judgment of God will be turned to days of rejoicing.[41] Zechariah seems to suggest, therefore, that the memory of suffering in the past is not a legitimate reason for fasting in the present. The biblical approach to fasting seems to be focused on present crises and/or future concerns.

D. Fasting in the Writings

1. Fasting on Behalf of Enemies – Psalms 35.13

Psalm 35 is a song of lament in which the psalmist prays for deliverance from his enemies. The psalm presents the enemies as ruthless, pitiless, brutal, and slanderous antagonists. They 'fight' against the writer of the psalm (v. 1). They 'devise evil' against him (v. 4) and set traps for him (v. 7). They gnash at him with their teeth (v.

---

[41] Another interpretation of God's answer (the interpretation adopted by Judaism) is that these fast days should continue, but they should be days of rejoicing instead of mourning. I cannot accept such an interpretation because, as all of Scripture demonstrates, fasting and rejoicing are mutually exclusive. That is why the Lord said, 'The fasts shall become ... cheerful feasts'. The Hebrew combination of the verb 'to be' (היה) followed by the preposition 'to' (ל) indicates a changing from one thing to another, hence the translation 'shall become' rather than 'shall be'. The fast day changes to a feast day, because one cannot fast and feast at the same time. Cf. Schmemann, who observes that the Eucharist as a 'Feast of the Church' is 'incompatible' with fasting (*Introduction to Liturgical Theology*, p. 215). Therefore, in the Orthodox Church, the Eucharist is never observed in the midst of a fast.

16) and 'devise deceitful words', hoping to bring him to destruction (v. 20). What is even more troubling is that the psalmist had treated them with kindness in the past, but they are now repaying him with evil:

> Malicious witnesses rise up;
> They ask me of things that I do not know.
> They repay me evil for good,
> To the bereavement of my soul.
> But as for me, when they were sick,
> My clothing was sackcloth;
> I afflicted myself with fasting;
> And my prayer kept returning to my bosom.
> I went about as though it were my friend or brother;
> I bowed down mourning,
> As one who sorrows for a mother (Ps. 35.11-14).

David recalls that, when his enemies were sick, he had fasted and prayed for their healing.[42] David had demonstrated a deep commitment to their good. John Goldingay remarks, 'in this situation, eating is too much of a frivolity. The psalm assumes that merely to feel sadness is not enough; because we are physical creatures and not just minds and spirits, it would be odd not to express sorrow in (e.g.) abstention from food and thus afflicting one's spirit or one's self.'[43] David had responded to his opponents' crisis as if they were his friends or brothers, and he had fasted and prayed as he would have done for his own mother.[44] These enemies, however, have disregarded David's kindness.

The fasting of David for his enemies anticipates Jesus' command: 'Love your enemies, and pray for those who persecute you' (Mt. 5.44). Moreover, his fasting foreshadows the teaching of the

---

[42] The authorship of Psalm 35 is not certain, but the superscription attributes the psalm to David.

[43] John Goldingay, *Psalms* (Baker Commentary on the Old Testament Wisdom and Psalms; 3 vols.; Grand Rapids, MI: Baker Academic, 2006), I, p. 496.

[44] The verb forms suggest that the psalmist's fasting for them had occurred at some time in the past, before the events for which he complains here. See Goldingay, *Psalms*, I, pp. 496-97. Samuel L. Terrien, *The Psalms: Strophic Structure and Theological Commentary* (Eerdmans Critical Commentary; Grand Rapids, MI: Eerdmans, 2003), p. 310, even asserts that these enemies had at one time been the psalmist's friends. However, the phrasing, 'like friends', suggests otherwise.

early Christian document that we call the *Didache*: 'pray for your enemies, and fast on behalf of those who persecute you' (1.3).

2. Hungry for God – Psalms 42.3

Psalms 42 and 43 should be read together[45] as a lament that expresses the psalmist's longing to return to the house of God where the he can enjoy God's presence once again.

> As the deer pants for the water brooks,
> So my soul pants for you, O God.
> My soul thirsts for God, for the living God;
> When shall I come and appear before God?
> My tears have been my food day and night,
> While they say to me all day long, Where is your God?
> (Ps. 42.1-3).

The psalmist is hungry and thirsty for the presence of God. In fact, he is so consumed with his desire to 'come and appear before God', that he has lost his appetite. His fasting is generated by his intense affection for God and for God's presence. Instead of eating, he weeps; but his 'salty tears do not bring satisfaction, only a greater thirst for God'.[46] The fasting continues 'day and night' as a manifestation of urgent longing. 'Instead of eating, all the suppliant does is cry'.[47] The absence of God is a spiritual crisis for the psalmist, and he responds to that crisis with fasting.

3. Fasting and Waiting – Psalms 69.10

The psalmist is confronted with a desperate situation, symbolized in terms of sinking in deep mire and drowning in a flood (vv. 1-2). Apparently, he is accused falsely by hateful enemies (v. 4), who seek to shame him and destroy him. Therefore, the psalmist sets his complaint before the Lord. He has wept until he can hardly weep any more (v. 3). His prayers, his weeping, and his mourning are all a

---

[45] James Luther Mays, *Psalms* (Interpretation; Louisville, KY: John Knox Press, 1994), p. 173; and Terrien, *The Psalms*, p. 350, argue that Psalms 42 and 43 were originally a single psalm. However, Goldingay, *Psalms*, suggests that Psalm 43 may have been 'composed to accompany' Psalm 42 (II, p. 21). In either case, the two psalms should be read together.

[46] Stephen J. Lennox, *Psalms: A Bible Commentary in the Wesleyan Tradition* (Indianapolis, IN: Wesleyan Pub. House, 1999), p. 133.

[47] Goldingay, *Psalms*, II, p. 24.

part of 'waiting' upon God (v. 3), but even his seeking after God has brought criticism upon him:

> Because a passion for your house has consumed me,
> And the reproaches of those who reproach you
> have fallen on me.
> When I wept and fasted,
> It turned into reproach for me.
> When I made sackcloth my clothing,
> I became a byword to them.
> Those who sit in the gate talk about me,
> And I am the song of the drunkards.
> As for me, my prayer is to you, O LORD,
> At a favorable moment.
> O God, in your abundant faithfulness,
> answer me with your sure deliverance (Ps. 69.9-13).

Although the psalmist is suffering, he identifies the central point of contention as something outside himself. He is zealous for the house of God, and he has opposed those who 'reproach' God (v. 9). Therefore, his fasting and prayer is not aimed at personal needs. Instead, he fasts for the honor of God.[48] The psalmist responds to the enemy's attacks by praying, fasting, weeping, and wearing sackcloth (a sign of mourning); however, even his pious actions bring ridicule down upon him. His enemies are so ruthless that they revile him, talk about him, and write songs of mockery about him.

The psalmist reacts to the crisis in proper fashion, and even though his enemies, his friends, and even his family do not appreciate his spirituality, his focus continues to be upon God. He says, 'My prayer is to you, O LORD' (v. 13). We may learn from the psalmist's experience that our fasting and prayer may not always be accepted by everyone. However, if our fasting is directed toward the Lord, he will hear our cries and answer us according to his faithful love (v. 13).

4. Fasting and Misery – Psalms 102.4

Psalm 102 is the prayer of someone whose strength is failing because of ongoing distress. The psalmist is suffering physically from the long period of fasting:

---

[48] See Goldingay, *Psalms*, II, p. 344.

> Hear my prayer, O LORD; let my cry come to you.
> Do not hide your face from me in the day of my distress;
>   Incline your ear to me;
>   In the day when I call answer me quickly.
> For my days pass away like smoke,
>   And my bones have been scorched like a hearth.
> My heart has been stricken and withered like grass,
>   Indeed, I forget to eat my bread (Ps. 102.1-4).

The crisis is so acute that the psalmist forgets to eat. Worries, anxieties, and antagonists consume every waking moment. The psalmist goes on to say, 'For I eat ashes like bread, and mingle tears with my drink, because of your indignation and anger; for you have lifted me up and thrown me aside' (Ps. 102.9-10). Ashes represent mourning and grief; and apparently, they get into the mouth while the psalmist is praying.

Although the outlook is bleak, the psalm concludes with statements of hope, because the Lord is 'enthroned forever' (v. 12) and will 'regard the prayer of the destitute' (v. 17). Even while suffering, the psalmist has confidence that the Lord will 'hear the groans of prisoners' and will 'set free those who were doomed to die' (v. 20).[49]

5. Fasting and Weakness – Psalms 109.24

Once again, David[50] pleads for deliverance from the accusations of his enemies who, out of hatred, lie and attack him even while he prays for them (vv. 2-4).

> For I am poor and needy,
>   And my heart is pierced within me.
> I am gone like a shadow at evening;
>   I am shaken off like a locust.
> My knees are weak through fasting;
>   My body has become gaunt.
> I am an object of scorn to my accusers;

---

[49] We will not discuss Ps. 107.18, which speaks about people who have become so ill that they 'loathe' any kind of food. Abstinence on account of illness is not fasting as we have defined the term. Terrien likens their illness to *anorexia nervosa* (*Psalms*, p. 739), but there are many other kinds of illness that also produce a loss of appetite and/or nausea.

[50] The authorship of Psalm 109 is not certain, but the superscription attributes the psalm to David.

When they see me, they shake their heads.
Help me, O LORD my God!
Save me according to your steadfast love (Ps. 109.22-26).

David has fasted so long that his strength is gone. He has become 'gaunt', and people 'shake their heads' at him. He prays that the curses hurled at him from his enemies will be turned back upon them, but he refuses to take vengeance into his own hands. He prays, 'Let them know that this is your hand; you, O LORD have done it' (v. 27). David's fasting is generated by a crisis caused by hateful adversaries, but his goal in fasting is that God will be honored and glorified. Furthermore, David does not reckon his fasting to be efficacious of itself; his hope finds its justification in the character of God – God's 'steadfast love' (vv. 21, 26).

6. Spiritual Priorities – Job 23.10-12

One day Job was prosperous, happy, and surrounded by family and friends; but the next day he was destitute, miserable, and alienated because of his troubles. His 'comforters' interrogated him in order to discover what sin he must have committed to bring his calamities upon him. As they debated the question, the friends argued that Job's troubles must have been caused by his disregard for God's law, while Job continued to defend his integrity.

> But he knows the way that I take:
> When he has tested me, I will come forth as gold.
> My foot has held fast to his steps,
> I have kept his way, and have not turned aside.
> I have not departed from the commandment of his lips;
> I have treasured the words of his mouth
> more than my daily portion[51] (Job 23.10-12).

Job was confident that his righteousness would be vindicated eventually. He insisted that he had always walked in God's 'way' and acted in accord with God's commandments. Furthermore, Job in-

---

[51] Fasting is not clearly indicated here, and the word 'food' is not in the Hebrew text; however, the word חק ('something prescribed') can mean a 'proper portion of food' according to Ludwig Köhler and Walter Baumgartner, *The Hebrew and Aramaic Lexicon of the Old Testament* (2 vols.; Leiden: Brill, Study edn, 2001), I, p. 114. Cf. Francis Brown *et al.*, *The New Brown, Driver, Briggs, Gesenius Hebrew and English Lexicon: With an Appendix Containing the Biblical Aramaic* (trans. Edward Robinson; Peabody, MA: Hendrickson, 1979), p. 349.

sisted that he had 'treasured' spiritual things more than material goods and pleasures. To Job, the word of God was more valuable than a daily portion of food.[52] While Job's confession does not state categorically that he fasted, it does stand in agreement with the spirit of Deut. 8.3, which states, 'one does not live by bread alone, but by every word that comes from the mouth of the LORD'.

7. Life and Death Fasting – Esther 4.3, 16; 9.31

The setting for the book of Esther is the post-exilic Persian empire. The people of Judah had been exiled to Babylon, and many of them remained there even after Zerubbabel led a large contingent back to Judah in the days of Cyrus, king of Persia. The Jews in Persia were given a good deal of liberty, but they continued to practice Judaism and maintain their ethnic identity.

Esther's parents had died, and her cousin Mordecai had adopted her as his own daughter. When Esther came of age, she was chosen by King Ahasuerus to be his queen. In the mean time, Mordecai found himself in trouble when he refused to bow down to the Persian official, Haman. When Haman learned that Mordecai was a Jew, he plotted to have all of the Jews killed, and a decree was written and disseminated to every province, ordering the death of all the Jews. When the Jews heard the decree, they were terrified. 'In every province, wherever the king's command and his decree came, there was great mourning among the Jews, with fasting and weeping and lamenting, and most of them lay in sackcloth and ashes' (Est. 4.3).

Mordecai warned Esther of Haman's plot, and she determined that she would approach the king and seek to have the decree reversed, but to approach the king uninvited would normally result in a death sentence. Therefore, Esther proclaimed a fast for all the Jews:

> Then Esther said in reply to Mordecai, 'Go, gather all the Jews to be found in Susa, and hold a fast on my behalf, and neither eat nor drink for three days, night or day. I and my maids will also fast as you do. After that I will go to the king, though it is against the law; and if I perish, I perish' (Est. 4.15-16).

---

[52] Cf. Jesus' statement, 'My food is to do the will of him who sent me' (Jn 4.34).

Mordecai did as Esther requested, and all the people fasted both food and water for three days and three nights. Consequently, when Esther came before the king, he listened to all that she had to say, and the Jews were saved. Haman, who had conspired to kill the Jews, was hanged on the same gallows that he had prepared for Mordecai's execution. In memory of God's miraculous deliverance of the Jewish people, the annual days of Purim were established. From that day until now, the Jews have fasted on the day before Purim:[53]

> Letters were sent wishing peace and security to all the Jews, to the one hundred twenty-seven provinces of the kingdom of Ahasuerus, and giving orders that these days of Purim should be observed at their appointed times, as the Jew Mordecai and Queen Esther enjoined on the Jews, just as they had laid down for themselves and for their descendants regulations concerning their fasts and their lamentations (Est. 9.30-31).

The fast of Esther and the Jews was an attempt to ameliorate a crisis in which their lives were threatened. Planning and preparation for Esther's mission were not sufficient to meet the threat. Even prayer was not sufficient under these urgent conditions – they must fast. Furthermore, their fasting was of the most radical kind; they abstained from all food and drink for a period of three days. Clearly, their fast was not for the purpose of spiritual formation, growth in grace, self-denial, sanctification, or any other transformative purpose. Their fast was intended to get God's attention so that God might intervene and avert the crisis. Their fasting was a matter of life and death. God heard their prayers and worked behind the scenes to give favor to Esther and to orchestrate a reversal of the circumstances.

8. King Darius Fasts for Daniel – Daniel 6.18-20

Daniel faced a threat that was similar to Esther's, but it was only Daniel's life that was in danger. Knowing that Daniel prayed to his God daily, his enemies convinced King Darius to issue a decree forbidding any prayer that was not directed toward Darius. As we would expect, Daniel disobeyed the command and continued to

---

[53] It should be noted that the fast of Purim was commanded by Esther, not by the Lord.

pray to the Lord three times a day. He was arrested, and the king, although he approved of Daniel, was required by his own decree to throw Daniel into the den of lions. Darius, however, was not pleased with the scenario:

> Then the king went to his palace and spent the night fasting; no food was brought to him, and sleep fled from him. Then, at daybreak, the king got up and hurried to the den of lions. When he came near the den where Daniel was, he cried out anxiously to Daniel, 'O Daniel, servant of the living God, has your God whom you faithfully serve been able to deliver you from the lions?' Daniel then said to the king, 'O king, live forever! My God sent his angel and shut the lions' mouths so that they would not harm me' (Dan. 6.18-22).

Darius, grieving over Daniel's punishment, spent the night fasting. Although Darius was not a Jew, he knew that Daniel was a just man who should not have been thrown to the lions. Therefore, he was motivated by the urgency of the crisis to fast for Daniel's safety. Daniel was saved; and his enemies were executed because of their treachery.

9. Fasting and Confession – Daniel 9.3

While reading the prophecies of Jeremiah, Daniel was made aware of two important details. First, he learned that the Jews' exile in Babylon should last for seventy years (Dan. 9.2; Jer. 25.8-14). Second, he observed that the reason for the exile was the Jews' refusal to heed the warnings and calls to repentance that had been issued by the earlier prophets (Dan. 9.4-6, 10). Because of their unfaithfulness to the covenant, they had brought upon themselves the calamity of the exile, just as it had been predicted in the law of Moses (Dan. 9.13; Deut. 28.49-68). Therefore, Daniel, perhaps realizing that the seventy years was near completion, began to fast and pray and confess to God the sins of his people:

> Then I turned to the LORD God, to seek an answer by prayer and supplication with fasting and sackcloth and ashes. I prayed to the LORD my God and made confession, saying, 'Ah, LORD, great and awesome God, keeping covenant and steadfast love with those who love you and keep your commandments, we have sinned and done wrong, acted wickedly and rebelled, turn-

ing aside from your commandments and ordinances. We have not listened to your servants the prophets, who spoke in your name to our kings, our princes, and our ancestors, and to all the people of the land' (Dan. 9.3-6).

Daniel's approach to God included five components: (1) prayer, which is a general term that denotes any kind of appeal to God; (2) supplication, which is a plea for grace; (3) fasting; (4) wearing of sackcloth; and (5) putting ashes on the head. The combination of fasting, sackcloth, and ashes was the normal sign of deep sorrow of any kind, such as mourning, grief, or repentance.

The content of the prayer reveals that Daniel's objective was that his people might be forgiven for their rebellion against the law of God. He begins his prayer with a statement of confidence in God's covenant faithfulness; then he proceeds to offer a detailed confession of sins, expressed in the plural 'we'. In sixteen verses, Daniel uses the plural forms 'we', 'us', and 'our' more than twenty-five times.[54] Daniel repents on behalf of all the Jews who had disobeyed God's commandments, sinned against God's law, disregarded God's prophets, and trampled upon God's covenant. In order to signify the urgency and seriousness of his confession, Daniel fasted along with his prayer.

The length of Daniel's fast is not recorded, but while he continued in prayer and fasting, the angel Gabriel came to him with a message from God. Surprisingly, the message was not a simple declaration of forgiveness or restoration; rather, it was a mysterious prediction: 'Seventy weeks are decreed for your people and your holy city: to stop the transgression, to put an end to sin, and to atone for iniquity, to bring in everlasting righteousness, to seal both vision and prophet, and to anoint a most holy place' (Dan. 9.24). Daniel's fasting resulted in a visit from God's messenger and a prophecy regarding God's remedy for Israel's sin. There is no indication that Daniel fasted with the intent of receiving a visionary experience,[55] but the fast brought Daniel to a place of humility and

---

[54] The use of the plural 'reflects the features of the corporate prayer of the Psalter'. John Goldingay, *Daniel* (Word Biblical Commentary; Dallas, TX: Word Books, 1989), p. 233. Goldingay explains that the communal prayer of confession was 'a postexilic phenomenon' (p. 235).

[55] The statement by Andrew E. Hill, 'Daniel', in T. Longman and D.E. Garland (eds.), *The Expositor's Bible Commentary* (Grand Rapids, MI: Zondervan,

receptivity. Nowhere in Scripture are we commanded to seek after revelations or visions; nevertheless, Pentecostal evangelist Franklin Hall is correct in his affirmation, 'Yes, prophecies and great revelations are the results of fasting and prayer'.[56]

10. The Daniel Fast – Daniel 10.2-3

About three years after his vision of chapter nine, Daniel designated a time of prayer and seeking the Lord in order to 'gain understanding' and to 'humble' himself before the Lord (Dan. 10.12). When he had prayed for three weeks, he received another vision from the Lord:

> In the third year of King Cyrus of Persia a word was revealed to Daniel, who was named Belteshazzar. The word was true, and it concerned a great conflict. He understood the word, having received understanding in the vision. At that time I, Daniel, had been mourning for three weeks. I had eaten no rich food, no meat or wine had entered my mouth, and I had not anointed myself at all, for three full weeks (Dan. 10.1-3).

Daniel describes his period of eating a limited diet as a time of 'mourning' (אבל), which is a sorrowful response to a death, a tragedy, bad news, or awareness of a personal spiritual need. Daniel probably abstained in response to the desperate conditions in Jerusalem, his homeland, as reported Neh. 1.4.[57]

In order to underline the gravity of his request for understanding and the seriousness of his attempt to humble himself, Daniel restricted his diet and he did not anoint himself with fragrant oil (which symbolized joy). He ate no 'rich food, no meat or wine'. By rich food, Daniel probably refers to the 'royal fare' to which he was entitled as a member of the king's court.[58] The dating of his fast would mean that he also avoided the rich foods that would have been part of the Feast of Unleavened Bread. The text does not reveal why Daniel did not fast from all food as he had done earlier. It

---

2008), that fasting was somehow a 'preparation' for 'receiving a revelation from God' (p. 162) is wrongheaded. People who fast may receive revelations, but nowhere in the Bible does anyone fast for the purpose of receiving a revelatory or visionary experience.

[56] Franklin Hall, *The Fasting Prayer* (San Diego, CA: Franklin Hall, 1947), p. 108. Cf. Wallis, *God's Chosen Fast*, p. 71-76.

[57] Goldingay, *Daniel*, p. 290.

[58] Cf. Hill, 'Daniel', p. 179.

should be noted that neither the word 'fast' nor its synonym ('to afflict oneself') is found in Daniel 10; therefore, Daniel's practice should properly be described as abstinence rather than fasting.

Daniel's experience suggests that if one is unable to practice normal fasting, abstinence from certain rich foods can be beneficial.[59] It can add urgency to prayers and depth to spiritual passion. Abstinence can strengthen humility and help to direct prayer toward God.[60]

11. Seeking God for the Right Way – Ezra 8.21-23

Because of Israel's continuing idolatry, the Lord judged them and allowed them to be defeated by the Babylonians, who carried the Israelites into exile in Babylon. The Babylonian empire was eventually conquered by the Persian empire, and God moved upon the heart of the Persian king Cyrus to allow the Israelites to return to Judah. There they would rebuild the city of Jerusalem along with the temple of the Lord (Ezra 1.1-11).

The first group of about 42,000 exiles to return to Judah was led by Zerubbabel, who became governor, and by Joshua, who became high priest. When they arrived in Jerusalem, they reconstructed the altar on the temple mount, and they laid the foundation for the rebuilding of the temple itself. After a time, the new temple was completed, and the people celebrated Passover as they had done in the past (Ezra 6.19).

Subsequent to the rebuilding of the temple, another group of exiles returned to Judah under the leadership of Ezra the scribe. Regarding Ezra, we read that 'the good hand of his God was upon him. For Ezra had set his heart to study the law of the LORD and to practice it, and to teach the statutes and ordinances in Israel' (Ezra 7.9-10). Artaxerxes, the new king of Persia issued a decree of support for Ezra's return to Judah.

Ezra gathered about 5,000 exiles and encamped at the river of Ahava. In preparation for the journey, Ezra called upon the people to fast and pray that God would guide them on their journey back to Jerusalem:

---

[59] See Wallis, *God's Chosen Fast*, pp. 21-24.
[60] The New Testament exemplar for the partial fast is John the Baptist, who ate 'locusts and wild honey' (Mt. 3.4). It is said as well that John's disciples fasted (Mt. 9.14; Mk 2.18; Lk. 5.33).

I proclaimed a fast there, at the river Ahava, that we might afflict ourselves before our God, to seek of him a right way for ourselves, our children, and all our possessions. For I was ashamed to request from the king troops and horsemen to protect us from the enemy on the way, because we had said to the king, The hand of our God is favorably disposed to all those who seek him, but his power and his anger are against all those who forsake him. So we fasted and sought our God concerning this, and he listened to our entreaty ... Then we journeyed from the river Ahava on the twelfth of the first month to go to Jerusalem; and the hand of our God was upon us, and he delivered us from the hand of the enemy and the ambushes by the way (Ezra 8.21-31).

Ezra's prayer for guidance is ultimately a request for safety, but on their journey through the desert, safety was connected to their route and the timing of their movements from one encampment to another. Having no military escort, Ezra's party depended upon the Lord's guidance as the means of avoiding bandits and robbers along the pathway through the wilderness.[61] Ezra's concern for safe travel to Jerusalem was heightened by the presence of the wives and children, who were unable to defend themselves against violent attack. Therefore, the prayer for divine guidance was urgent.[62]

In order to ensure the effectiveness of the Jews' prayers, Ezra called for a corporate fast. He was well aware of the dangers that lay ahead and the need for God's help. Ezra stated that they 'afflicted' themselves through fasting. Their self-affliction would intensify their prayers and certify to God their earnestness. The Lord responded to their prayer and fasting by providing safe passage all the way to Jerusalem.

12. Mourning over Unfaithfulness – Ezra 9-10

Once Ezra and his company reached Jerusalem, they began to adjust to the new and more difficult living conditions. Many of the Jews took advantage of the new situation by initiating contact with the people of the land and even intermarrying with them in violation of the Law of Moses. When Ezra was informed of these

---

[61] Cf. McKnight, *Fasting*, p. 48.
[62] Franklin, *Fasting*, p. 175-78, takes special note of Ezra's mention of the 'little ones'.

transgressions, he was deeply concerned, recognizing the spiritual dangers inherent in intermarriage with non-Jews. Thus, he fell down before God:

> When I heard this, I tore my garments and my mantle, and pulled hair from my head and beard, and sat appalled ... And at the evening sacrifice I rose from my fasting, with my garments and my mantle torn, and fell upon my knees and spread out my hands to the LORD my God, saying: 'O my God, I am ashamed and blush to lift my face to you, my God, for our iniquities have risen higher than our heads, and our guilt has mounted up to the heavens' (Ezra 9.3-6).

While Ezra prayed and confessed the sins of his people, they gathered around him and 'wept bitterly' (Ezra 10.1). Apparently, his fasting made an impression not only upon God but also upon the people (which, incidentally, would not have been possible had his fasting been kept secret). They joined in Ezra's confession, and they decided to make a covenant with God to divorce their foreign wives. Ezra approved and made them swear an oath, but he continued to fast:

> Then Ezra withdrew from before the house of God, and went to the chamber of Jehohanan the son of Eliashib, where he spent the night, neither eating bread nor drinking water; for he was mourning over the faithlessness of the exiles (Ezra 10.6).

'Fasting was Ezra's way of demonstrating his own complicity in Israel's moral wandering, and it was also his way of identifying with his fellow wanderers from God in order to lift them up before the God of mercy.'[63]

Ezra sent out a proclamation throughout all of Judah, asking the returned exiles to gather at Jerusalem within three days. When they had assembled, Ezra addressed the multitude and rebuked them for their violation of the Law of Moses. The people confessed and repented of their transgressions. Then, 'they pledged themselves to put away their wives, and their guilt offering was a ram of the flock for their guilt' (Ezra 9.19).

---

[63] McKnight, *Fasting*, p. 32.

On the Day of Atonement and in Joel, the people are exhorted to fast and repent for their own sins. However, both Daniel and Ezra fast and confess on behalf of their people Israel (Dan. 9.3; Ezra 10.6-11). The confessions of Daniel and Ezra represent a kind of corporate solidarity in which the entire community bears the guilt of sin, even if certain individuals are not guilty for the specific sins that are being confessed. The fasting of Daniel and Ezra on behalf of the people also reflects the same kind of pastoral intercession that is evident in the earlier story of Moses, when he pleaded on behalf of the Israelites (Deut. 9.18-19).

13. Fasting in the Wake of Bad News – Nehemiah 1.4

After the Babylonian exile, groups of Jews returned to Judea under the leadership of Zerubbabel and Ezra; and after some struggles, the temple was rebuilt. However, conditions in Judea continued to be deplorable. In Babylon, a man named Nehemiah learned that the people of Judea remained 'in great trouble and shame'; the walls of Jerusalem were still 'broken down'; and the gates of the city, which had been 'destroyed by fire', had not been restored. The report so affected Nehemiah, that he fasted and prayed and mourned:

> When I heard these words I sat down and wept, and mourned for days, fasting and praying before the God of heaven. I said, 'O LORD God of heaven, the great and awesome God who keeps covenant and steadfast love with those who love him and keep his commandments; let your ear be attentive and your eyes open to hear the prayer of your servant that I now pray before you day and night for your servants, the people of Israel, confessing the sins of the people of Israel, which we have sinned against you. Both I and my family have sinned' (Neh. 1.4-6).

Nehemiah's fasting was an expression of his passionate concern for his fellow Jews. Reminiscent of the prayer of Daniel, Nehemiah affirms God's covenant faithfulness (Neh. 1.5) and admits that Israel's exile was on account of multiple transgressions (Neh. 1.8). After repenting for Israel's sin, Nehemiah pleads for 'success' and 'mercy' from God.

The Lord soon answered Nehemiah's prayers. Nehemiah was cupbearer to the king of Persia, and in the course of his duties, the king noticed Nehemiah's sad face. When the king asked about the cause of Nehemiah's sadness, he explained to the king the troubling situation in Judea. The king not only gave Nehemiah leave to go to Judea, but he also gave him authorization and support for the project of rebuilding the walls of Jerusalem.

14. Fasting after Feasting – Nehemiah 9.1

Nehemiah was able to rebuild the walls of Jerusalem in fifty-two days (Neh. 6.15). Once the project was completed, the people gathered together to celebrate and to read from the book of the Torah (Neh. 8.1). Ezra the scribe read to the people from morning until noon, and all the people gave their full attention to the Torah:

> And Nehemiah, who was the governor, and Ezra the priest and scribe, and the Levites who taught the people said to all the people, 'This day is holy to the LORD your God; do not mourn or weep' (for all the people wept when they heard the words of the law). Then he said to them, 'Go your way, eat the fat and drink sweet wine … for this day is holy to our LORD; and do not be grieved, for the joy of the LORD is your strength …' And all the people went their way to eat and drink … and to make great rejoicing (Neh. 8.9-12).

Ezra's reading from the Torah included the instructions for celebrating the Feast of Tabernacles; and, realizing that the time for the feast was at hand, the people celebrated for the next eight days, as the Torah commanded. Each day, Ezra would read another passage from the Torah.

The Feast of Tabernacles was a time of rejoicing, but as soon as the feast days were completed, the Jews entered a time of mourning and repentance. The reading of the Torah had produced a sense of guilt among the people and a desire for repentance (Neh. 8.9). Therefore, they proclaimed a fast:

> The people of Israel were assembled with fasting and in sackcloth, and with earth on their heads. Then those of Israelite descent separated themselves from all foreigners, and stood and confessed their sins and the iniquities of their ancestors. They stood up in their place and read from the book of the law of the LORD their God for a fourth part of the day, and for another fourth they made confession and worshiped the LORD their God (Neh. 9.1-3).

This corporate fast for repentance bears similarities to the fast that was called for by Joel. The people mourned and grieved over their sins, and their fasting was a sign of the sincerity of their repentance. They confessed their own sins as well as the sins of their ancestors, showing that the first step to restoration is the willingness to bear corporate responsibility for unfaithfulness.

Too often, we are tempted to assert our own righteousness while casting blame toward others who appear to be more sinful than ourselves. The Old Testament would seem to suggest that our way forward is to join in corporate confession and repentance without self-righteous excuses.

15. Mourning for Saul – 1 Chronicles 10.12

The last books in the Hebrew Bible are the books of 1 and 2 Chronicles. The first nine chapters of 1 Chronicles consist of the genealogies of the Israelites, beginning with Adam and concluding with the family of King Saul. Chapter ten retells the narrative of Saul's death that is found in 1 Samuel 31.

> But when all Jabesh-gilead heard everything that the Philistines had done to Saul, all the valiant warriors got up and took away the body of Saul and the bodies of his sons, and brought them to Jabesh. Then they buried their bones under the oak in Jabesh, and fasted seven days. So Saul died for his unfaithfulness; he was unfaithful to the LORD in that he did not keep the command of the LORD; moreover, he had consulted a medium, seeking guidance, and did not seek guidance from the LORD. Therefore the LORD put him to death and turned the kingdom over to David son of Jesse (1 Chron. 10.11-14).

The fasting of the men of Jabesh-gilead was a sign of their grief. They mourned the death of Saul, their king and their benefactor in times past.[64]

The story of Saul's death, followed by the mourning and fasting of the men of Jabesh-gilead is essentially unchanged from its form in 1 Samuel 31, except for an additional comment at the end. This text in 1 Chronicles includes the reason for Saul's death. The text states that Saul 'died for his unfaithfulness', and because 'he did not

---

[64] For more information on the background to this text, see the earlier discussion of the parallel narrative in 1 Sam. 31.13.

keep the command of the Lord; moreover, he had consulted a medium'. Therefore, the Lord turned Saul's kingdom over to David.

16. Fasting for Victory – 2 Chronicles 20.3
When Jehoshaphat was king of Judah, the Moabites and Ammonites assembled their armies and attacked Judah:

> Messengers came and told Jehoshaphat, A great multitude is coming against you from Edom, from beyond the sea; they are already at Hazazon-tamar (that is, En-gedi). Jehoshaphat was afraid; he set himself to seek the LORD, and proclaimed a fast throughout all Judah. Judah assembled to seek help from the LORD; from all the towns of Judah they came to seek the LORD (2 Chon. 20.2-4).

Only recently, Jehoshaphat had barely escaped out of a battle against the Arameans in which Ahab, king of Israel, had lost his life. Now, this new threat made Jehoshaphat afraid; therefore, he immediately chose to 'seek the LORD' and to proclaim a fast all across the land of Judah. The people gathered at the temple to humble themselves before the Lord and pray for deliverance.

As they fasted, King Jehoshaphat stood before the people and prayed to the Lord, admitting that he was powerless against the enemy. He pleaded for God's help. Then the Spirit of the Lord came upon a man named Jahaziel, and he prophesied, 'Thus says the LORD to you: Do not fear or be dismayed at this great multitude; for the battle is not yours but God's' (2 Chron. 20.15). The Lord instructed Jehoshaphat to appoint singers who would go before the army, praising the Lord. The next day, when the army and the singers went forth as instructed, the Lord gave them a great victory over all their enemies, and they returned to Jerusalem with rejoicing.

The fasting of Jehoshaphat was generated out of his sense of urgency. The crisis of war was at the door, and Judah desperately needed God's help. The fast demonstrated to God that Jehoshaphat and his people were reliant upon God and not upon themselves.[65] The fast produced humility and receptivity to the Holy Spirit, creating an environment in which the Spirit could speak a prophetic

---

[65] In times of fasting like this one, every person would be obligated to fast, 'For he who would not share in the distress would have no part in the consolation' (Hirsch, 'Asceticism', p. 166).

word to the community.[66] John Wesley, taking the fast of Jehoshaphat as a model, states, 'in like manner, particular persons, who take heed unto their ways, and desire to walk humbly and closely with God, will find frequent occasion for private seasons of thus afflicting their souls'.[67] Similarly, Jentezen Franklin declares that we can experience the same kind of victory that God gave to Israel. Franklin writes, 'Press in like Jehoshaphat in times of great distress – you and your whole family, perhaps even your entire church. God will deliver you and show you His plan.'[68]

---

[66] The same kind of crisis fasting that is found in 2 Chron. 20.3 is observed in the apocryphal books: Judith 4 and 2 Maccabees 13.
[67] Wesley, 'Upon Our Lord's Sermon on the Mount: Discourse Seven', p. 308.
[68] Franklin, *Fasting*, (p. 51).

3

FASTING IN THE NEW TESTAMENT

Fasting represents the Church's eschatological expectation: *'the people of God standing in readiness, awaiting the* Parousia *of the Lord'.* – Alexander Schmemann[1]

A. Fasting in the Gospels

1. Jesus Fasts Forty Days – Matthew 4.1-4

In the Gospel according to Matthew, fasting is mentioned in four passages. Jesus fasted forty days and nights at the inauguration of his public ministry (Mt. 4.1-4); he taught the proper motivation for fasting (Mt. 6.6-18); he explained that his disciples would not fast while he was with them, but they would fast later (Mt. 9.14-15); and he prescribed fasting as an aid to difficult exorcisms (Mt. 17.21).

As soon as Jesus came up out of the waters of baptism, the Spirit of God descended upon him, and 'a voice came from heaven, saying, "This is my beloved son, in whom I am well pleased"' (Mt. 3.17). The reader might expect that Jesus would commence his ministry without delay. After all, he had been named already as the Messiah (Mt. 1.17, 18), the savior (Mt. 1.21), the king of the Jews (Mt. 2.2), and the Spirit baptizer (Mt. 3.11). At his baptism, he was endowed with the Holy Spirit and affirmed by the Heavenly Father. However, Jesus must face one more qualifying event:

---

[1] Alexander Schmemann, *Introduction to Liturgical Theology* (trans. Asheleigh E. Moorhouse; Library of Orthodox Theology; Portland, ME: American Orthodox Press, 1966), p. 157.

> Then Jesus was led up by the Spirit into the wilderness to be tempted by the devil. He fasted forty days and forty nights, and afterwards he was hungry. The tempter came and said to him, 'If you are the Son of God, command these stones to become loaves of bread'. But he answered, 'It is written, "A person does not live by bread alone, but by every word that comes out of the mouth of God"' (Mt. 4.1-4).

After his temptation, 'Jesus began to preach and to say, "Repent, for the kingdom of heaven is at hand"' (Mt. 4.17).

Fasting as preparation for ministry is not surprising when we consider the challenges facing ministers and when we recognize the weaknesses inherent in all human leaders. The value of fasting, however, is not quite so obvious in the case of Jesus. The reason for Jesus' fasting is not stated, and Jesus had already been anointed with the Holy Spirit before he went into the wilderness to fast. Therefore, the fast was not for the purpose of preparing him for the coming of the Spirit. His anointing with the Spirit, however, was not the only preparation that Jesus must endure before the inauguration of his ministry – he must also be tested.[2] Thus, the fast of Jesus was an occasion for testing; and as Israel was tested in the wilderness for forty years, Jesus was tested in the wilderness for forty days. His forty days without food provided an opening for the devil, who said to Jesus, 'If you are the Son of God, command these stones to become loaves of bread'. Although he was very hungry, Jesus refused to succumb to temptation. He was ready for the test; and he responded to the devil by quoting from Old Testament, citing Deut. 8.3, 'A person does not live by bread alone but by every word that comes forth from the mouth of God'. Rather than turn the stones into bread in order to satisfy his physical hunger, Jesus affirmed the life-giving power of the word of God. Jesus knew that even as all living things came into existence by God's word, they continue to be sustained by that same living word. Later on, Jesus would explain the primacy of spiritual hunger over physical hunger when he taught, 'Blessed are those who hunger and thirst for righteousness, for they will be filled' (Mt. 5.6). Fasting,

---

[2] Cf. Piper, *A Hunger for God: Desiring God through Fasting and Prayer*, p. 54.

therefore, is an expression of our hunger for the life-giving word of God.[3]

In his successful resistance to temptation, Jesus reversed the scenario that played out in Genesis, when Adam and Eve were similarly tempted. The serpent invited Eve to taste the forbidden fruit, and she ate it and gave it to Adam who also ate. In the garden, Adam and Eve were tested through their human appetites, and they failed;[4] but in the wilderness, Jesus was tempted through his human appetites, and he succeeded, going on to bring deliverance to all who would hear and obey his word. As soon as he emerged from his temptation, he began his ministry of preaching and healing.

2. When You Fast – Matthew 6.16-18

Matthew 5–7, often called 'The Sermon on the Mount', contains many of the key teachings of Jesus. Throughout the Sermon, Jesus corrects, expands, and deepens many of the views found in Jewish tradition that were taught by the rabbis of his day. One of his concerns was to demonstrate that righteousness was defined by something deeper than an outward show of piety. Righteousness, a matter of the heart, flowed from a right relationship with God and resulted in right relationships with neighbors. As an example, Jesus pointed to the Pharisees, who were well known to practice faithfully every detail of the Law, and said, 'unless your righteousness exceeds the righteousness of the scribes and Pharisees, you will by no means enter the kingdom of heaven' (Mt. 5.20).

Three religious practices that were important marks of righteousness in Jesus' day were almsgiving, prayer, and fasting;[5] and in Mt. 6.1-18 Jesus addresses the motivations behind those practices. The 'hypocrites' (apparently a veiled allusion to the Pharisees) were motivated by human approval and applause, but Jesus warns, 'Beware of practicing your righteousness before other people to be noticed by them; otherwise you have no reward with your Father who is in heaven' (Mt. 6.1). Thus, regarding each act of piety, Jesus instructs his followers to examine their motives. He says, 'When you give, do not give to be seen by others, or you will have no reward from your heavenly Father. When you pray, do not pray with the

---

[3] Franklin, *Fasting*, p. 123.
[4] Cf. Franklin, *Fasting*, pp. 21-22, 109; Wallis, *God's Chosen Fast*, p. 77.
[5] Cf. the apocryphal text: 'Prayer is good when accompanied by fasting, almsgiving, and righteousness' (Tobit 12.8).

goal of receiving praise from others, or you will have no reward from your heavenly Father' (Mt. 6.2-6, paraphrased).

Jesus gives similar instructions regarding fasting:

> When you fast, do not put on a gloomy face like the hypocrites, for they neglect their appearance so that they will be noticed by others when they are fasting. Truly I say to you, they have their reward in full. But you, when you fast, anoint your head and wash your face so that your fasting will not be noticed by others, but by your Father who is in secret; and your Father who sees in secret will reward you (Mt. 6.16-18).

It was important that Jesus teach his disciples the deeper meaning of righteousness. Apparently, the scribes and Pharisees were somewhat like the Israelites to whom Isaiah prophesied. They were intent on obeying the letter of the Law, but they were oblivious to the Spirit of the Law. They were liturgically correct, but they were spiritually bankrupt. They viewed giving, praying, and fasting as inherently meritorious acts that would invariably guarantee the favor of God. Furthermore, they valued too highly the approval of other people. In light of Jesus' words, John Wesley advised, 'Let us beware of mocking God, of turning our fast, as well as our prayers, into an abomination unto the Lord ... by seeking the praise of men'.[6] Jesus corrected their theology by insisting that the heavenly Father only rewards those who give and pray and fast with the right motives.

It would be easy to misinterpret Jesus' instruction that we fast unto the Father who is 'in secret' to mean that our fasting must be kept secret and that fasting is entirely an individual practice, but that is not the meaning here. The fasting is not in secret; rather, it is the Father who is in secret. To fast to the Father who is in secret means that we do not fast with the intent of putting our piety on display – we do not make a show of our fasting. It means that we do not fast for the approval and praise of other people. Fasting can hardly be kept secret or private for several reasons. First of all, family members, co-workers, and others who are close to us will take notice if we do not eat. When we are asked why we are not eating, we should give a straightforward answer. Second, the Jews to which Jesus

---

[6] Wesley, 'Upon Our Lord's Sermon on the Mount: Discourse Seven', p. 316.

spoke practiced well-known corporate fast days, and everyone was expected to fast. Thus, the fasting was not a secret.[7] The fasts mentioned in the Bible were often corporate fasts, and the people involved were not concerned about secrecy. In fact, the people would often gather together for prayer while they were fasting. For example, Joel commanded, 'Blow the trumpet in Zion; declare a holy fast; call a sacred assembly' (Joel 2.15). The 'prophets and teachers' in Acts 13 who fasted and worshiped together were not trying to keep their fasting a secret.

Throughout the Bible and Christian history, fasting has been mostly a corporate activity that was not kept secret. In the liturgical churches, annual fast days were observed by everyone. In the Protestant churches, fast days were often called on the occasion of tragedies or natural disasters. Everyone participated and gathered in the churches for prayer and worship. In addition to the corporate fasts, individual fasts have always been practiced in times of prayer, grief, suffering, and danger. However, the emphasis on fasting as an individual spiritual discipline came to us primarily through the monastic movement, which will be discussed below. The monastic lifestyle emphasized the individual ascetic progress towards perfection.

Although fasting is not a commandment or a requirement, Jesus assumes that, because of fasting's spiritual benefits, we will fast. In Matthew 6, he teaches on almsgiving, prayer, and fasting. In referring to each practice, Jesus uses the word 'when' rather than 'if'. He says, 'when you give …', 'when you pray …', and 'when you fast …'.[8] The fact that Jesus 'dealt with fasting as a spiritual exercise distinct from praying' affirms the importance of fasting.[9] Within the context of the first century, it was not necessary for Jesus to command his disciples to give, to pray, or to fast. These three acts of devotion were built into the fabric of Jewish life, and Jesus was confident that his disciples would perform them regularly.[10]

---

[7] Cf. Piper, *A Hunger for God: Desiring God through Fasting and Prayer*, pp. 72-73.

[8] The Greek ὅταν with the present subjunctive signifies 'whenever', usually referring to actions that are repeated (Bauer, *A Greek-English Lexicon*, p. 592). Wesley, 'Upon Our Lord's Sermon on the Mount: Discourse Seven', p. 313, interprets Jesus' words as 'an unquestionable command'.

[9] Wallis, *God's Chosen Fast*, p. 27.

[10] Cf. Franklin, *Fasting*, p. 11.

3. Fasting When the Bridegroom Is Taken – Matthew 9.14-15

Although Jesus expected his followers to fast, he did not ask them to fast while he remained on the earth with them. Fasting was such a common spiritual practice that the disciples' lack of fasting was noted by observers:

> The disciples of John came to him, asking, 'Why do we and the Pharisees fast, but your disciples do not fast?' And Jesus said to them, 'The attendants of the bridegroom cannot mourn as long as the bridegroom is with them, can they? But the days will come when the bridegroom is taken away from them, and then they will fast' (Mt. 9.14-15).

Jesus is not saying that the fasting of the Pharisees and the disciples of John had been inappropriate. In fact, their fasting was commendable in anticipation of the coming of the Messiah. However, there is now no reason for them to fast, because the Messiah has come.[11] Jesus explained that the bridegroom's attendants do not fast while the bridegroom is with them because it is a time of joy and celebration, and mourning would not be appropriate. When the bridegroom departs, the celebration will be ended, and then will be the proper time for sorrow. In the same way, Jesus (the bridegroom) is with his disciples, and it is a time of joy. When Jesus departs from them, then it will be appropriate for them to fast.[12]

We may find eschatological connections in Jesus' words here. We are now in a period in which Jesus is absent from us (though he is present through the Holy Spirit). Jesus went away, and he promised to return, but he has not returned yet. While the bridegroom is away, we fast, just as he said the disciples would fast after the bridegroom departed. 'The fast of this age is not merely an act of mourning for Christ's absence, but an act of preparation for His return'.[13] We are living in a time of anticipation, awaiting the return of Jesus, at which time we will be invited to the Marriage Supper of the Lamb. Therefore, in some ways, we are grieving over his ab-

---

[11] Cf. Craig Blomberg, *Matthew* (New American Commentary; Nashville, TN: Broadman Press, 1992), p. 158.

[12] Cf. Ryan, *The Sacred Art of Fasting*, pp. 36-37.

[13] Wallis, *God's Chosen Fast*, p. 32.

sence and long to see him face to face when we will receive the fullness of his presence.[14]

4. Fasting and Evil Spirits – Matthew 17.21

Matthew reports an event in which the disciples were unable to expel an evil spirit from a young boy. Jesus responds that the disciples could not cast out the evil spirit because of their 'little faith' (ὀλιγοπιστίαν). Then he adds, 'This kind goes out only by prayer and fasting' (Mt. 17.21). Matthew 17.21 is not present in the best manuscripts of the Greek New Testament.[15] Scholars believe that it was added by a scribe in an attempt to harmonize the Matthean and Markan texts. However, even though Jesus' statement about fasting may not have been part of the original text, it demonstrates that the early church believed that fasting is necessary for the strengthening of certain kinds of prayer.

5. Fasting When the Bridegroom Is Taken – Mark 2.18-20

Fasting is mentioned only twice in Mark's Gospel. The first reference to fasting comes as a question from people who observed that Jesus' disciples did not fast.

> Now John's disciples and the Pharisees were fasting; and people came and said to him, 'Why do John's disciples and the disciples of the Pharisees fast, but your disciples do not fast?' Jesus said to them, 'The wedding guests cannot fast while the bridegroom is with them, can they? As long as they have the bridegroom with them, they cannot fast. The days will come when the bridegroom is taken away from them, and then they will fast on that day' (Mk 2.18-20).

We will not repeat the comments that we made earlier regarding Mt. 9.14-15, but we will just mention an interesting thread found in Mark's account. In Mark, the question about the disciple's lack of fasting is both preceded and followed by other texts regarding food.

---

[14] We will not discuss Mt. 15.32, which states, 'Then Jesus called his disciples to him and said, I have compassion on the crowd, because they have been with me now three days, and have nothing to eat; and I am unwilling to send them away hungry, lest they faint on the way'. The word translated 'hungry' is νῆστις, which can be rendered 'fasting', but the hunger of the multitude is not caused by a fast but by the unavailability of food.

[15] The mention of fasting in Mt. 17.21 appears in the fifth-century codices C and W.

Not only is the spirituality of the disciples suspect because they do not observe the rules of piety, but the spirituality of Jesus is also questioned because he 'eats and drinks with tax collectors and sinners' (Mk 2.16). Furthermore, the disciples are accused of disregarding the Law by plucking grain on the Sabbath day (Mk 2.23-24). In each case where propriety is in doubt, Jesus clarifies and redefines pious behavior.[16] He eats with sinners because it is the sick, not the well, who need a physician. His disciples do not fast because fasting is inappropriate (and even unlawful) during a time of rejoicing. The disciples are allowed to pluck grain because 'The Sabbath was made for humanity, and not humanity for the Sabbath' (Mk 2.27).[17]

6. Fasting and Evil Spirits – Mark 9.29

Mark reports an incident in which the disciples were unable to expel an evil spirit from a young boy. The disciples asked Jesus why they were unable to cast out the evil spirit, and Jesus replied, 'This kind can come out by nothing but prayer and fasting' (Mk 9.28-29, cf. Mt. 17.21 above). Many manuscripts of the Greek New Testament do not include the words 'and fasting', but they are present in later manuscripts.[18] Even though Jesus' statement about fasting may not have been part of the original text, it shows us that the early church believed that fasting is necessary for the strengthening of certain kinds of prayer, particularly when it comes to exorcism.

7. Fasting as Worship – Luke. 2.37

Fasting is mentioned four times in the Gospel according to Luke. The setting for the first reference to fasting is when Mary and Joseph brought the infant Jesus 'to Jerusalem to present him to the LORD' (Lk. 2.22) and to offer a sacrifice. When they arrived at the temple, they were met by Simeon, a man who had the Spirit upon

---

[16] In an attempt to relate Mk 2.21-22 to Jesus' comments on fasting, R. Alan Culpepper, *Mark* (The Smyth & Helwys Bible Commentary; Macon, GA: Smyth & Helwys, 2007), p. 88, argues that fasting 'belongs to an old order that cannot even be grafted onto the new'. Culpepper sees the entire section of Mark as a defense of Jesus' authority.

[17] We will not discuss Mk 8.3, which states, 'And if I send them away fasting to their own houses, they will faint on the way: for some of them came a long way'. The 'fasting' of the multitude is caused by the unavailability of food. It is not a case of intentional abstinence as an act of piety.

[18] The reference to fasting is apparently present in the third-century papyrus $\mathfrak{P}^{45}$ and the fourth-century codex A.

him. He had been told by the Holy Spirit that he would live to see the Christ, and he declared to Mary and Joseph that the baby Jesus was the Christ, the savior of Israel. As soon as Simeon finished speaking, the young family encountered an elderly woman named Anna:

> There was also a prophet, Anna the daughter of Phanuel, of the tribe of Asher. She was of a great age, having lived with her husband seven years after her marriage, then as a widow to the age of eighty-four. She never left the temple but worshiped there with fasting and prayer night and day. At that moment she came, and began to praise God and to speak about the child to all who were looking for the redemption of Jerusalem (Lk. 2.36-38).

Anna's experience suggests that fasting can be practiced as an element of worship.[19] She 'worshiped' God with fasting and prayer. The word 'worship' (λατρεύω) is sometimes translated 'serve'. It means 'to perform religious rites as a part of worship'.[20] We know that the word signifies more than just outward physical rituals because we are encouraged to 'worship (λατρεύω) in the Spirit' (Phil. 3.3) and because the saints in heaven 'worship (λατρεύω) [God] day and night' (Rev. 7.15).

Anna's attentiveness to God was characterized by regular times of fasting and prayer. Her fasting, however, was not for repentance, mourning, or for a particular urgent prayer. Rather, her fasting was an act of worship that diverted her attention away from the earthly and set her gaze toward the heavenly. Apparently, she fasted in anticipation of the promised Messiah, who would redeem Israel.[21] Her fasting was rewarded by a revelation of the coming of the redeemer, and she was able to see with her own eyes the savior. She then preached to others that the redeemer had come.

---

[19] Cf. Baab, *Fasting*, p. 77.

[20] J.P. Louw and E.A. Nida, *Greek-English Lexicon of the New Testament: Based on Semantic Domains* (2 vols.; New York: United Bible Societies, 2nd edn, 1989), I, p. 533; cf. T. Friberg, B. Friberg, and N.F. Miller, *Analytical Lexicon of the Greek New Testament* (Baker's Greek New Testament Library; Grand Rapids, MI: Baker Books, 2000), p. 244; and Bauer, *A Greek-English Lexicon*, p. 468.

[21] See Piper, *A Hunger for God: Desiring God through Fasting and Prayer*, pp. 87-88.

8. Jesus Fasts Forty Days – Luke 4.2

Like Matthew, Luke reports the forty-day fast of Jesus that occurred immediately following his baptism (see the discussion of Mt. 4.1-4 above):

> Jesus, full of the Holy Spirit, returned from the Jordan and was led by the Spirit in the wilderness, where for forty days he was tempted by the devil. He ate nothing at all during those days, and when they were over, he was hungry. The devil said to him, 'If you are the Son of God, command this stone to become a loaf of bread'. Jesus answered him, 'It is written, A person does not live by bread alone but by every word of God' (Lk. 4.1-4).[22]

The reason for Jesus' fasting is not stated, but the original readers of the gospels would remember the fasts of Moses and Elijah. Moses fasted forty days while on Mt. Sinai receiving the Torah, and Elijah fasted forty days prior to his own encounter with God. Moses and Elijah were the two Old Testament prophets most prominent in Jewish tradition. Later in the Gospel of Luke, they appear with Jesus at his transfiguration. The forty-day fast of Jesus, therefore, designates him as the new Moses, the deliverer of Israel and giver of the new covenant. It also indicates that Jesus is the fulfillment of the Old Testament prophetic ministry. As with Moses and Elijah, the fasting of Jesus signifies the spiritual nature of the kingdom of God.[23]

Luke makes it clear that Jesus was 'full' of the Holy Spirit; therefore, as we stated in relation to Mt. 4.1-4, the fast was not for the purpose of preparing him for the coming of the Spirit. It was the Holy Spirit who led Jesus into the wilderness to fast, to pray, and to be tested. As soon as he emerged from his temptation, he declared, 'The Spirit of the LORD is upon me, because he has anointed me to preach good news to the poor. He has sent me to preach deliverance to the captives …' (Lk. 4.18). After his victory over temptation, Jesus was ready to bring victory to others also.

---

[22] The phrase 'word of God' is not found in the best Greek manuscripts.

[23] Franklin, *Fasting*, p. 110, writes, 'The first thing Jesus felt in His earthly ministry for you and me was hunger. The last thing that He felt on this earth was thirst' (Jn 19.28).

9. Fasting when the Bridegroom Is Taken – Luke 5.33-35

For the third time in the gospels, we read about the questions that were aimed at Jesus' disciples regarding their lack of fasting:

> Then they said to him, 'Why do the disciples of John fast often and make prayers, and likewise those of the Pharisees, but yours eat and drink?' And he said to them, 'Can you make the friends of the bridegroom fast while the bridegroom is with them? But the days will come when the bridegroom will be taken away from them; then they will fast in those days' (Lk. 5.33-35).

In Luke's Gospel, the question about the disciples' lack of fasting occurs within the larger context of Jesus' choosing of the twelve. He calls Simon Peter, James, and John; then he finds Levi, who invites Jesus to a 'great feast' (Lk. 5.29). While Jesus and his disciples are eating, the question of fasting is posed. Soon afterwards, Jesus names the twelve (Lk. 6.13-16). Therefore, the accusation against Jesus' disciple may imply a questioning of their sincerity as genuine followers. After all, how serious can these disciples be if they do not practice the standard rituals of spiritual discipline? Jesus does not consider fasting to be an accurate measure of spiritual commitment. Fasting is not necessary while he is present with them, but he asserts that they will fast after he is taken away.

10. Pharisaical Fasting – Luke 18.12

Fasting was a common practice in first-century Judaism, and the Pharisees were known to fast on Mondays and Thursdays of every week. We read about their regular fasting in the following narrative:

> Also he spoke this parable to some who trusted in themselves that they were righteous, and despised others: 'Two men went up to the temple to pray, one a Pharisee and the other a tax collector. The Pharisee stood and prayed thus with himself, "God, I thank you that I am not like other men – extortioners, unjust, adulterers, or even as this tax collector. I fast twice a week; I give tithes of all that I possess". And the tax collector, standing afar off, would not so much as raise his eyes to heaven, but beat his breast, saying, "God, be merciful to me a sinner!" I tell you, this man went down to his house justified rather than the other; for everyone who exalts himself will be humbled, and he who humbles himself will be exalted' (Lk. 18.9-14).

The irony of this story is that although fasting is normally practiced as an expression of humility and self-abasement, the Pharisee found his fasting to be a reason for self-exaltation and pride. John Wesley evaluates the Pharisee, saying that he lacks 'nothing of godliness, but the power; nothing of religion, but the spirit; nothing of Christianity, but the truth and the life'.[24] Therefore, it was not the Pharisee who went home 'justified', even though he performed all of the duties and rituals that were required by Jewish tradition. Instead, it was the tax collector – despised as a traitor by the Jews – who was justified, because he humbled himself and begged for mercy. Fasting, like other religious rituals, can be a valuable aid to spiritual growth; but it must not be seen as meritorious or as an end in itself. The story does not suggest that Jesus was against fasting but that Jesus 'was against the arrogant self-righteousness of a man who did the right things but whose heart remained pompous before God'.[25] Thus, the teaching of Jesus regarding fasting is consistent with that of the Old Testament prophets.

B. Fasting in the Acts of the Apostles

1. Saul of Tarsus – Acts 9.9-18

Saul (who would be known later as Paul) was traveling on the road to Damascus, and he encountered Jesus Christ in a vision. Saul talked with Jesus and was converted, but he was physically blinded by the brightness of Jesus' appearance. After getting up from the ground, his friends led him into Damascus, where 'he was three days without sight, and he neither ate nor drank' (Acts. 9.9).

During these three days, the Lord appeared to a Christian by the name of Ananias, who lived in Damascus.

> And the LORD said to him, 'Arise and go to the street called Straight, and inquire at the house of Judas for a man from Tarsus named Saul, for behold, he is praying, and he has seen in a vision a man named Ananias come in and lay his hands on him, so that he might regain his sight' ... And Ananias departed and entered the house, and after laying his hands on him said, 'Brother Saul, the LORD Jesus, who appeared to you on the road

---

[24] Wesley, *The Works of the Rev. John Wesley*, V, pp. 26-27.
[25] McKnight, *Fasting*, p. 71.

by which you were coming, has sent me so that you may regain your sight, and be filled with the Holy Spirit'. And immediately there fell from his eyes something like scales, and he regained his sight, and he arose and was baptized; and he took food and was strengthened (Acts 9.7-19).

The reason for Saul's fasting is not stated explicitly, but we might infer that he is fasting and praying both for divine direction and for physical healing.[26] Having been blinded by the vision of Jesus, it would be quite natural that Saul would be praying for a reversal of his blindness. Also, the Lord told Ananias that Saul 'is praying, and he has seen in a vision a man named Ananias come in and lay his hands on him, so that he might regain his sight' (9.12). Apparently, Saul had seen in a vision the answer to his prayer.

Saul's fasting might also be an involuntary reaction to his life-altering encounter with Jesus Christ.[27] Having talked face-to-face with Jesus and having been told to await further instructions (9.6), Saul's emotions would be in turmoil. Perhaps the weight of the sacred experience simply overshadowed Saul's desire for food and drink, and perhaps his entire attention was focused upon seeking for God's direction in his life. Saul's prayer for healing and illumination may have been an all-consuming passion.

It is not insignificant that Saul's fasting also had the effect of preparing him to be filled with the Holy Spirit. Although Saul had seen a vision of his healing only, Ananias knew that Saul's greater need was the endowment of the Holy Spirit. Therefore, when he prayed for Saul, he said, 'the LORD Jesus ... has sent me so that you may regain your sight, and *be filled with the Holy Spirit*' (Acts 9.17, emphasis added).

2. The Fasting of Cornelius – Acts 10.30

Cornelius was a Gentile soldier, a centurion, described as 'a devout man who feared God with all his household; he gave alms generously to the people and prayed constantly to God' (Acts 10.2). As he prayed one afternoon, an angel of God appeared to him and instructed him to send for Peter, who would come and speak to him and his associates. Cornelius relates his experience to Peter:

---

[26] See Franklin, *Fasting*, p. 47.
[27] Cf. McKnight, *Fasting*, p. 34.

> So Cornelius said, 'Four days ago I was fasting until this hour; and at the ninth hour I prayed in my house, and behold, a man stood before me in bright clothing, and said, "Cornelius, your prayer has been heard, and your alms are remembered in the sight of God. Send therefore to Joppa and call Simon here, whose surname is Peter. He is lodging in the house of Simon, a tanner, by the sea. When he comes, he will speak to you"' (Acts 10.30-32).[28]

Prayer, almsgiving, and fasting were important acts of piety to both Jews and Christians, an essential part of spiritual life and worship. The behavior of Cornelius matches the common expectations for god-fearing behavior. His actions of fasting and prayer demonstrate his intense hunger for God,[29] which is rewarded later when Peter visits and presents the gospel to him and his companions. The Holy Spirit falls upon the assembled crowd and they speak in tongues and glorify God (Acts 10.44-45). As in the case of Saul, fasting preceded the gift of the Spirit.

3. The Fasting of Church Leaders – Acts 13.1-4

We learn from the gospels that, in addition to their annual fast days, the Jews fasted two days out of every week. The early Christians, being mostly Jewish, continued a similar practice of regular fasting.

> Now in the church at Antioch there were prophets and teachers: Barnabas, Simeon who was called Niger, Lucius of Cyrene, Manaen a member of the court of Herod the ruler, and Saul. While they were worshiping the LORD and fasting, the Holy Spirit said, 'Set apart for me Barnabas and Saul for the work to which I have called them'. Then after fasting and praying they laid their hands on them and sent them off. So, being sent out by the Holy Spirit, they went down to Seleucia; and from there they sailed to Cyprus (Acts 13.1-4).

The early church in Antioch included several people who were called 'prophets and teachers' (Acts 13.1). Among them were Barnabas and Saul. We read in Acts 13 that these prophets and leaders

---

[28] The phrase regarding fasting is absent in the best Greek manuscripts, and may not have been part of the original text of Acts. It is found as early as the fourth to fifth centuries in $\mathfrak{P}^{50}$ and A^2.

[29] Franklin, *Fasting*, pp. 82-83.

at Antioch were praying and fasting, and 'as they worshiped the LORD and fasted', the Holy Spirit spoke to them, selecting Barnabas and Saul for missionary work.

Here, as in Luke 2, fasting and prayer are practiced as a dimension of worship. In this case the Greek word (λειτουργέω) means the 'expression of religious devotion',[30] is similar in meaning to the word discussed earlier in relation to Luke 2 (λατρεύω) but is a bit more formal. Earlier, the apostles had appointed seven men who would supervise the church's distribution to widows, so that the apostles might give themselves wholly to their primary duties, which were 'prayer and the ministry of the word' (Acts 6.4). Here in Acts 13, the use of 'worship' (λειτουργέω) indicates that fasting was also considered to be an essential duty. It was a practice that was necessary for fulfilling the roles of 'prophets and teachers' (13.1). That is, fasting and prayer should be a regular part of worship for leaders in the Church. Inasmuch as the prophets and teachers were ministering 'to the LORD' in their fasting and prayer, it seems important to observe that fasting, as worship, is directed toward God and is intended to bring glory and honor to God who is worshiped.

The text does not indicate in what manner the Spirit spoke to the worshipers in Antioch, but it was likely through some sort of prophetic word. The hearers of the Spirit's message understood it to be a call to go forth and spread the gospel to other cities. Therefore, in obedience to the charismatic word, they sent forth Barnabas and Saul as missionaries.

Regarding the purpose of fasting, the group of prophets and teachers were fasting as a part of their worship to the Lord, and there is no indication that they were asking for God's direction or for a prophecy or any other kind of revelation. God, however, perceiving their hearts to be receptive to his word, spoke to them and provided clear indications that it was time for Barnabas and Saul to launch out into a new kind of ministry. Perhaps it was their fasting that brought them to a place of openness to the charismatic word of the Holy Spirit. In any case, their fasting was one element in their overall practice of approaching God in worship, and God responded by granting them special revelation by the Spirit.

---

[30] Bauer, *A Greek-English Lexicon*, p. 858.

This passage also includes a second reference to fasting. As soon as the Holy Spirit had spoken and set apart Barnabas and Saul as missionaries, the other leaders at Antioch acted to obey the Spirit's directions: 'When they had fasted and prayed, they sent them on their way' (Acts 13.3). Apparently, their earlier fasting as worship was not enough to prepare Barnabas and Saul for their task as missionaries. They must also take time to fast and pray in order that they might be spiritually equipped for the work that lay ahead of them and so that God might go with them. Moreover, the other leaders must lend their support for their brothers by entering into the fast along with them.[31] This passage, therefore, suggests that fasting can function both as a preparation for ministry and as a sign of corporate solidarity with others who are entering ministry.

4. Fasting and Ordination – Acts 14.23

Barnabas and Saul traveled to Cyprus and throughout Asia Minor preaching the gospel and planting churches. After about a year and a half, they revisited the churches, encouraging them to be steadfast in the face of persecution (Acts 14.22). Recognizing the importance of good leadership, Barnabas and Saul appointed elders. We read, 'So when they had appointed elders in every church, with prayer and fasting they entrusted them to the LORD in whom they had believed' (Acts 14.23). Just as the church at Antioch had ordained them with fasting and prayer, Barnabas and Saul ordained those who were chosen to serve as elders in the new churches. Derek Prince observes that two significant events, the sending out of apostles and the appointment of elders, were both performed with fasting.[32] The text suggests that fasting and prayer were not a magical guarantee of success. On the contrary, fasting and prayer were means of entrusting the elders to the Lord, and the Lord would empower the elders for ministry. Fasting as a part of ordination serves to recognize the weaknesses and frailty of all human leaders. Fasting should produce in the leader a dependency upon the Lord and upon his Holy Spirit.

---

[31] According to John Wesley, *The Works of the Rev. John Wesley*, XIII, p. 213, the fasting was to impart a 'blessing' upon Barnabas and Saul.

[32] Derek Prince, *Fasting* (New Kensington, PA: Whitaker House, 1993), pp. 23-24.

5. Fasting for Evil – Acts 23.12

Paul's evangelistic work among the Gentiles gave him a reputation for disregarding the Law of Moses (Acts 21.21). Therefore, when he entered the Temple in Jerusalem to celebrate the Passover, a number of Jewish people created a riot, and Paul was arrested by the Romans. The Romans set Paul before the Jewish Sanhedrin, where Paul gave his testimony, setting off a sharp conflict between the Sadducees and the Pharisees on the council. On account of Paul's notoriety, a group of Jews decided to kill him:

> And when it was day, some of the Jews banded together and bound themselves under an oath, saying that they would neither eat nor drink till they had killed Paul. Now there were more than forty who had formed this conspiracy. They came to the chief priests and elders, and said, 'We have bound ourselves under a great oath that we will eat nothing until we have killed Paul' (Acts 23.12-14).

The plan to kill Paul was discovered by Paul's sister, who came and reported it to Paul in jail. Paul then sent one of the Roman soldiers to inform his superiors of the plot:

> And he said, 'The Jews have agreed to ask that you bring Paul down to the council tomorrow, as though they were going to inquire more fully about him. But do not yield to them, for more than forty of them lie in wait for him, men who have bound themselves by an oath that they will neither eat nor drink till they have killed him; and now they are ready, waiting for the promise from you' (Acts 23.20-21).

After hearing about the Jewish conspiracy to assassinate Paul, the Romans moved him secretly and brought him to Caesarea, where he was safe.

This account of Paul's ordeal reveals that fasting can be used for evil purposes (cf. 1 Kings 21). The men who conspired together believed that they were doing the work of God by plotting the elimination of a traitorous Jew, whose preaching was harmful to their people. Their strong belief, therefore, caused them to resort to extreme measures, including fasting, as a way to ensure the success of their plan. Fasting, even when misdirected, is a sign of sincerity and urgency.

6. The Fast – Acts 27.9

After Paul's arrest, he was imprisoned in Caesarea, awaiting trial. The Jewish leaders came and presented their case against him. Paul's incarceration dragged on, while the governor Festus continued to entertain complaints about Paul from the Jews. Eventually, Paul felt constrained to exercise his option as a Roman citizen to appeal to Caesar, which meant that he was put on a ship headed for Rome. Against Paul's advise, the ship set sail at time of the year that was known to be perilous on the Mediterranean Sea:

> Now when much time had been spent, and sailing was now dangerous because the Fast was already over, Paul advised them, saying, 'Men, I perceive that this voyage will end with disaster and much loss, not only of the cargo and ship, but also our lives' (Acts 27.9-10).

This text says very little about fasting, but it confirms the importance of the Day of Atonement. That fast day is so well known that it can be referred to simply as 'the fast' (τὴν νηστείαν). Inasmuch as the Day of Atonement would have fallen near the end of September, the favorable season for sailing was nearing its end.[33]

7. Fasting in the Storm – Acts 27.20-24

Paul's prediction about stormy weather came to pass, and the ship – and Paul's safety – was soon in jeopardy.

> Now when neither sun nor stars appeared for many days, and no small tempest beat on us, all hope that we would be saved was finally given up. But after long abstinence from food, Paul stood in the midst of them and said, 'Men, you should have listened to me, and not have sailed from Crete and incurred this disaster and loss. And now I urge you to take heart, for there will be no loss of life among you, but only of the ship. For there stood by me this night an angel of the God to whom I belong and whom I serve, saying, "Do not be afraid, Paul; you must be brought before Caesar; and indeed God has granted you all those who sail with you"' (Acts 27.20-24).

---

[33] Cf. Luke Timothy Johnson, *The Acts of the Apostles* (Sacra Pagina Series, 5; Collegeville, MN: Liturgical Press, 1992), p. 447.

Before the ship had sailed, Paul had warned the captain that lives would be lost unless they remained in Crete (Acts 27.10). The captain ignored Paul's warning and sailed directly into a violent storm that threatened to sink the ship. The storm was so ferocious that 'all hope' of being saved was lost. Paul, however, turned to God; and, after he had fasted and prayed for a long time, an angel of God appeared to him and promised that no lives would be lost.

In this narrative, Paul's fasting is generated by a severe crisis and its goal is divine intervention. Paul fasts in order to add urgency and passion to his prayers. The decision to fast and pray is not difficult when one's life hangs in the balance. In this case, Paul's intense and persistent prayer, strengthened by fasting, moved God to action, bringing deliverance not only to Paul but to all of the men on the ship.

8. Time to Stop Fasting – Acts 27.33-35

The storm continued for many days; and, apparently, the sailors were unwilling to rest on Paul's word of assurance. Therefore, they continued to fast and pray for fourteen days:

> Just before daybreak, Paul urged all of them to take some food, saying, 'Today is the fourteenth day that you have been in suspense and remaining without food, having eaten nothing. Therefore I urge you to take some food, for it will help you survive; for none of you will lose a hair from your heads'. Having said this, he took bread and gave thanks to God in the presence of all, and he broke it and began to eat (Acts 27.33-35).

After a long struggle against the storm, and with assurance from the Lord that all would be saved, Paul encouraged the sailors to eat so that they might regain their strength. The danger was not yet past and further challenges lay ahead; therefore, they would need their full energy to escape with their lives. Paul's admonition suggests that there are times when fasting is not appropriate or even detrimental.

C. Fasting in the Epistles

1. Fasting and Marriage – 1 Corinthians 7.5

In 1 Corinthians 7, Paul discusses several issues related to marriage, possibly in response to questions that had been posed to him by the believers in Corinth. It is likely someone was teaching that celibacy was to be preferred over marriage; and perhaps they were even teaching that all sex was sinful.³⁴ Paul insists, however, that sexual relations are not sinful when in the context of marriage; and, moreover, husbands and wives should not abstain from sex except for 'a time', which would be devoted to prayer and fasting.

> Let the husband render to his wife the affection due her, and likewise also the wife to her husband ... Do not deprive one another except with consent for a time, that you may give yourselves to fasting and prayer; and come together again so that Satan does not tempt you because of your lack of self-control (1 Cor. 7.3-5).³⁵

While this passage is a teaching on marriage, not on fasting, the connection between fasting and prayer is instructive.³⁶ It illustrates the early Christian view that when fasting, believers should also abstinence from all other earthly pleasures, including sex. Although fasting was an important Christian practice, husbands and wives should consider each other when making decisions about when to fast and when not to fast.

2. Fasting and the Labors of Ministry – 2 Corinthians 6.5

Paul spends a good deal of time in 2 Corinthians defending his ministry and his authority as an apostle. As evidence of his devotion to the service of Jesus Christ, Paul declares, 'But in all things we commend ourselves as ministers of God: in much patience, in tribulations, in needs, in distresses, in stripes, in imprisonments, in tumults, in labors, in sleeplessness, in fastings' (2 Cor. 6.4-5).

Paul's ministry created numerous hardships, which included 'sleeplessness' and 'fasting'.³⁷ These two hardships may have been

---

³⁴ See Craig Blomberg, *1 Corinthians* (NIV Application Commentary; Grand Rapids, MI: Zondervan, 1994), pp. 132-34.

³⁵ Many new translations omit the words 'and fasting' (νηστεία) because they are not found in the best Greek manuscripts. See Gordon D. Fee, *The First Epistle to the Corinthians* (The New International Commentary on the New Testament; Grand Rapids, MI: Eerdmans, 1987), p. 272.

³⁶ Cf. Wallis, *God's Chosen Fast*, p. 84.

³⁷ J.P. Louw and Eugene Albert Nida, *Greek-English Lexicon of the New Testament: Based on Semantic Domains* (2 vols.; New York: United Bible Societies, 2nd edn, 1989), conclude, 'In the two occurrences of ἀγρυπνία in the NT (2 Cor 6.5; 11.27), failure to sleep was evidently the result of external circumstances which prevented normal sleep' (I, p. 260).

self-imposed or they may have been forced upon Paul by the conditions under which he ministered. The Greek word νηστεία ('fasting') means simply to be without food, and it is only from the context that we may determine if the absence of food was a voluntary or involuntary situation. The fact that the other hardships mentioned in verses four through five were involuntary might suggest that his fastings were also involuntary.[38] Furthermore, if Paul's fastings were voluntary, then why did he not mention prayers, which would naturally accompany fastings? It might be best to leave the question open and to observe only that Paul fasted, either by necessity or as a voluntary practice.

In any case, the fastings of Paul are instructive. Inasmuch as voluntary fasting is a kind of self-imposed testing, it would seem to be unnecessary, or even harmful, when a person lives in circumstances of dire need. For example, the Christian tradition of abstaining from meat on fast days is irrelevant to a person who has only rice to eat. If fasting is the afflicting of ourselves so that our prayers might be more intense and focused, then fasting is not needed in situations where people are already genuinely afflicted as Paul was.

3. Fasting and Paul's Troubles – 2 Corinthians 11.27

Later in 2 Corinthians, Paul rehearses his trials, adding a bit more detail to some aspects of his suffering. Once again, he mentions fasting:

> From the Jews five times I received forty stripes minus one. Three times I was beaten with rods; once I was stoned; three times I was shipwrecked; a night and a day I have been in the deep; in journeys often, in perils of waters ... in weariness and toil, in sleeplessness often, in hunger and thirst, in fastings often, in cold and nakedness – besides the other things, what comes upon me daily: my deep concern for all the churches (2 Cor 11.23-28).

The comments above regarding 2 Cor. 6.5 apply here as well. It appears that Paul's hardships in ministry are involuntary impositions.

---

[38] Ralph P. Martin, *2 Corinthians* (Word Biblical Commentary; Waco, TX: Word Books, 1986), suggests that all of the hardships mentioned here are 'voluntary renunciations'; therefore, in this context, fasting should also be understood as voluntary (p. 175). However, I fail to see how tribulations, needs, distresses, stripes, and imprisonments qualify as 'voluntary'.

It is puzzling, however, that Paul mentions here both 'hunger and thirst' along with 'fastings'. The repetition of hunger and fasting may be for emphasis, or it may indicate that fasting is to be understood as something separate from hunger. If the latter is true, then fastings would signify voluntary abstinence from food.[39] Either way, Paul makes it clear that he endured many hardships and sufferings, and he did so for the sake of the gospel. His trials may not have been voluntary, but he entered into them willingly, choosing to suffer with Christ.

Paul's example inspired Oral Roberts to engage in regular times of fasting. Roberts wrote 'My entire being cried out for the Lord's power ... Through that time of fasting and prayer ... I soon understood the apostle Paul's hard-learned lesson that God's strength shall be made perfect in our weakness'.[40]

---

[39] Martin, *2 Corinthians*, leaves the question open (p. 380).
[40] Oral Roberts, *Expect a Miracle: My Life and Ministry, an Autobiography* (Nashville, TN: Thomas Nelson, 1995), p. 68.

4

TOWARD A BIBLICAL THEOLOGY OF FASTING

> Fasting confirms and increases *'seriousness of spirit, earnestness, sensibility and tenderness of conscience, deadness to the world, and*
> *consequently the love of God, and every holy and heavenly affection'*. – John Wesley[1]

The preceding examination of fasting in the Old and New Testaments reveals that people in the Bible fasted for a variety of reasons and for different lengths of time. All together, the Bible includes more than eighty references to fasting, more than twenty of which are in the New Testament.[2]

A number of scholars have attempted to discern a single core meaning of fasting, such as humility, mourning, or self-discipline. Each of those suggested meanings has much to commend it, but a single meaning cannot do justice to the diversity of the biblical text. Our study of the biblical text reveals that fasting is a natural human response to an intense affective experience, such as the experience of fear, danger, grief, suffering, humility, or awe. In the Bible, the function of fasting is to produce humility and single-mindedness in

---

[1] Wesley, 'Upon Our Lord's Sermon on the Mount: Discourse Seven', p. 310.
[2] The Hebrew צום (47), ענה נפש (11), Aramaic טות (1), Greek νηστεύω (14), νηστεία (5), νῆστις (2), and ἄσιτος (1) total 81. We can also add the references to Moses, who neither ate nor drank (Exod. 34.28; Deut. 9.9); Hannah, who 'did not eat' (1 Sam. 1.7); an unnamed prophet (1 Kgs 13.8-22); the psalmist (Ps. 42.3); and Paul and his shipmates (Acts 27).

the person fasting, which will result in added effectiveness in spiritual pursuits.

I will suggest five distinct functions of fasting in the Bible, but I admit that the categories could be stated differently and that these functions may overlap at certain points.

A. Urgency in Prayer

In the Bible, fasting is most often an expression of urgency in prayer, suggesting that 'Fasting ushers us into a reflective place where we can listen to God and pray wholeheartedly for things that really matter'.[3] In the Old Testament, when a person was faced with any dire need, they were encouraged to pour out their souls to God with all of their hearts through a prayer of lament. The person may suffer from illness, an attack of an enemy, a tragedy or some other crisis. These laments would include prayers of repentance (Psalm 51), prayers for healing (Psalm 38), prayers for divine wisdom and guidance (Psalm 86), prayers for aid in crisis (Psalm 3), and lamenting over the dead (2 Sam. 1.17-27).[4] All of these would be prayers of lament, which are expressions of the person's desire to reach out and get God's attention. Therefore, the person cries out to God, 'Oh, God, you are my God', as an indicator of the covenant relationship between the person and God. David Lambert agrees that fasting is a form of lament:

> petitionary prayer in the Hebrew Bible usually arises from the state of affliction or crisis. Voicing that affliction, prayer captures the attention of YHWH and rouses him, as a God of mercy, to pity and hence action. While prayer constitutes a verbal articulation of the distress, fasting provides an equally expressive – indeed, given the difficulty of rendering pain in words, perhaps an even more expressive – physical manifestation. It therefore shares in the dialogical nature of prayer.[5]

---

[3] Baab, *Fasting*, p. 10.

[4] McKnight's argument that fasting is not about 'results' goes against a multitude of biblical texts in which prayers are offered with the clear purpose and desire of obtaining a positive result. See, McKnight, *Fasting*, pp. xix-xxi.

[5] Lambert, 'Fasting as a Penitential Rite: A Biblical Phenomenon?', pp. 479-80, 487. Lambert's examination of the biblical text leads him to conclude that fasting as penance is foreign to biblical thought (pp. 478-80).

Biblical prayer is based upon the Old Testament paradigm of God's saving activity that reaches as far back as the exodus. In Exodus 2, the Israelites were suffering under the oppression of the Egyptians, and they cried out to God. Their groans reached up to heaven, and God remembered his covenant with Abraham (Exod. 2.23-25). God appeared to Moses and said, 'I have surely seen the oppression of my people … and have heard their cry … and I have come down to deliver them' (Exod. 3.7-8). The prayer of lament is an effort to cry out to God and reach God's ears,[6] and as a part of that cry, Old Testament believers would instinctively involve the whole person (including the body) as a way to make their cries more effective.[7] Therefore, fasting is an aid to urgent prayer because it involves the total person.

We usually think of prayer as a product of the mind. Prayers that are formed in the mind may then be expressed through the voice, the uttering of words. In times of urgent need, however, the mind and the voice are not enough to articulate the affections and passions that flow from the heart. Biblical prayer (and spirituality as a whole) involves the total person in order to get God's attention and to move God to action; therefore, fasting accompanies prayer as a way of involving the total person.[8] Pentecostal evangelist Franklin Hall writes, 'When a consecrated Christian goes into fasting, the fast becomes prayer to him in every sense of the meaning of prayer'.[9]

We might identify at least four specific types of prayer that were often accompanied by fasting: prayers of repentance, prayers for healing, prayers for God's guidance and illumination, and prayers for divine aid in time of crisis.[10]

---

[6] Cf. Ryan, *The Sacred Art of Fasting*, p. 22.

[7] Cf. McKnight, *Fasting*, p. xiii.

[8] It should be pointed out that for Pentecostals, glossolalia is another way that prayer is expressed to God, especially in those times when we do not know how we should pray. Through the gift of tongues, the Spirit prays through us with 'groanings that cannot be uttered' (Rom. 9.26, 27). Prayers in tongues (much like fasting) are often more primal and more deeply affective than prayers composed of words from our known languages.

[9] Hall, *The Fasting Prayer*, p. 35.

[10] John Wesley stated that fasting is a means 'of obtaining whatever blessings we stand in need of' (Wesley, 'Upon Our Lord's Sermon on the Mount: Discourse Seven', p. 311).

1. Prayers of Repentance

a. Confession of One's Own Sins

Biblical fasting as an aid to repentance was practiced by the entire Jewish community on the annual Day of Atonement, and it was encouraged whenever the people had failed in their covenant responsibilities. Prayers of confession and repentance might also be offered in the form of intercession for others, as was the case with Moses, Ezra, Nehemiah, and Daniel.

The Day of Atonement was prescribed in the Torah as an annual day of repentance for the Israelites; and fasting from both food and water was one of the day's essential requirements. Sacrifices would be made and the scapegoat would be sent into the wilderness bearing the sins of the people. In regard to fasting, Leviticus uses the terminology 'afflict yourselves', which emphasizes the humbling of oneself that is necessary for true repentance.

The connection between repentance, fasting, and the Day of Atonement manifests itself in the contemporary Jewish practice of reading the book of Jonah on the Day of Atonement. The people of Ninevah 'called a fast', and they repented of their evil and sought to change God's verdict against them (Jon. 3.5-10).

Repentance is accompanied by fasting in a number of other biblical texts. In 1 Samuel 7, for example, Samuel calls the Israelites together to Mizpah where he challenges them to confess their sins and discard their idols. The Israelites 'fasted on that day, and they said, "We have sinned against the LORD"' (1 Sam. 7.6). The prophet Joel also summons the people of Israel to repent in hope that God will forgive and restore favor to Israel. Joel calls out saying, 'Lament, O priests; wail, O ministers of the altar! ... Consecrate a fast; proclaim a solemn assembly. Gather the elders ... and cry out to the LORD' (Joel 1.13-14).

A similar fast was observed in Nehemiah when 'The people of Israel were assembled with fasting ... they made confession and worshiped the LORD their God' (Neh. 9.1-3). The people mourned and grieved over their sins, and their fasting was a sign of the sincerity of their repentance. They confessed their own sins as well as the sins of their ancestors, showing that the first step to restoration is the willingness to bear corporate responsibility for unfaithfulness.

In the biblical texts, fasting often accompanies repentance, but nowhere is it suggested that fasting is meritorious or that it accomplishes forgiveness.[11] Texts like Isaiah 58, Jeremiah 14, and Luke 18 demonstrate that fasting alone is not sufficient to produce true repentance or to effect forgiveness. The fasting on the Day of Atonement did not, in itself, provide forgiveness of sins. Forgiveness was secured by the offering of sacrifices, the release of the scapegoat, and by the genuine repentance of the people. The people of Ninevah, in addition to their fasting, 'believed in God', called on God, and 'repented' of their wickedness and violence. Joel includes fasting as one of the aids to repentance, along with weeping, mourning, and prayers for divine mercy. Fasting, however, does not accomplish anything apart from their returning to the Lord and their prayers for grace. Like weeping, fasting is an outward expression of the inward pain that is caused by their sin and their unfaithfulness to God. The fact that fasting accompanies repentance suggests that fasting, like prayer, both moves God and transforms the worshiper. After all, repentance is a human response to God's offer of grace. Thus, fasting does not atone for sin or earn God's favor; rather, it produces in the worshiper a willing heart and a humility of mind that enables true repentance to take place.[12]

b. Confession on Behalf of Others

Fasting is employed not only by those who repent of their own sins, but by those who intercede for others. When Moses reflected upon his second divine encounter on Mt. Sinai he explained that he had fasted 'because of' Israel's sin (Deut. 9.18-19). Moses believed that their idolatry, as manifested in the golden calf episode, had angered God to the point that God would 'destroy' the Israelites. Therefore, Moses fasted as a means of intercession for the Israelites. He pleaded with God to have mercy upon the sinful people, and God heard Moses' prayer.

Daniel, Ezra, and Nehemiah also fasted and prayed and confessed to God the sins of their people. Daniel says, 'Then I turned to the LORD God ... with fasting and sackcloth and ashes. I prayed ... and made confession' (Dan. 9.3). When Ezra learned that the

---

[11] Contra the Roman Catholic view as exemplified by Murphy, *The Spirituality of Fasting*, p. 17.
[12] Cf. Baab, *Fasting*, pp. 57-58.

post-exilic Jews had intermarried with the people of the land, he fell down before God in fasting and repentance (Ezra 9.3-6). 'He spent the night, neither eating bread nor drinking water; for he was mourning over the faithlessness of the exiles' (Ezra 10.6). Nehemiah's confession is reminiscent of the prayer of Daniel. Nehemiah affirms God's covenant faithfulness (Neh. 1.5) and admits that Israel's exile was on account of multiple transgressions (Neh. 1.8).

On the Day of Atonement and in Joel, the people are exhorted to fast and to repent for their own sins. However, Daniel, Ezra, and Nehemiah fast and confess on behalf of their people Israel. Their confessions represent a kind of corporate solidarity in which the entire community bears the guilt of sin, even if certain individuals are not guilty for the specific sins that are being confessed. The fasting of Daniel, Ezra, and Nehemiah on behalf of the people also reflects the same kind of pastoral intercession that is evident in the earlier story of Moses when he pleaded on behalf of the Israelites (Deut. 9.18-19). Too often, we are tempted to assert our own righteousness while casting blame toward others who appear to be more sinful than ourselves. The Old Testament would seem to suggest that our way forward is to join in corporate confession and repentance without self-righteous excuses.

2. Prayers for Healing

Many of the urgent prayers recorded in the Bible are pleas for healing. In Psalm 35, David recalls that when his enemies were sick he had fasted and prayed for their healing. He says, 'But as for me, when they were sick, My clothing was sackcloth; I afflicted myself with fasting' (Ps. 35.13). He had demonstrated a deep commitment to their good. He had responded to their crises as if they were his friends or brothers, and he had fasted and prayed as he would have done for his own mother.

When David's baby grew sick, he 'prayed to God for the child, and he fasted, and he went in and lay all night upon the ground' (2 Sam. 12.16). David's elders came and tried to get him to eat, but he refused. David fasted and prayed for seven days, pleading with God for the life of the child. It is evident that David considered fasting to be an important companion to his prayers for the healing of his child. He said, 'While the child was alive, I fasted and wept; for I said, "Who knows, the LORD may be gracious to me, that the child may live'" (2 Sam. 12.22). He believed that fasting would verify his repentance, his humility, his sincerity, his pain, and his urgency.

Even though David prayed and fasted earnestly, the child died. When presented with a crisis, David fasted. However, the fact that the child died indicates that fasting has no automatic magical power that causes God do our bidding. Fasting does not guarantee that we will get what we ask.

3. Prayers for God's Guidance

On many occasions, biblical characters prayed in order to discern God's will. Fasting is often reported to accompany these prayers for divine direction, wisdom, or illumination. On some occasions, the purpose of the prayer and fasting may not be stated explicitly, but when God responds to the prayer and fasting, he does so by providing illumination, wisdom, or direction.

In Judges 20, for example, the Israelites had been defeated, even though they believed their cause to be just. Therefore, they joined together in a corporate fast, which lasted from morning to evening (12 hours). After they wept and fasted and pleaded for guidance, the Lord answered them. Not only did the Lord give them specific direction, but he also gave them a word of hope. The Lord directed them to enter the fray once again; and this time they would win the victory.

At the end of the Babylonian exile, Ezra gathered about 5,000 of the Jews who agreed to return with him to Judea. In preparation for the journey, Ezra called upon the people to fast and pray that God would guide them on their journey back to Jerusalem. In order to ensure the effectiveness of their prayers, Ezra called for a corporate fast. He was well aware of the dangers that lay ahead and the need for God's help. The fasting of the Jews would intensify their prayers and certify to God their earnestness.

Others who received divine direction after fasting and praying include Elijah (1 Kings 19), Nehemiah (1.4), Daniel (10.2-3), Cornelius (Acts 10.30), the leaders at Antioch (Acts 13), and Paul (Acts 27). On one occasion, as the prophets and teachers at Antioch 'ministered unto the LORD and fasted, the Holy Ghost said, "Set apart for me Barnabas and Saul for the work to which I have called them"' (Acts 13.2). Fasting made their hearts receptive and open to the Holy Spirit, who spoke to them and provided clear indications that it was time for Barnabas and Saul to launch out into a new kind of ministry.

4. Prayers for Divine Aid in Crisis

In the Bible, fasting was often utilized when praying for divine intervention in time of crisis. In addition to the urgent needs for healing, forgiveness, and guidance, a broad range of other crises may present themselves to God's people. In the case of Hannah, for example, she was ridiculed repeatedly on account of her childlessness until she could not bear it any longer. At that point, Hannah 'wept and would not eat' (1 Sam. 1.7). She presented herself at the tabernacle of the Lord. Deeply distressed, she wept before the Lord and said, 'If you will look on my affliction ... and give me a son, then I will give him to the LORD all the days of his life' (1 Sam. 1.11). Hannah's self-imposed affliction (fasting) was an outward sign of her physical affliction and inward pain. Hannah came to a place where she needed to get in touch with God. Compared to the constant pain that Hannah endured, food became unimportant to her. She had suffered all that she could bear, so she prayed, fasted, and wept. Because of her insistence, which was authenticated by fasting, the Lord remembered her, and she soon gave birth to a son. Whenever our barrenness and the enemy's taunting become unbearable, fasting will help us to communicate our pain to God in prayer.

Also on the personal level, the psalmist reports that he fasted when threatened by deadly adversaries. In Psalm 102, the crisis is so acute that the psalmist forgets to eat. Worries, anxieties, and antagonists consume every waking moment. Although the outlook is bleak, the psalm concludes with statements of hope, because the Lord is 'enthroned forever' (v. 12) and will 'regard the prayer of the destitute' (v. 17).

Similarly, David's fasting in Psalm 109 is generated by a crisis caused by hateful adversaries. He prays that the curses hurled at him from his enemies will be turned back upon them, but he refuses to take vengeance into his own hands. He prays, 'Let them know that this is your hand; you, O Lord have done it' (v. 27). His goal in fasting is that God will be honored and glorified. David does not reckon his fasting to be efficacious of itself; his hope finds its justification in the character of God – God's 'steadfast love' (vv. 21, 26).

A crisis occurred on the national level when Jehoshaphat was king of Judah.[13] The Moabites and Ammonites assembled their armies and attacked Judah; 'Jehoshaphat was afraid; he set himself to seek the LORD, and proclaimed a fast throughout all Judah' (2 Chron. 20.3) The king and the people fasted and pleaded for God's help. Then the Spirit of the Lord came upon a man named Jahaziel, who prophesied, 'Thus says the LORD to you: "Do not fear or be dismayed at this great multitude; for the battle is not yours but God's"' (2 Chron. 20.15). The Lord gave instructions for the battle, and Judah won a great victory over all its enemies.

The fasting of Jehoshaphat was generated out of his sense of urgency. The crisis of war was at the door, and Judah desperately needed God's help. The fast demonstrated to God that Jehoshaphat and his people were reliant upon God and not upon themselves. The fast produced humility and receptivity to the Holy Spirit, creating an environment in which the Spirit could speak a prophetic word to the community.

In Jewish tradition, the story of Esther is esteemed as a great example of crisis-oriented fasting. The setting for the book of Esther is the post-exilic Persian empire. When Esther came of age, she was chosen by King Ahasuerus to be his queen. Haman, an enemy of the Jews, plotted to have all of the Jews killed, and a decree was written and disseminated to every province, ordering the death of all the Jews. The Jews responded with fasting and weeping and lamenting, and most of them lay in sackcloth and ashes' (Est. 4.3). Furthermore, Esther proclaimed a three-day fast for all the Jews (Est. 4.15). When Esther approached the king, he listened to all that she had to say, and the Jews were saved. Haman, who had conspired to kill the Jews, was hanged on the same gallows that he had prepared for Mordecai's execution. In memory of God's miraculous deliverance of the Jewish people, the annual days of Purim were established. From that day until now, the Jews have fasted on the day before Purim (Est. 9.30-31).

The fast of Esther and the Jews was an attempt to ameliorate a crisis in which their lives were threatened. Planning and preparation for Esther's mission were not sufficient to meet the threat. Even

---

[13] Another national fast was observed in Jer. 36.6-9 in response to the impending Babylonian invasion.

prayer was not sufficient under these urgent conditions – they must fast. Furthermore, their fasting was of the most radical kind; they abstained from all food and drink for a period of three days. Clearly, their fast was not for the purpose of spiritual formation, growth in grace, self-denial, sanctification, or any other transformative purpose. Their fast was intended to get God's attention so that God might intervene and avert the crisis. Their fasting was a matter of life and death. God heard their prayers and worked behind the scenes to give favor to Esther and to orchestrate a reversal of the circumstances.

In the New Testament, we read that the apostle Paul fasted when faced with a deadly storm. He was on a ship that was headed for Rome when a storm arose that was so severe that all hope was lost. However, after fasting, Paul stood up in the midst of the sailors and declared that an angel of God had appeared to him, promising that no lives would be lost (Acts 27.21-25). Paul's experience confirms the Old Testament practice of fasting in times of crisis, whether that crisis be personal or communal. Crisis-oriented fasting has strong support in the biblical text.

B. Fasting as Mourning

In the Bible, fasting can be an expression of mourning. We observed in relation to David's fasting for the healing of his child that it was customary among the Jews to fast as a sign of mourning for the dead. One example of that practice is found in 1 Samuel 31, when King Saul and his sons are killed in battle. The men of Jabesh-gilead came and rescued the bodies of Saul and his sons. They brought them to Jabesh, burned them (to prevent any further humiliation) and buried their bones under a tree at Jabesh. Then they fasted for seven days as a symbol of their grief and mourning over their slain king (cf. 1 Chron. 10.12).

News of the death of Saul and Jonathan soon reached the ears of David, who had returned to Ziklag after his defeat of the Amalekite raiders. David responded to the news with much grief. He tore his clothing, and he and his men 'mourned and wept and fasted until evening, for Saul and for Jonathan his son … because they were fallen by the sword' (2 Sam. 1.11). David was a challenger to Saul's throne and an object of Saul's hatred; therefore, we might expect him to have rejoiced over the death of his adversary. However, David held the office of king in great respect, and he mourned greatly over the death of Saul, 'the LORD's anointed' and over Jonathan, David's close friend. In honor of the slain king, David and his men fasted from morning until evening. The text gives no indication that David's grief was artificial or insincere. Therefore, his fasting resulted naturally from the intense shock of hearing about Saul's death. When grief is overwhelming, the appetite is diminished.

Soon after the death of Saul, Abner, one of Saul's men, changed sides and swore allegiance to David. However, David's general, Joab, murdered Abner, and David was devastated at Joab's disregard for the covenant that David had made with Abner. King David wept and mourned for Abner, and he fasted until sundown (2 Sam. 3.31-36). On this occasion, David's mourning and fasting was a matter of honor and duty rather than affection.

C. Fasting and Worship

1. Fasting and Divine Encounter

When Moses first met the Lord on the far side of the desert, the Lord instructed him to bring the Israelites to Mt. Sinai where they would 'worship God' (Exod. 3.12). Moses did just as the Lord commanded him, and with the Israelites encamped at the foot of the mountain, Moses went up to meet God. Moses encountered God's glory and fell down before the Lord, fasting for forty days and forty nights. To attain God's presence is the goal of worship, and for Moses, fasting and worship were joined for forty days.

Moses was sustained by God in a miraculous fashion. Evidently, the presence of God was so powerful, that Moses was nourished by the divine energy. The fact that his face glowed with light when he came down from the mountain was evidence that Moses' body was to some extent transformed by the experience. The fasting of Moses teaches us that although the consumption of food and water is the normal requirement for human existence, the power and presence of God are sufficient to overcome that normal requirement. It is likely that Moses fasted because the divine presence overwhelmed his desire for food. Therefore, Moses' story demonstrates that profound worship experiences can be more captivating than the allure of physical appetites. There are times when food becomes unimportant in comparison to the attraction of the divine presence, when God's glory overpowers every other sight, sound, and sensation.

The experience of Elijah mirrored that of Moses. Elijah fasted for forty days and nights as he journeyed to Mt. Sinai, where he encountered God's glory just as Moses had (1 Kgs 19.7-8). The Lord passed by in wind, earthquake, and fire; then Elijah heard the voice of the Lord. As I mentioned earlier, like Moses, Elijah fasted for forty days and forty nights. Like Moses, Elijah encountered God's presence on the mountain. Like Moses, Elijah was directed by the voice of God. Later on, like Moses, Elijah was taken from the earth by God himself. As in the case of Moses, Elijah's fasting was apparently a sign of God's miraculous, sustaining power. Like Moses, Elijah did not live by bread alone, but by the word of God.

Fasting and worship are connected also in Psalm 42. The psalmist is hungry and thirsty for the presence of God. In fact, he is so consumed with his desire to 'come and appear before God', that he has lost his appetite. His fasting is generated by his intense affection for God and for God's presence. Instead of eating, he weeps. The fasting continues 'day and night' as a manifestation of urgent longing. The psalmist's longing for God foreshadows the similar longing of Pentecostal worshipers, who seek for the presence and glory of God.[14]

New Testament texts about fasting align it closely with worship. We read in Acts 13 that the prophets and leaders at Antioch were praying and fasting, and 'as they worshiped the LORD and fasted', the Holy Spirit spoke, calling Barnabas and Saul to a specific work of ministry. Here, fasting and prayer are practiced as a dimension of worship. This Greek word (λειτουργέω) also indicates that fasting was considered to be an essential duty. It was a practice that was necessary for fulfilling the roles of 'prophets and teachers' (Acts 13.1). That is, fasting and prayer should be a regular part of worship for leaders in the Church.[15] Inasmuch as the prophets and teachers

---

[14] See Lee Roy Martin, 'Longing for God: Psalm 63 and Pentecostal Spirituality', *Journal of Pentecostal Theology* 22.1 (2013), pp. 54-76.

[15] It is texts like this one that demonstrate the weakness of McKnight's definition of fasting: 'Fasting is the natural, inevitable response of a person to a grievous sacred moment' (McKnight, *Fasting*, p. xviii). Ordination is a sacred moment

were ministering 'to the LORD' in their fasting and prayer, it seems important to observe that fasting, as worship, is directed toward God and is intended to bring glory and honor to God who is worshiped.[16]

2. Fasting as Part of a Worshipful Life

Worship includes remarkable moments of divine encounter; but, as a way of life, worship extends beyond the remarkable and into the habitual. Therefore, regular times of fasting can serve as an expression of customary and constant worship.[17] Persistent worship is evident in the New Testament story of the prophet Anna. Mary and Joseph brought the infant Jesus 'to Jerusalem to present him to the LORD' (Lk. 2.22) and to offer a sacrifice. There, they encountered Anna, who at the age of eighty-four, 'never left the temple, serving night and day with fastings and prayers' (Lk. 2.37). The word 'serving' (Greek λατρεύω) means 'to perform religious rites as a part of worship', and in many cases is best translated 'worship'. Anna's attentiveness to God was characterized by regular times of fasting and prayer.[18] Her fasting, however, was not for repentance, mourning, or for a particular urgent prayer. Rather, her fasting was an act of worship that diverted her attention away from the earthly and set her gaze toward the heavenly.

Although Jesus did not command or require his disciples to fast, he assumed that they would fast because of its spiritual benefits.[19] In Matthew 6, he taught on almsgiving, prayer, and fasting. In referring to each practice, Jesus used the word 'when' rather than 'if'. He said, 'when you give ...', 'when you pray ...', and 'when you fast ...' Within the context of the first century, it was not necessary for Je-

---

but not a 'grievous' moment. Other texts show that fasting is not always a 'response', it is often observed out of hope and in anticipation of future sacred moments. McKnight's definition is suggestive, but it is too simplistic; and, as a presupposition to his exegesis, it unduly influences his interpretation of the biblical text.

[16] Fasting as worship may be inferred from Zech. 7.5, when the Lord asked the Jews, 'When you fasted ... did you fast unto me?'

[17] Although the Day of Atonement came only once a year, it represented a continual and regular observance that was tied intimately to the worship of the tabernacle/temple.

[18] The verb translated 'never left' is imperfect tense and 'fasting' is a present participle, both having a durative or ongoing aspect.

[19] Cf. Curtis C. Mitchell, 'The Practice of Fasting in the New Testament', *Bibliotheca Sacra* 147.588 (1990), p. 458.

sus to command his disciples to give, to pray, or to fast. These three acts of righteousness were built into the fabric of Jewish life, and Jesus was confident that his disciples would perform them regularly.

Furthermore, he explained that his disciples would fast after he had been taken away from them (Mt. 9.14-15; Mk 2.18-20; Lk. 5.33-35). The 'taking away' of Jesus suggests that fasting as worship can have eschatological significance. When Jesus was taken from the earth, the Church entered a period of Jesus' absence (though he is present through the Holy Spirit). Jesus went away, and he promised to return, but he has not returned yet. While the bridegroom is away, his disciples fast. The Church is living in a time of hope, awaiting the return of Jesus, at which time the Marriage Supper of the Lamb will mark the end of the time of fasting. In much the same way that Anna fasted in anticipation of the coming Messiah, the Church fasts in anticipation of the return of that same Messiah.

The fastings of Paul point to another aspect of the worshipful life. His record of suffering (which included fasting) was an important part of his apostolic defense (2 Cor. 6.5; 2 Cor. 11.27). Paul makes it clear that he endured many hardships and sufferings, and he did so for the sake of the gospel. His trials may not have been voluntary, but he entered into them willingly, choosing to suffer with Christ as an act of worship. The modern, western view of worship as a reflective, cognitive activity does not take into account the biblical insistence on bodily (and affective) participation in worship. Perhaps Paul's fasting is part of his own outworking of his exhortation to the Roman believers: 'present your bodies a living and holy sacrifice, acceptable to God, which is your spiritual service of worship' (Rom. 12.1).[20] Through fasting, Paul's body became a living sacrifice, offered in worship.

D. Fasting and Ministry

Fasting played an important role in the ministries of biblical characters like Moses, Elijah, Daniel, Ezra, Nehemiah, Jesus, and Paul. Some of them fasted at the inauguration of their ministries, and others fasted at key moments in their ministries. The prophet Joel

---

[20] The Greek word translated 'spiritual service of worship' is λατρεία, which is a cognate of the verb λατρεύω, used in Lk. 2.37 in reference to Anna's fasting.

called for a time of fasting that would be followed by the outpouring of the Holy Spirit and universal prophetic ministry. Saul of Tarsus (later called Paul) was filled with the Holy Spirit while fasting (Acts 9.17). Although fasting did not play a role in Saul's conversion on the road to Damascus, it was instrumental in the subsequent outworking of his call to ministry. In the book of Acts, fasting plays a key role in authorizing, ordaining, leading, and empowering ministry.

1. Calling and Direction in Ministry

The fasting of the prophets and teachers in Antioch (Acts 13) appears to have been a continuing element in the performance of their ministries, but during one observance of fasting, the Holy Spirit singled out Barnabas and Saul for a specific calling to ministry. The text does not indicate in what manner the Spirit spoke, but it was likely through some kind of prophetic word. The hearers of the Spirit's message understood it to be a call to go forth and spread the gospel to other cities. Therefore, in obedience to the charismatic word, they sent forth Barnabas and Saul as missionaries.

From the Gospels, we learn that the ministry of Jesus Christ was preceded by forty days of fasting and testing. Unlike Saul, however, Jesus did not fast as preparation for the Spirit. The Holy Spirit came upon Jesus at his baptism, and then the Spirit led him into the wilderness where he fasted. Jesus' forty-day fast placed him in the company of Moses and Elijah, who had fasted while encountering God's presence. Jesus, however, instead of encountering the glory of God, encountered the attack of the devil. Jesus' fasting, therefore, was part of his testing; and his passing of the test was evidence that he was prepared for his messianic ministry. Given the difficulty of ministry today, I would suggest that fasting might play a similar role in preparing ministers for the tests that they will face.

2. Ordination and the Community

Although it is God who calls women and men to ministry, it is the Church, the community of faith that participates in that calling as a context, a witness, a sender, a supporter, and as an encourager. Every minister represents the Church, and the Church participates in every ministry.

Therefore, as soon as the Holy Spirit had spoken and set apart Barnabas and Saul as missionaries, the other leaders at Antioch acted to obey the Spirit's directions: 'When they had fasted and prayed, they sent them on their way' (Acts 13.3). Apparently, their earlier fasting as worship was not enough to prepare Barnabas and Saul for their task as missionaries. They must also take time to fast and pray in order that they might be spiritually equipped for the work that lay ahead of them and so that God might go with them. Moreover, the other leaders must lend their support for their brothers by entering into the fast along with them. This passage, therefore, suggests that fasting can function both as a preparation for ministry and as a sign of corporate solidarity with others who are entering ministry.

After Barnabas and Saul had established a number of churches in Asia Minor, they 'appointed elders in every church, with prayer and fasting they entrusted them to the Lord in whom they had believed' (Acts 14.23). Just as the church at Antioch had ordained them with fasting and prayer, Barnabas and Saul ordained those who were chosen to serve as elders in the new churches. Fasting and prayer were means of entrusting the elders to the Lord, and the Lord would empower the elders for ministry. Fasting as a part of ordination serves to recognize the weaknesses and frailty of all human leaders. Fasting should produce in the leader a dependency upon the Lord and upon his Holy Spirit.

E. Fasting and Dependence upon God

Fasting is an assertion of dependence upon God; and through fasting, we learn that God, not food, sustains us. The devil tempted Jesus by saying, 'If you are the Son of God, then turn these stones into bread' (Mt. 4.3). Although Jesus had not eaten for forty days and was very hungry, he refused to surrender to temptation. He answered the devil by citing Deut. 8.3, 'A person does not live by bread alone but by every word that comes forth from the mouth of God'. Rather than turn the stones into bread in order to satisfy his physical hunger, Jesus affirmed the life-giving power of the word of God. Jesus knew that even as all living things came into existence by God's word, they continue to be sustained by that same living word.

The larger context of Deut. 8.3 indicates that Israel's hunger in the wilderness was a time of testing, orchestrated by God so that he might discipline them 'as a man disciplines his son' (Deut. 8.5). Through this discipline, the Lord would learn what was in their hearts; he would discover whether they would be faithful to him or not (8.2). He assured them that he was bringing them to a good land where they would 'eat food without scarcity' and they would 'lack nothing' (8.9). They were warned of the dangers of forgetting that everything they have comes from God. God spoke and water flowed from the rock. God spoke and manna rained down from heaven. Therefore, even the bread itself was created by God's word. Everything they had needed for survival had been given to them by the word of God. However, if they should ever begin to trust in themselves or turn to other gods, they would 'surely perish' (8.19).

We are tempted to believe that food is our source of life and strength and that we obtained it by our own ingenuity. Fasting humbles us and tests our commitment to the word of life.[21] Fasting reveals what is in our hearts. Fasting reminds us to praise God for the 'good land' that he has given us. Through fasting we learn that it is the spiritual, not the physical, that sustains us.

F. Biblical Critique of Fasting

Our study of the biblical text reveals at least five functions of fasting: (1) Fasting is an aid to any kind of urgent prayer (2) Fasting is an expression of mourning (3) Fasting is an expression of worship (4) Fasting plays a key role in authorizing, ordaining, leading, and empowering ministry (5) Fasting is an expression of dependence upon God and his Word. In addition to these functions of fasting, the Bible offers a critique of those who fast for the wrong reasons or with improper expectations. Therefore, the Lord does not accept all fasting.

1. Fasting while Oppressing the Weak
Fasting, like all religious practices, can become an empty ritual, performed out of habit or duty. A legalistic attitude toward religious rites, in which the rules surrounding a practice receive more attention than the theological functions of the practice, can erode the spiritual benefits to the point that deep reform is needed. The Old Testament prophets accused the Israelites of reaching that point. In Isaiah 58, the practice of fasting was singled out as a ritual that illustrated Israel's spiritual disease. If we are to prevent our fasting from

---

[21] Cf. Buchanan, 'Go Fast and Live: Hunger as Spiritual Discipline', p. 17.

degenerating into a valueless ritual, we must pay close attention to Isaiah's guidelines for the fast that is pleasing to God.

The Israelites fasted, but they claimed their fasting had gone unrewarded! They complain to God: 'We have fasted, so why have you not seen us? (Isa. 58.3). God replies that he could not take notice of their fasting because they were oppressing their neighbors. Rather than humbling themselves and pursuing God's desire, they were pursuing their own selfish desires. Rather than afflicting themselves as an outward sign of inward mourning, they fought among themselves and oppressed the weak (Isa. 58.3-4).

Apparently, the Israelites had followed the proper liturgy in their fasting – afflicting themselves, bowing down, lying in sackcloth and ashes – but the Lord insists that their fasting did not please him. The fast that pleases God will cause those in power to release their wicked and oppressive grip on the weak. The fast that pleases God will include radical hospitality: those who prosper will share with the hungry, provide shelter for the homeless, and give clothing to the naked. Fasting pleases God only when it is accompanied by the practice of justice and righteousness (Isa. 58.6-13).

2. Fasting while Worshiping Idols

Jeremiah offers a rebuke similar to that of Isaiah, but his assessment of Israel's spiritual condition emphasizes a different sin. Jeremiah's prophecy resembles Isaiah 58 in many ways. The people were calling upon the Lord, but he was unwilling to hear their prayers. Idolatry was rampant, and God had threatened judgment. However, while Isaiah emphasized Israel's sins of injustice and selfishness (failure to love one's neighbor), Jeremiah stressed Israel's sin of idolatry (failure to love God). Therefore, Jeremiah says of the Israelites, 'they have loved to wander' (Jer. 36.10). Without a complete return to God, fasting would do them no good. They could fast, they could pray, they could offer sacrifices, but they still have their idols. They must give up those idols and worship the Lord alone before the Lord would honor their fasting and prayer.

Fasting does not compensate for spiritual deficiencies in other areas. It is not a cure-all for our spiritual ills, but it is one spiritual practice that helps us to get in touch with our ourselves (our addictions, our weaknesses) and to get in touch with God (his strength, his purposes).

3. Fasting on Display

Fasting was an important mark of piety in first-century Judaism, and Jesus instructs his followers to examine their motivations behind the practice. They should not fast with the objective of being noticed by others; rather, they should fast to the Father who is 'in secret' (Mt. 6.16-18). Jesus' command that we fast to the Father who is 'in secret' does not mean that our fasting must be kept secret and that fasting is entirely an individual practice. Fasting is not in secret; rather, it is the Father who is in secret. To fast to the Father who is in secret means that we do not fast with the intent of putting our piety on display – we do not make a show of our fasting. It means that we do not fast for the approval and praise of other people.

The kind of fasting that Jesus calls for stands in contrast to the fasting of the Pharisee who boasted that he fasted twice a week (Lk. 18.12). Fasting is normally practiced as an expression of humility and self-abasement, but the Pharisee found his fasting to be a reason for self-exaltation and pride. Fasting, like other religious rituals, can be a valuable aid to spiritual growth; but it must not be seen as meritorious or as an end in itself.[22]

4. Fasting at Inappropriate Times

As helpful as fasting can be, there are times when fasting is not appropriate. In 1 Samuel 14, we read that Saul had commanded his soldiers to fast, thinking that God would honor their self-denial. Saul failed to realize that the soldiers would need as much energy as could be mustered if they were to defeat the enemy. Normally, fasting is observed in conjunction with resting. The Day of Atonement, for example, is a 'sabbath of solemn rest' (Lev. 16.31). Although fasting is an important aid to prayer and a helpful method for dealing with crisis, there are times when fasting is counterproductive.

Zechariah points to another type of fasting that is inappropriate – memorial fasting. By the time of Zechariah, the Jews had established four new fasts as days of mourning over the calamities that led up to the exile. However, in light of the Lord's promise to rebuild the temple and to restore Judah, these fast days that commemorated the judgment of God would be changed into days of

---

[22] Cf. Wesley, 'Upon Our Lord's Sermon on the Mount: Discourse Seven', p. 317.

feasting filled with rejoicing. Zechariah seems to suggest, therefore, that the memory of past suffering is not a legitimate reason for fasting.[23]

Jesus points out that fasting is a time of mourning and/or expectation; therefore, fasting is inappropriate during times of feasting, celebration, and fulfillment. When questioned as to why his disciples did not fast, Jesus replied that the guests at a wedding do not fast while the bridegroom is present (Mt. 9.14-15; Mk 2.18-20; Lk. 5.33-35). Once the bridegroom has departed, the guests may fast. The apostle Paul, for example, fasted and prayed during the storm that threatened to destroy the ship in which he sailed. However, as soon as Paul was assured by the Lord that everyone's lives would be saved, he encouraged his shipmates to eat and regain their strength (Acts 27.33-35). Paul's fasting was appropriate in a time of mourning, seeking, and hoping; but once he had been assured of safety, he considered fasting to be no longer necessary.

G. Other Observations about Fasting in the Bible

The survey of fasting in the Bible has revealed a number of helpful insights regarding the nature and function of fasting. In addition to those that have already been noted, I would make a few other observations about the biblical fasts:

1. Fasting could be a private matter, but fasting was often a public activity, involving a group of people or the entire community.
2. Fasting was sometimes observed on behalf of others rather than for oneself.
3. Fasting can be a part of the liturgical calendar (annual fasts and weekly fasts), but most of the fasts mentioned in Scripture came in response to a crisis.
4. Fasting can be of various durations, depending upon the situation. Normally, fasting lasted from 12 hours to 3 days.
5. Biblical fasts include fasting from both food and drink (the total fast), fasting from food (the normal fast), and fasting

---

[23] The memorial fast of Purim seems to contradict the spirit of Zechariah's prophecy, but it should be noted that the fast of Purim was commanded by Esther, not by the Lord.

from meat, wine, and delicacies (abstinence/partial fast/ Daniel fast). Daniel's experience suggests that if one is unable to practice normal fasting, abstinence from certain rich foods can be beneficial. It can add urgency to prayers and depth to spiritual passion. A partial fast can strengthen humility and help to direct prayer toward God.
6. Biblical fasting is a companion to prayer.[24] It cannot be emphasized too much that fasting alone will not accomplish the spiritual results that come with fasting combined with prayer, meditation on Scripture, and waiting upon God. Those who fast must take time to go apart and pray and seek God during their fast.
7. The purpose of fasting in the Bible is to involve the body (hence the whole person) in communion with God. It is not enough to express prayer through words. Pain, lament, and cries must be shared with God through bodily action.
8. Fasting developed in Christianity as an act of self-denial and self-discipline. The theology of fasting as a discipline might be expressed through Paul's reflections to the Corinthian church: 'I keep under my body and bring it into subjection' (1 Cor. 9.27); and 'all things are lawful for me, but I will not be brought under the power of any' (1 Cor. 6.12). For Paul, those who have no self-control cannot be considered Christians; they are people 'whose end is destruction, whose god is their belly' (Phil. 3.19).

H. Conclusion

Nowhere in the New Testament are we commanded to fast. However, we are commanded to humble ourselves before God, and fasting is one of the ways that we humble ourselves. 'When we fast, we throw ourselves on the mercy of God. We acknowledge that we have nothing without God, we are utterly dependent on God, and God alone is our treasure and hope.'[25] Since fasting is a type of self-humiliation, it points to Jesus' statement that 'whoever exalts himself shall be abased and he that humbles himself shall be exalted'

---

[24] Cf. Wesley, 'Upon Our Lord's Sermon on the Mount: Discourse Seven', pp. 312, 318.
[25] Baab, *Fasting*, p. 32.

(Lk. 14.11). Peter writes, 'God resists the proud but gives grace to the humble. Therefore, humble yourselves under the mighty hand of God, that God may exalt you in due time' (1 Pet. 5.5, 6). James puts it in these words, 'Afflict yourselves, and mourn, and weep; let your laughter be turned to mourning, and your joy to heaviness. Humble yourselves in the sight of the LORD, and he will lift you up' (Jas 4.6-10). James uses the term, 'afflict yourselves', which often refers to fasting; still, he does not mention fasting explicitly.

Not only are we commanded to humble ourselves, but we are promised a reward if we do so. Jesus, Peter, and James declare that whoever will humble himself or herself will be exalted. The Greek word used in these texts (ὑψόω) means to elevate or place above. In the context of the above Scriptures it means the giving of dignity, or 'enhancement in honor, fame, position, power, fortune'.[26]

Those who draw near to God through fasting will be rewarded with God's intimate presence. Moses met with God face to face while fasting (Exod. 34.28). Daniel received visions while fasting (Dan. 9.3-27; 10.1-21). Elijah heard the still small voice of God while fasting (1 Kgs 19.12). Jesus was ministered to by angels while fasting (Mt. 4.11). While fasting, Anna was allowed to see the redeemer (Lk. 2.37, 38). Paul was baptized in the Holy Spirit while fasting (Acts 9.9-18). While fasting, Cornelius saw a vision that led him to Peter (Acts 10.3, 30). The Holy Spirit spoke to the early church leaders when they fasted (Acts 13.2). An angel brought a message to Paul when he had fasted (Acts 27.21-24). Not everyone who fasts receives revelations, angelic visitations, or visions, but if you draw near to God through fasting, God has promised to 'draw near to you' (Jas 4.8).

---

[26] Bauer, *A Greek-English Lexicon*, p. 858.

5

FASTING IN CHRISTIAN HISTORY

Fasting enables us spiritually to see that spiritual air in which Christ, the Sun who knows no setting, does not rise, but shines without ceasing.
– St. Symeon the New Theologian[1]

A. Fasting in Early Christianity

The practice of fasting has been an important component of the spirituality of Judaism and Christianity from their beginnings. The Israelites of the Old Testament practiced fasting, and so did the Jews and Christians of the New Testament. Early Christians fasted for a variety of reasons.[2] They fasted in commemoration of the death of Jesus, in preparation for baptism, as a weapon against temptation,[3] for the reception of revelations,[4] and out of concern for the poor.[5] They understood that fasting was acceptable to God only when observed in conjunction with righteousness and justice.[6]

---

[1] Symeon, *Symeon the New Theologian: The Discourses* (The Classics of Western Spirituality; New York: Paulist Press, 1980), p. 168.

[2] On early Christian fasting, see David W.T. Brattston, 'Fasting in the Earliest Church', *Restoration Quarterly* 53.4 (2011), pp. 235-45.

[3] See Polycarp, who writes, 'persevering in fasting, beseeching the all-seeing God in our supplications "to lead us not into temptation," even as the Lord said, "The spirit is willing, but the flesh is weak"' (*Letter to the Philippians* 7). Cf. Clement of Alexandria, *Stromata* 7.12.

[4] See *The Shepherd of Hermas*, Vis. 2.2.1; 3.10.6-7; *The Acts of Peter* 2.1.1; 2.2.5; 2.6.17-18; *The Acts of Thomas* 9.86.

[5] E.g. *The Shepherd of Hermas*, Sim. 5.1-3.

[6] Cf. *The Epistle of Barnabas* 3.1-5, which cites Isa. 58.4-10.

In the *Didache: The Teaching of the Twelve Apostles,* one of the earliest Christian documents, believers are advised to fast every Wednesday and Friday. Those particular days were selected in order to separate the Christians from the Jews, who fasted on Tuesdays and Thursdays. The *Didache* states, 'But let not your fasts be with the hypocrites [i.e. the Jews], for they fast on the second and fifth day of the week. Rather, fast on the fourth day and the Preparation [Friday]' (*Didache* 8.1). The Friday fast coincided with the crucifixion of Jesus; therefore, fasting on Friday connected the early believers with the sufferings of Jesus.

The *Didache* also calls for fasting for another reason, one that is rarely mentioned in discussions of fasting: 'pray for your enemies, and fast on behalf of those who persecute you' (*Didache* 1.3). This expansion of Jesus' command to 'love your enemies, and pray for those who persecute you' (Mt. 5.44), makes prayer for one's enemies a serious matter indeed. To say a prayer for one's enemy is a difficult task, but to fast for that enemy requires an even deeper commitment to peace.

Very early on, many Christians fasted for the purpose of saving food, which could then be given to the poor. In a time when people had very little income but desired to share with others, fasting was a way of saving food that could be given away to those in need.[7] Even today, some people fast for this reason, and others fast as a way of expressing solidarity with the poor and with those who are hungry around the world.[8] Speaking in the same spirit but more broadly, Augustine wrote, 'fasting without kindness and mercy is worth nothing to the one who is fasting'.[9]

The practice of fasting developed more complexity over the years, and conflicting views of fasting were expressed, particularly during the patristic period.[10] Some proponents of fasting believed

---

[7] Jewish tradition also encouraged the sharing of food on fast days (Sanh. 35a and Ber. 6b). Cf. Wesley, 'Upon Our Lord's Sermon on the Mount: Discourse Seven', p. 318.

[8] Cf. 'PCUSA Fasting Monthly to Identify with Poor', *Christian Century* 125. 21 (2008), p. 18.

[9] 'On the Beginning of Lent', Sermon 207.1, *The Works of St. Augustine: A Translation for the 21st Century* (ed. John E. Rotelle; trans. Edmund Hill; Hyde Park, NY: New City, 1995), III/6, pp. 109-10.

[10] Cf. Herbert Musurillo, 'The Problem of Ascetical Fasting in the Greek Patristic Writers', *Traditio* 12 (1956), p. 2.

that all fasting should be voluntary, while others proposed that all Christians should be required to fast, especially on certain important days.[11]

There was also a tension over the meaning of fasting in relation to the theology of body and spirit. Christians who were influenced by Greek dualism believed that the materiality of food was the cause of much evil;[12] therefore, Christians should eat as little as possible and fast as often as possible.[13] Furthermore, according to these and other extremists, all forms of pleasure are evil; consequently, food should not be enjoyed,[14] and even married Christians should remain celibate.[15] On the other extreme, however, *The Gospel of Thomas* insists that fasting is unnecessary to believers who have been purified from sin.[16]

For some of the Fathers, fasting was a means of developing the discipline needed for spiritual growth, while for others it was a form of penance that should be practiced regularly according to the church calendar. The idea that fasting should be a regular component of spiritual discipline was a key ingredient in the monastic movement. The first step toward monasticism was when certain individuals began to separate themselves and to practice rigorous asceticism alone. Later, however, groups of these individuals who believed the Church was being secularized began to form into

---

[11] Cf. Leo the Great, who wrote that the Lenten fast 'is imposed on all the faithful without exception': 'Sermon 49.1', in Philip Schaff and Henry Wace (eds.), *Nicene and Post-Nicene Fathers. Second Series* (14 vols.; Peabody, MA: Hendrickson Publishers, 1994), XII, p. 160.

[12] Margaret R. Miles, *Fullness of Life: Historical Foundations for a New Asceticism* (Philadelphia, PA: Westminster Press, 1981), p. 19. Cf. Murphy, *The Spirituality of Fasting*, pp. 42-43.

[13] E.g. Tertullian, *De Ieiunio Adversus Psychicos* (*On Fasting: In Opposition to the Materialists*), which is the earliest extended Christian treatment of fasting. Negative views of the body are also present later in Augustine, who wrote, for example, that the body weighs down the soul ('On the Value of Fasting', Sermon 400, *Works of St. Augustine*, III/10, p. 473).

[14] See Basil, who writes, 'eating should be for necessity and not for pleasure' (*Longer Rules* 19). See also his *Shorter Rules* 126-40. Augustine would later write that food is necessary, but enjoyment of it inevitably leads to sin (*Confessions* 10.31).

[15] Cf. Augustine, 'On the Beginning of Lent', Sermon 210.9, *Works of St. Augustine*, III/6, p. 123.

[16] Berghuis, *Christian Fasting: A Theological Approach*, pp. 87-89. At some points, the *Gospel of Thomas* seems to present contradictory views regarding fasting.

communities that lived separate from normal society. Dietary rules varied from one monastic community to another, but even the most lenient community required painfully rigorous fasting. St. Antony, the father of monasticism, ate only one meal per day, consisting only of bread, salt, and water.[17] These 'monks' practiced fasting as a path of self-denial, mortification of the flesh, and the individual attainment of perfection.[18] Thus, there developed two functions of fasting: the personal monastic fast that was practiced according to the 'rhythm of the individual's ascetical life'[19] and the communal fast that was attached to the Christian calendar.

Early liturgical fasting began as a part of the preparation of baptismal candidates for Easter, because the early churches would baptize their converts every Easter. Before the Easter baptismal service, the baptismal candidates would go through a time of prayer and fasting in preparation for baptism. The *Didache* states, 'But before the baptism let the baptizer fast, and the baptized, and whoever else can; but you shall order the baptized to fast one or two days before' (*Didache* 7.4).[20] Later, when adult baptisms became rare, the idea of a season of penance was applied to all believers, and Easter came to represent a time of yearly symbolic rebaptism. The Lenten fast of one or two days soon developed into a five-day fast, and eventually it was formalized by the Council of Nicaea as a universal forty-day fast (325 CE). Thus, over the centuries, the practice of fasting in conjunction with the Christian calendar became well-established and was codified and made mandatory by the church councils. Along with codification, the number of fast days increased over time.

B. Fasting in the Roman Catholic Church

Although Roman Catholicism allows for individual, voluntary fasting, it has emphasized the fast days of the liturgical calendar. The

---

[17] Berghuis, *Christian Fasting: A Theological Approach*, p. 121.
[18] Miles, *Fullness of Life: Historical Foundations for a New Asceticism*, pp. 135-63, categorizes aceticism into four types, rejects the 'body as a problem' approach, and suggests new ways to practice asceticism today based upon the 'body as human condition'. Cf. the positive approach to the body by Murphy, *The Spirituality of Fasting*, pp. 58-65.
[19] Schmemann, *Introduction to Liturgical Theology*, p. 198.
[20] Cf. Justin Martyr, *First Apology*, 61.2.3.

ancient fasts of Wednesday and Friday have been consolidated into the observation of abstinence on Friday, in which no meat products are consumed. Each of the four seasons are begun with fasting on the Ember Days. The forty days of Lent are the most important fast days, and Good Friday is the most essential fast of the entire Easter season. It is also expected that worshipers will fast during the morning hours prior to receiving the Lord's Supper.[21]

Thomas Aquinas summarizes the purposes of fasting: 'First, in order to bridle the lusts of the flesh ... Secondly, we have recourse to fasting in order that the mind may arise more freely to the contemplation of heavenly things ... Thirdly, in order to satisfy for sins'.[22] First, the Roman Catholic Church views fasting as a means to control the flesh and subjugate the human appetites (the passions), which are considered detrimental to the spiritual life.[23] This approach to fasting as mortification reflects an underlying dualism between body and spirit.[24] Second, fasting as an aid to prayer and contemplation suggests that fasting enables the believer to focus more intently upon God. Third, Roman Catholics observe fasting as an element of penance. For Catholics, fasting is a meritorious work that is associated with 'satisfaction' for sin.[25] The focus on penance

---

[21] Oddly enough, the practice of fasting before Eucharist seems to contradict Paul's instructions to the Corinthian church, in which he commanded them to 'eat at home' so as not to be hungry when coming to church (1 Cor. 11.20-34). However, most practices of communion leave no opportunity for abuse by people who desire to overeat, though some churches celebrate the Lord's Supper in the context of an Agape Meal.

[22] Thomas Aquinas, *Summa Theologica* (II, 2, Q 147, Art 1). For an extensive study of Aquinas' view on fasting, see Stephen Loughlin, 'Thomas Aquinas and the Importance of Fasting to the Christian Life', *Pro Ecclesia* 17.3 (2008), pp. 343-61.

[23] Representative of Roman Catholic view is Gregory Bainbridge, 'Is Fasting Obsolete?', *Worship* 34.9 (1960), pp. 573-78. In contrast to Roman Catholicism, Judaism insists that 'the appetites and passions' are not rooted in evil; therefore, 'The appeal to mortify the flesh for the sake of pleasing Heaven could not find voice in the synagogue' (Hirsch, 'Asceticism', p. 165).

[24] For a more positive assessment of asceticism, see Miles, *Fullness of Life: Historical Foundations for a New Asceticism*, pp. 9-154.

[25] Karl Rahner, 'Penance', in Karl Rahner (ed.), *Encyclopedia of theology: the concise Sacramentum mundi* (New York: Seabury Press, 1975), pp. 1187-1204. Fasting is a work of penance (p. 1187) that serves as a means of satisfaction. Rahner states that satisfaction is necessary because, in RC theology, forgiveness of sin committed after baptism does not cancel 'all consequences, and penalties of sin' (p. 1190). Satisfaction (including fasting) is one way that a Christian 'experiences the seriousness of divine justice' (p. 1190).

is understandable given the Roman Catholic emphasis on the cross.[26]

In the past, the Roman Catholic church insisted on strict observance of their fast days, but they allowed exceptions for people who engaged in hard labor (and other occupations). Vatican II, however, radically altered the Roman Catholic requirements regarding fasting, so that it has become a voluntary practice. Msgr. Charles Murphy laments the decline in fasting, arguing that it was a marker of 'religious identity' that has now been lost.[27]

C. Fasting in the Eastern Orthodox Church

The Eastern Orthodox Church requires a fasting regimen that is even more extensive and stringent than the Roman Catholic one. The Orthodox have two kinds of fasts, the normal fast from all food and 'ascetic fasting' (similar to the Roman Catholic 'abstinence'). Ascetic fasting involves abstinence from meat products, fish, eggs, dairy, olive oil, and alcohol.

Ascetic fasting is required on every Wednesday and Friday unless a fast-free period has been declared. The Orthodox also observe a total fast in preparation for receiving the Lord's Supper. They abstain from all food and drink from the night before communion until they partake of the Lord's supper. The season of Lent, which they call the Great Lent, is their most severe period of fasting. During the first week of Lent, they eat only two meals, one on Wednesday evening and the other on Friday evening. Ascetic fasting is practiced on weekdays in the second through sixth weeks of Lent; but on Saturdays and Sundays, wine and oil are permitted. On Good Friday, the strictest fast day of the year, all Orthodox Christians are strongly urged to fast. To commemorate the death and resurrection of Mary, the mother of Jesus, the Eastern Orthodox Church observes a two-week fast called the Dormition Fast. The Orthodox also observe the Nativity Fast, which consists of ascetic fasting dur-

---

[26] Robert F. Taft, 'Lent: A Meditation', *Worship* 57.2 (1983), p. 125.

[27] Murphy, *The Spirituality of Fasting*, pp. 1-12. Cf. Eamon Duffy, 'To Fast Again', *First Things* 151 (2005), p. 4-6. Not all Catholics would agree with Murphy and Duffy. For example, Ryan, *The Sacred Art of Fasting*, appreciates the new rules, and insists that they have saved fasting from 'legalism, minimalism, and externalism' (p. 3).

ing the forty days prior to Christmas. Other fasts include the Eve of Theophany, the Exaltation of the Cross, and the Beheading of John the Baptist.

In contrast to the Roman Catholic emphasis on the cross, the Eastern Orthodox Church emphasizes the resurrection, and for them, the fasting of Great Lent is an anticipation of Easter; it is a time of expectation, awaiting the resurrection. Fasting is an expression of the eschatological position of the Church, already a part of the kingdom of God, which has not yet been fully realized. The Eucharistic Fast is 'the essential mode of our preparation for the messianic banquet at Christ's table in His Kingdom'.[28]

Unlike the Roman Catholics, the Eastern Orthodox do not believe the passions to be antithetical to spiritual life.[29] Instead they view the passions as a vital part of the whole person, formed in the image of God. The passions, therefore, are not to be subjugated, but they are to be directed toward God. In that light, the first Sunday of preparation for Lent centers on the word 'desire' and features the biblical story of Zacchaeus, whose strong desire to see Jesus resulted in salvation. The Orthodox emphasize that becoming a Christian begins with desire – the desire for God. Therefore, they fast in order to enhance that spiritual desire. Through fasting, the passions of the body are transformed and redirected toward a desire for God.[30]

D. Fasting in Early Protestantism

The Protestant Reformation produced many criticisms of the Roman Catholic medieval practices of fasting. The reformers viewed Roman Catholic fasting as legalistic and works-centered. Martin Luther, for example, recognized the usefulness of fasting as a spiritual discipline, but he resisted in the strongest terms the Roman Catholic view of fasting as meritorious.[31] Ulrich Zwingli famously initiated the Swiss Reformation by speaking in favor of eating sausages

---

[28] Alexander Schmemann, *Great Lent* (Crestwood, NY: St. Vladimir's Seminary Press, Rev. edn, 1974), pp. 49-50.

[29] Cf. Baab, *Fasting*, p. 59.

[30] Schmemann, *Great Lent*, pp. 17-18.

[31] See Berghuis, *Christian Fasting: A Theological Approach*, p. 129. On the Lutheran view of fasting, see Fischer, 'Fasting and Bodily Preparation: A Fine Outward Training', pp. 887-901.

during Lent. He observed that the Lenten Fast was unbiblical and that Christians should be free to eat or to fast according to their own consciences.[32]

For the most part, Protestants encouraged fasting primarily in response to tragedies and crises, when appointing ministers, and when faced with doctrinal disputes. John Calvin saw Joel 1-2 as a pattern for public confession and repentance.[33] Therefore, whenever French Protestants would call for a fast, everyone would gather at the church for prayer, reading of Scripture, singing of psalms, and listening to sermons. The convocation would last from morning to late afternoon, at which time the people would be dismissed to their homes and discontinue the fast.[34]

From the Reformation until now, the practice of fasting has suffered from infrequent attention among Protestants. Consequently, it is rarely observed by Protestant Christians today. Despite its lack of attention from mainstream Protestantism, fasting has survived because of its periodic emphasis within movements that might be characterized as revivalistic, pietistic, holiness, and Pentecostal. For example, fasting was practiced and encouraged by many notable leaders, including George Whitefield, Jonathan Edwards, Charles Finney, D.L. Moody, Andrew Murray, A.W. Tozer, and John Wesley (to be discussed below). Jonathan Edwards insisted that 'ministers, above all persons, ought to be much in prayer and fasting', and all Christians should fast often for the advancement of God's kingdom.[35] Charles Finney wrote that whenever he sensed that his preaching had become powerless and ineffective, he would fast: 'I would then set apart a day for private fasting and prayer ... After humbling myself, and crying out for help, the power would return upon me with all its freshness. This has been the experience of my life.'[36] Andrew Murray explained that prayer and fasting go together:

---

[32] Berghuis, *Christian Fasting: A Theological Approach*, pp. 135-36. Cf. R.A. Mentzer, 'Fasting, Piety, and Political Anxiety among French Reformed Protestants', *Church History* 76.2 (2007), pp. 334-35.

[33] John Calvin, *Institutes of the Christian Religion*, 3.3.17; cf. 4.12.15.

[34] Mentzer, 'Fasting, Piety, and Political Anxiety among French Reformed Protestants', pp. 338-56.

[35] Jonathan Edwards *et al.*, *The Works of Jonathan Edwards* (2 vols.; London: William Ball, 1839), I, pp. 424, 426.

[36] Charles G. Finney, *Power from on High* (Salem, OH: Schmul Pub. Co., 2001), p. 6. Cf. Franklin, *Fasting*, p. 69.

'*prayer needs fasting* for its full growth'; and 'prayer is the reaching out after God and the unseen; fasting, the letting go of all that is of the seen and temporal'.[37]

The efforts of these leading figures, however, did not make fasting an essential, or even desirable, component of Protestant and Evangelical spirituality in the twentieth century. However, fasting was brought to widespread acceptance by Richard Foster's highly acclaimed book, *Celebration of Discipline: The Path to Spiritual Growth*, published in 1978, in which he showed that fasting is not a practice limited to extremists or liturgical churches.[38] The observance of fasting as an aid to self-examination and spiritual formation was subsequently promoted in books by popular Evangelical authors such as Dallas Willard, Elmer Towns, and John Piper.[39] The works of Towns and Piper coincided with the promotion of fasting by Campus Crusade founder Bill Bright.[40] In the 1990's, Bright organized a campaign for fasting that included massive seminars and conferences.

Like most other American fads, the widespread enthusiasm for fasting dissipated soon after the conferences ended, but a more limited interest in fasting persists.[41] Books on fasting continue to appear, and these newer works represent a broad spectrum of traditions.[42] In many places today, fasting is promoted within the context of a larger concern for spiritual formation and growth.

---

[37] Andrew Murray, *With Christ in the School of Prayer* (Christian Classics; Virginia Beach, VA: CBN University Press, 700 Club edn, 1978), pp. 98-99 (emphasis original). Cf. Hickey, *The Power of Prayer and Fasting*, p. 7.

[38] Richard J. Foster, *Celebration of Discipline: The Path to Spiritual Growth* (San Francisco: Harper & Row, 1st edn, 1978).

[39] Dallas Willard, *The Spirit of the Disciplines: Understanding How God Changes Lives* (San Francisco: Harper & Row, 1988); Elmer L. Towns, *Fasting for Spiritual Breakthrough* (Ventura, CA: Regal Books, 1996); Piper, *A Hunger for God: Desiring God through Fasting and Prayer*.

[40] Cf. Baab, *Fasting*, p. 65.

[41] Cf. Christine J. Gardner, 'Hungry for God: Why More and More Christians Are Fasting for Revival', *Christianity Today* 43.4 (1999), p. 37.

[42] See, for example, Presbyterian pastor Baab, *Fasting*; Anabaptist minister McKnight, *Fasting*; Pentecostal pastor Franklin, *Fasting*; and Roman Catholic scholar Murphy, *The Spirituality of Fasting*.

E. Fasting according to John Wesley

The Pentecostal revival emerged from the Wesleyan–Holiness movement; therefore, the construction of a Pentecostal approach to fasting demands consideration of Wesley's views. True to his roots in the Anglican Church,[43] where liturgical fasting was observed, Wesley practiced regular fasting; and, through his sermons and personal letters, he encouraged others to fast. Consistent with his strong emphasis upon a disciplined lifestyle, he fasted twice a week and asked his ministers to do so as well. As early as 1725, Wesley resolved to fast every Wednesday;[44] and in 1731, he decided to observe the liturgical fasts of the Anglican Church, which included fasting on Wednesday, Friday,[45] and prior to receiving the Lord's supper.[46] He reasoned that the common disregard for the fasts was not 'a lawful excuse for neglecting them'.[47]

Expecting all Methodists to practice fasting as a part of their spiritual formation,[48] he wrote the following in 'The General Rules of the Methodist Church':

> It is expected of all who desire to continue in these societies that they should continue to evidence their desire of salvation,
> *Thirdly*: By attending upon all the ordinances of God, such are:
> The public worship of God.
> The ministry of the Word, either read or expounded.
> The Supper of the Lord.
> Family and private prayer.
> Searching the Scriptures.
> Fasting or abstinence.[49]

---

[43] On the Anglican view of fasting, see Massey Hamilton Shepherd, 'Fasting among Churchmen', *Anglican Theological Review* 40.2 (1958), pp. 81-94.

[44] Wesley, *The Journal of the Rev. John Wesley*, I, p. 51.

[45] Wesley, *The Works of the Rev. John Wesley*, VII, p. 288. Wesley writes, '[In 1731] I began observing the Wednesday and Friday Fasts, commonly observed in the ancient church; tasting no food till three in the afternoon' (Wesley, *The Works of the Rev. John Wesley*, I, pp. 99-100). Cf. Wesley, *The Journal of the Rev. John Wesley*, II, pp. 257-58. Cf. Wesley, *The Works of the Rev. John Wesley*, VIII, p. 274.

[46] Wesley, *The Journal of the Rev. John Wesley*, V, p. 455, 459.

[47] Wesley, *The Journal of the Rev. John Wesley*, I, p. 101.

[48] See Wesley, 'Upon Our Lord's Sermon on the Mount: Discourse Seven', pp. 304-18.

[49] N.M. Alexander (ed.), *The Book of Discipline of the United Methodist Church* (Nashville, TN: The United Methodist Publishing House, 2008), p. 103.

Wesley used the terms 'ordinances of God' and 'means of grace' interchangeably in reference to fasting.[50] According to Wesley, fasting is a necessary means of grace, and 'the man who never fasts is no more in the way to heaven, than the man that never prays'.[51] Fasting is necessary for sanctification,[52] and without fasting, 'it is impossible to grow in grace'.[53] In light of the fact that the means of grace 'convey God's grace' to both Christians and non-Christians, Wesley also urged sinners to fast on their way to repentance.[54]

Fasting facilitates spiritual growth, and its neglect inevitably saps one's spiritual vitality. Wesley writes, 'Is not the neglect of this plain duty (I mean fasting, ranked by our Lord with almsgiving and prayer) one general occasion of deadness among Christians?'[55] He remarks concerning the backsliding of a certain parishioner, 'from the time he left off fasting … he sunk lower and lower, till he had neither the power nor the form of religion left'.[56]

Although Wesley encouraged frequent fasting,[57] he spoke out against extremism. He warned that one should fast only so much as one's health permits,[58] and he lamented the fact that, in the early days of Methodism, 'some in London carried this to excess, and fasted so as to impair their health'.[59] He also commented on a group of people who had fasted for six weeks, observing, 'What a mercy that half of them did not die in making the experiment!'[60]

Moreover, Wesley insisted that fasting, like the other means of grace, must be expressions of love that are generated by faith. One can fast and still have no 'religion as avails before God'.[61] Fasting, therefore is not an 'end' but a 'means', and Wesley is careful to distinguish between the two.[62] He notes that there is no 'natural or

---

[50] Wesley, *The Works of the Rev. John Wesley*, VII, p. 117.
[51] Wesley, *The Works of the Rev. John Wesley*, VII, p. 289.
[52] Wesley, *The Works of the Rev. John Wesley*, VI, p. 51.
[53] Wesley, *The Works of the Rev. John Wesley*, VI, p. 333, cf. p. 510.
[54] Wesley, *The Journal of the Rev. John Wesley*, II, p. 330.
[55] Wesley, *The Journal of the Rev. John Wesley*, V, p. 17.
[56] Wesley, *The Journal of the Rev. John Wesley*, IV, p. 124.
[57] He wrote, 'Love fasts when it can, and as much as it can' (Wesley, *The Works of the Rev. John Wesley*, XI, p. 440).
[58] Wesley, *The Journal of the Rev. John Wesley*, II, p. 291. Cf. Wesley, *The Works of the Rev. John Wesley*, V, p. 326; VIII, pp. 316-17.
[59] Wesley, *The Works of the Rev. John Wesley*, VII, pp. 288-89.
[60] Wesley, *The Journal of the Rev. John Wesley*, VIII, p. 72.
[61] Wesley, *The Works of the Rev. John Wesley*, VIII, p. 18.
[62] Wesley, 'Upon Our Lord's Sermon on the Mount: Discourse Seven', p. 305.

necessary connection between fasting, and the blessings God conveys thereby'.[63] Furthermore, fasting, important as it is, is positioned far from the center of the gospel. Wesley places love at the center, seated on the throne of the heart, around which are 'all holy tempers', such as the fruit of the Spirit. In an 'exterior circle' are all the 'works of mercy', and still farther from the center are the 'works of piety', which include fasting.[64]

The motives for fasting and the attitude of the one fasting were important considerations for Wesley. He wrote the following regarding fasting:

> First, let it be done unto the Lord, with our eye singly fixed on Him. Let our intention herein be this, and this alone, to glorify our Father which is in heaven; to express our sorrow and shame for our manifold transgressions of his holy law; to wait for an increase of purifying grace, drawing our affections to things above; to add seriousness and earnestness to our prayers; to avert the wrath of god, and to obtain all the great and precious promises which he hath made to us in Jesus Christ.[65]

Wesley also warns that we must beware 'of fancying we merit anything of God by our fasting'.[66] Accordingly, he argues strongly against the Roman Catholic view of penance. Wesley insists that fasting does not constitute 'satisfaction' in any sense, and it is in no way 'meritorius'.[67]

Wesley taught that fasting was beneficial for many reasons, but the chief benefit was as an aid to prayer.[68] Insisting that prayer is more effective when accompanied by fasting, he wrote, 'God will hearken to the prayer that goeth not out of feigned lips; especially when fasting is joined therewith';[69] and, 'When two or three agree to

---

[63] Wesley, 'Upon Our Lord's Sermon on the Mount: Discourse Seven', p. 310.
[64] Wesley, *The Works of the Rev. John Wesley*, VII, p. 60.
[65] Wesley, 'Upon Our Lord's Sermon on the Mount: Discourse Seven', p. 316.
[66] Wesley, 'Upon Our Lord's Sermon on the Mount: Discourse Seven', p. 316.
[67] Wesley, *The Works of the Rev. John Wesley*, X, pp. 124-25. Cf. XII, p. 101.
[68] Wesley, 'Upon Our Lord's Sermon on the Mount: Discourse Seven', p. 310. Regarding Jesus' promise, 'Seek, and you shall find' (Mt. 7.7), Wesley writes, 'Seek, in the way he hath ordained, in searching the Scriptures, in hearing his word, in meditating thereon, in fasting, in partaking of the Supper of the Lord, and surely ye shall find' (Wesley, *The Works of the Rev. John Wesley*, V, p. 401).
[69] Wesley, *The Works of the Rev. John Wesley*, XIII, p. 7.

seek God by fasting and prayer, it cannot be that their labour should be in vain'.[70]

Wesley often fasted for the 'success of the gospel'[71] and for God's mercy upon 'a guilty land'.[72] He fasted for his 'King and country'.[73] He sometimes ended the year with fasting and a watchnight service.[74] Wesley fasted in regard to personal decisions,[75] in preparation for church conferences,[76] on behalf of the poor,[77] and as part of the ordination process.[78] Wesley fasted for healing of the sick, and he believed that certain illnesses were beyond the reach of physicians; they could be cured only by prayer and fasting.[79] He tells the story of a man who, for reasons unknown, became 'raving mad ... He continued so for several days, till some agreed to keep a day of fasting and prayer. His lunacy then ended as suddenly as it began.'[80]

Wesley wrote frequently in his journal about the blessedness of prayer on the fast days: 'Thursday the 28th we set apart for fasting and prayer ... We had all free access to the throne of grace; and a firm, undoubting confidence that He in whom we believed would do all things well.'[81] On other occasions, he wrote, 'God was in the midst of us';[82] and, 'It was a blessed time; the windows of heaven were open, and the skies poured down righteousness'.[83] Wesley described extended times of prayer and fasting in glowing terms: 'Then especially it is that God is often pleased to lift up the souls of

---

[70] Wesley, *The Works of the Rev. John Wesley*, XII, p. 396.
[71] Wesley, *The Journal of the Rev. John Wesley*, VI, p. 35; V, pp. 317, 413.
[72] Wesley, *The Journal of the Rev. John Wesley*, VI, p. 79. Cf. VI, p. 341; VII, p. 517.
[73] Wesley, *The Journal of the Rev. John Wesley*, IV, pp. 140, 418, 423; V, pp. 351, 496; VI, p. 212; VII, p. 471. Cf. Hall, *The Fasting Prayer*, who encouraged fasting 'for national repentance' (pp. 99, 109).
[74] Wesley, *The Journal of the Rev. John Wesley*, V, p. 223; VI, p. 7.
[75] Wesley, *The Journal of the Rev. John Wesley*, I, pp. 323-25.
[76] Wesley, *The Journal of the Rev. John Wesley*, VI, pp. 118, 363.
[77] Wesley, *The Journal of the Rev. John Wesley*, VII, p. 360. Wesley also insisted that the giving of alms should accompany fasting (Wesley, 'Upon Our Lord's Sermon on the Mount: Discourse Seven', p. 318).
[78] Wesley, *The Journal of the Rev. John Wesley*, VIII, pp. 328-29.
[79] Wesley, *The Journal of the Rev. John Wesley*, V, p. 165.
[80] Wesley, *The Journal of the Rev. John Wesley*, VI, pp. 207-208.
[81] Wesley, *The Journal of the Rev. John Wesley*, III, p. 432.
[82] Wesley, *The Journal of the Rev. John Wesley*, III, p. 456.
[83] Wesley, *The Journal of the Rev. John Wesley*, IV, p. 366. Cf. V, pp. 216, 329.

his servants above all the things of earth, and sometimes to rap them up, as it were, into the third heavens'.[84]

Wesley's views regarding the function and practice of fasting combined the biblical teachings with the best of the historic Christian approaches. Like other Christian traditions, he taught the value of regular, liturgical fasting; and he tended toward aceticism. However, he resisted formalism, legalism, and works-righteousness. Wesley agreed with the biblical perspective that fasting is an aid to all kinds of prayer; therefore, he often resorted to fasting as a response to crisis.

---

[84] Wesley, *Sermons*, p. 310.

6

FASTING IN EARLY PENTECOSTALISM

When we fast and pray, we should never lose sight of the fact that our fast must be for the glory of God, that Jesus shall continually have all praise, honor, and glory. – Franklin Hall[1]

A. Introduction

The Eastern Orthodox Church, the Roman Catholic Church, the Anglican Church, and many other traditions emphasize fasting as a vital element of corporate liturgical life and worship, but most Protestant churches relegate fasting to the discretion of the individual. Pentecostalism, however, occupies an interesting historical space in that it emerged out of the Wesleyan–Holiness movement and, consequently, inherited John Wesley's Anglican appreciation of fasting but without the liturgical formalization of the practice.[2]

The purpose of this chapter is to examine the theology and practice of fasting in early Pentecostalism. The results gained here will be combined with the biblical conclusions and the other historical data in order to shape a distinctively Pentecostal approach to fasting.

---

[1] Franklin Hall, *Atomic Power with God through Fasting and Prayer* (Phoenix, AZ: s.n., new edn, 1973), p. 24. Hall was a Pentecostal evangelist.

[2] Cf. Wesley's sermon on fasting: J. Wesley, *Sermons on Several Occasions* (2 vols.; London: Caxton Press, by Henry Fisher, 9th edn, 1829), pp. 304-18. Land, *Pentecostal Spirituality*, argues that in Pentecostalism, 'there is a core; a spiritual fundament present in the first part of the century with roots in the nineteenth and eighteenth centuries and, through Wesley, all the way back through eastern and western sources to the early church' (p. 207, n. 35).

Following the lead of recent works in constructive Pentecostal theology, this chapter examines the early Pentecostal periodical literature from the beginning of 1906 (when the Azusa St. revival began) to the end of 1915.³ According to Steven J. Land, who takes his cue from Walter J. Hollenweger, the first decade of the movement is crucial for establishing the 'heart' of the Pentecostal tradition.⁴ As with any renewal movement, Pentecostalism's core values and beliefs were generated in the heart and minds of its founders. That is not to say that contemporary constructive theology must follow the exact lines of the early tradition. However, if Pentecostal theology is to remain genuinely Pentecostal (rather than Evangelical plus glossolalia), any new paths that are constructed must be faithful extensions of the old ones.⁵

Periodical literature is the focus of my investigation for several reasons. First, the early Pentecostals produced few book-length works on theology. Most of the early theological discussions were carried on within the pages of numerous periodicals. Second, none of the early books included discussions of fasting. Third, the Pentecostal movement had no central authority that was tasked with formulating guidelines for Pentecostal theology and practice. The periodicals, published by Pentecostal leaders and often representing the various newly formed denominations, were the nearest things to authoritative theological voices.

Although the periodical research could be presented chronologically or by looking at one periodical after another, I have chosen to organize the material topically. I will examine the customs and conventions regarding the practice of fasting, then I will explore the function and meaning of fasting.

---

³ This method was pioneered by Kimberly E. Alexander, *Pentecostal Healing: Models in Theology and Practice* (JPTSup 29; Blandford Forum, UK: Deo Publishing, 2006); and was followed by Larry R. McQueen, *Toward a Pentecostal Eschatology: Discerning the Way Forward* (JPTSup, 39; Blandford Forum, UK: Deo Publishing, 2012); Green, *Toward a Pentecostal Theology of the Lord's Supper*; and Melissa L. Archer, *'I was in the Spirit on the Lord's day': A Pentecostal Engagement with Worship in the Apocalypse* (Cleveland, TN: CPT Press, 2014).

⁴ Land, *Pentecostal Spirituality*, p. 1; W.J. Hollenweger, *The Pentecostals* (Peabody, MA: Hendrickson, 1988), p. 551.

⁵ See Green, *Toward a Pentecostal Theology of the Lord's Supper*, pp. 74-76.

B. The Practice of Fasting in Early Pentecostalism

The early Pentecostals, having emerged from the Wesleyan–Holiness movement, naturally adopted fasting as an important practice.[6] In fact, the Pentecostal revival in Los Angeles is said to have arisen as a result of prayer and fasting. It is reported in the *Apostolic Faith* newspaper that the Azusa Street Mission began soon after William Seymour came to Los Angeles. A group of people had been praying together for about a year for revival. Their desire was to see sinners converted and the sick healed. They 'felt led of the LORD to call Bro. Seymour' in the same way that Cornelius sent for Peter in Acts 10. The spiritual preparation for the Azusa St. revival is described in the *Apostolic Faith* newspaper:

> Every afternoon at 3 o'clock they would pray for the induement of power. [Seymour] told them he did not have the Pentecost but was seeking it and wanted all the saints to pray with him till all received their Pentecost ... There was a great deal of opposition, but they continued to fast and pray for the baptism with the Holy Spirit, till on April 9th the fire of God fell in a cottage on Bonnie Brae. Pentecost was poured out upon workers and saints. Three days after that, Bro. Seymour received his Pentecost ... And the fire has been falling ever since. Hundreds of souls have received salvation and healing.[7]

1. Fasting as Both an Individual and Corporate Practice

Of the more than 50 reports of fasting that I uncovered in the early literature, about half refer to individual fasting, and about half refer to corporate fasting. When I speak of corporate fasting, I mean

---

[6] For example, holiness leader Phoebe Palmer 'followed Wesley's lead by reserving Fridays for fasting in order to maintain her spiritual zeal' (J.W. Williams, *Spirit Cure: A History of Pentecostal Healing* [New York: Oxford University Press, 2013], p. 5). See also Elizabeth Sisson, 'Faith, Fasting and Prayer', *Triumphs of Faith* 7 (Jan. 1887), p. 14; and Carry Judd, *The Prayer of Faith* (Beulah Heights, CA: Office of Triumphs of Faith, 1880), pp. 126-42. Both Elizabeth Sisson and Carry Judd (Montgomery) would later become Pentecostals, and they continued to emphasize fasting in their later publications.

[7] *Apostolic Faith* 1.4 (Dec. 1906), p. 1. Similarly, the Pentecostal outpouring upon what would become the Church of God (Cleveland) was preceded by fasting. According to A.J. Tomlinson, *The Last Great Conflict* (The Church of God Movement Heritage Series; Cleveland, TN: White Wing Publishing House, 2011), 'They prayed, fasted, and wept before the Lord until a great revival was the result'. Very soon people were baptized in the Holy Spirit, and 'a number of miraculous cases of healings were wrought by the power of God' (pp. 139-40).

fasting within small groups, local churches, or denominations. What is missing is the mention of any universal days of fasting among Pentecostals. Unlike other traditions, Pentecostalism as a whole has no established fast days, but individual groups and denominations have instituted their own customs. For example, Tuesdays and Fridays have been fast days in the Church of God in Christ.[8]

Individual fasts were encouraged for personal spiritual renewal[9] or sanctification.[10] People fasted when in need of divine guidance,[11] when desiring the baptism in the Holy Spirit,[12] and when seeking God for physical healing.[13] Sometimes people fasted as a means of intercession for others.[14]

---

[8] Church of God in Christ, *Church of God in Christ 105th Annual Holy Convocation, 11/40 Prayer Wall, Prayer Guidebook* (Memphis, TN: Church of God in Christ, Inc., 2012), p. 4.

[9] *The Household of God* 3.11 (Nov. 1907), p. 6. *The Household of God*, edited by former Quaker and Azusa St. participant William F. Manley, was published by John J. Scruby of Dayton, Ohio. *Church of God Evangel* 1.1 (Mar. 1, 1910), p. 8. The *Church of God Evangel* was begun in 1910 under the leadership of A.J. Tomlinson. It is the primary periodical of the Church of God (Cleveland, TN). *Apostolic Faith* 1.4, p. 3. *The Apostolic Faith* was published by William J. Seymour at the Apostolic Faith Mission. The newspaper reported on the Azusa Street revival in Los Angeles and included other news, articles, and letters from the Pentecostal movement worldwide.

[10] *Apostolic Faith* 1.4, p. 4. *The Christian Evangel* 51 (July 25, 1914), p. 2. The *Christian Evangel*, now published under the name *The Pentecostal Evangel*, is the weekly magazine of the Assemblies of God, USA. It began in 1913 in Plainfield, Indiana. *Church of God Evangel* 6.30 (July 24, 1915), p. 2.

[11] *Church of God Evangel* 6.35 (Aug. 28, 1915), p. 2. *Apostolic Faith* 1.8 (May 1907), p. 2.

[12] *Bridegroom's Messenger* 1.5 (Jan. 1, 1908), p. 4. *Church of God Evangel* 5.39 (Sept. 26, 1914), p. 7. *Bridegroom's Messenger* 1.3 (Dec. 1, 1907), p. 3. *Bridegroom's Messenger* 1.5, p. 4. *Bridegroom's Messenger* 1.8 (Feb. 15, 1908), p. 4. *Bridegroom's Messenger* 1.11 (Apr. 1, 1908), p. 3. *Confidence* 2.1 (Jan. 1909), p. 6. *Confidence* was published in England by A.A. Boddy, an Anglican vicar who was baptized in the Spirit in 1907. It featured news from England and from the emerging worldwide Pentecostal movement. *Apostolic Faith* 1.3 (Nov. 1906), p. 3. *Apostolic Faith* 1.4, p. 2. *Latter Rain Evangel* 1.6 (Mar. 1909), p. 23. *The Latter Rain Evangel*, edited by Anna C. Reiff, was published monthly by the Stone Church, an early Pentecostal congregation in Chicago led by William H. Piper and associated with the Assemblies of God. *Church of God Evangel* 1.6 (May 1, 1910), pp. 5-6.

[13] *Apostolic Faith* 1.6 (Feb.-Mar. 1907), p. 6.

[14] *Church of God Evangel* 1.19 (Dec. 1, 1910), p. 6. *Word and Witness* 8.10 (Dec. 20, 1912), p. 2. *Word and Witness*, published by E.N. Bell of Malvern, Arkansas, served as the primary periodical of the Church of God in Christ (white). In 1914, the magazine became one of two official organs of the Assemblies of God. The other was the *Christian Evangel*. *Church of God Evangel* 5.38 (Sept. 19, 1914), p. 8. *Church of God Evangel* 6.9 (Feb. 27, 1915), p. 4. *The Household of God*

Corporate fasting included the days of fasting preceding the Azusa St. revival,[15] and subsequent special fast days at the Mission.[16] Before conventions and other meetings, churches and denominations would call upon their constituents to fast.[17] A woman by the name of A.M. Flowers urged the entire Church to fast 'every Thursday';[18] and, in time of need, the Church might call a corporate fast day.[19] Children in an orphanage fasted together.[20] Small groups, larger groups, and entire denominations would designate fast days aimed at spiritual revival.[21]

2. Fasting in Conjunction with the Liturgical Calendar and in Times of Crisis

Early Pentecostals, particularly those who came out of liturgical churches, would sometimes fast in accordance with the Christian calendar. For example, the annual Easter convention at the Boland Street Mission (England) designated Good Friday as a fast day.[22] On another occasion, Ascension Day was observed as a fast day.[23] Pentecostals sometimes fasted in preparation for the sacraments of footwashing,[24] the Lord's Supper,[25] and ordination.[26] Regular fasting

---

4.12 (Dec. 1908), pp. 14-15. *Bridegroom's Messenger* 1.14 (May 15, 1908), p. 1. *Bridegroom's Messenger* was first published in 1907 in Atlanta, Georgia by evangelist G.B. Cashwell. Early contributors included leaders of what would become the Church of God (Cleveland, TN), the International Pentecostal Holiness Church, and the Pentecostal Free Will Baptist Church. Cashwell came from NC to Azusa St. in Nov. 1906 and was baptized in the Holy Spirit. He returned to his home in NC, and from there he evangelized and preached the Pentecostal message to the Southeastern United States. *The Whole Truth* 4.4 (Oct. 1911), p. 1. *The Whole Truth* was founded by C.H. Mason of the Church of God in Christ. *Church of God Evangel* 6.37 (Sept. 11, 1915), p. 2.

[15] *Apostolic Faith* 1.4, p. 1.
[16] *Apostolic Faith* 1.8, p. 2.
[17] *Confidence* 3.3 (Mar. 1910), p. 67. *Word and Witness* 8.10, p. 2. *Confidence* 1.2 (May 1908), p. 5. *Confidence* 1.3 (June 30, 1908), p. 5. *Confidence* 2.3 (Mar. 1909), p. 76. *Church of God Evangel* 5.38, p. 8.
[18] *Church of God Evangel* 6.9, p. 4.
[19] *Church of God Evangel* 6.27 (July 3, 1915), p. 2.
[20] *Confidence* 3.5 (May 1910), p. 114.
[21] *Apostolic Faith* 1.7 (Apr., 1907), p. 4. *Apostolic Faith* 2.13, May, 1908, p. 4. *Apostolic Faith* 1.10 (Sept. 1907), p. 1. *Latter Rain Evangel* 1.4 (Jan. 1909), p. 2. *The Whole Truth* 4.4, p. 1. *Church of God Evangel* 1.18 (Nov. 15, 1910), p. 1. *Church of God Evangel* 5.7 (Feb. 14, 1914), p. 7.
[22] *Confidence* 3.3, p. 67.
[23] *Confidence* 2.3, p. 76.
[24] *Church of God Evangel* 1.19, p. 6.
[25] *The Latter Rain Evangel* 9.2 (Oct., 1916), p. 23.

that was not necessarily associated with the Christian calendar was also encouraged.[27] For example, Henry L. Fisher, founder of the United Holy Church in North Carolina often fasted on Fridays.[28]

For the most part, fasting did not follow a liturgical calendar, but was undertaken on the occasion of a crisis or an important event. As mentioned above, people report that they fasted when sick, when in need of spiritual renewal, and when desiring divine direction. They fasted in anticipation of special meetings and whenever they believed that their prayers needed additional strength.

3. Other Aspects of the Practice of Fasting

It was observed above that early Pentecostals fasted both for themselves and for others. It was also noted that, on at least one occasion, children fasted for the most part of a day; and the account does not seem to suggest that the children's fasting was out of the ordinary.

In regard to the length of Pentecostal fasts, the early literature includes reports of fasting that lasted from one to fourteen days. Often, a single fast day was observed before conventions and other special meetings.[29] W.R. Paul Ham testified that he fasted one day in preparation for the sacrament of foot washing,[30] and one writer suggested that everyone should fast 'one day of every week'.[31] The Church of God called for a 'special day of prayer and fasting' because of a financial need,[32] and at an orphanage in India, the children fasted from morning to evening.[33]

Several persons wrote of fasting for three days, including G.W. Batman (resulting in sanctification),[34] a group of Christians in Indi-

---

[26] *The Whole Truth* 4.4, p. 3. *Minutes of the Seventh Annual Assembly* (Cleveland, TN: Church of God Publishing House, 1912), p. 18.

[27] *Church of God Evangel* 6.9, p. 4. *Church of God Evangel* 1.1, p. 8.

[28] Henry L. Fisher, 'Diary', March 3 and May 19, 1922; cited by Grant Wacker, *Heaven Below: Early Pentecostals and American Culture* (Cambridge, MA: Harvard University Press, 1st Harvard Univ. pbk. edn, 2003), p. 123. Also, C.H. Mason asked all ministers in the Church of God in Christ to fast two days per week, and the Assemblies of God designated one day per week for fasting.

[29] *Confidence* 3.3, p. 67. *Confidence* 1.2, p. 5. *Confidence* 1.3, p. 5. *Confidence* 2.3, p. 76. *The Whole Truth* 4.4, p. 1.

[30] *Church of God Evangel* 1.19, p. 6.

[31] *Church of God Evangel* 6.9, p. 4.

[32] *Church of God Evangel* 6.27, p. 2.

[33] *Confidence* 3.5, p. 114.

[34] *Apostolic Faith* 1.4, p. 4.

anapolis (resulting in physical healings),[35] and the participants at the Azusa St. Mission (resulting in 'an increase in power').[36]

On the fourth day of Cora Nelson's fast, Jesus appeared to her;[37] and it was six days of fasting that prepared G.B. Cashwell for his visit to Azusa St.[38] The Christian Alliance of Spokane, WA 'held a ten days' fast',[39] as did a group in New York City.[40]

The length of the fast was not always predetermined. Julia Divine, 'fasted and prayed many days' before she was baptized in the Holy Spirit,[41] and Anna Bauers vowed that she would not eat until her baby was healed of diphtheria. After 'three days and nights' of fasting, the baby was healed instantaneously.[42] R.J. Scott fasted for three days before the Lord appeared to him and gave him instructions regarding his immediate future.[43] Margaret Gill and a friend fasted and prayed for four days until she was healed of an incurable illness,[44] and a man from Berlin wrote that after 14 days of fasting, he received the baptism in the Holy Spirit.[45]

Extremism is also found among the early Pentecostals, but it is rebuked sharply:

> A sad case of fanatical delusion some little time ago occurred in one of the Western States (U.S.A.) Three persons starved themselves to death under the impression that they could fast for forty days. It seems as if some will accept no guidance from sane members of the body. The details tell us of the course of events, viz.: (1) Separation in fanaticism from others; (2) a shutting of themselves up apart; (3) a giving of themselves to teachings not in accord with the whole WORD; (4th) [*sic*] disaster and death.[46]

---

[35] *Apostolic Faith* 18 (Portland, OR) (Jan. 1909), p. 1. *The Apostolic Faith* (Portland, OR) was begun by Florence Crawford in 1908 as a continuation of the paper of the same name from the Apostolic Faith Mission in Los Angeles. It was published by the Apostolic Faith Mission in Portland.
[36] *Apostolic Faith* 1.8, p. 2.
[37] *Church of God Evangel* 5.39, p. 7.
[38] *Apostolic Faith* 1.4, p. 2.
[39] *Apostolic Faith* 1.7, p. 4.
[40] *Apostolic Faith* 2.13, May, 1908, p. 4
[41] *Church of God Evangel* 1.6, pp. 5-6.
[42] *The Household of God* 4.12, pp. 14-15.
[43] *Apostolic Faith* 1.8, p. 2.
[44] *Apostolic Faith* 1.6, p. 6.
[45] *Confidence* 2.1, p. 6.
[46] *Confidence* 3.12 (Dec. 1910), p. 278.

It is suggested that the antidote to fanaticism is to be found in submission to the community's orthodox interpretation of Scripture.

4. A Summary of the Practice of Fasting among Early Pentecostals

Early Pentecostals practiced both individual and corporate fasting, but there is no mention of universally established fast days. Individual fasts were encouraged for personal spiritual renewal or sanctification, but sometimes people fasted as a means of intercession for others. People fasted when in need of divine guidance, when desiring the baptism in the Holy Spirit, and when seeking God for physical healing.

Before conventions and other meetings, churches and denominations would call upon their constituents to fast. In time of need, the Church might call a corporate fast day; and small groups, larger groups, and entire denominations would designate fast days aimed at spiritual revival. Early Pentecostals would sometimes fast in accordance with holy days such as Good Friday or Ascension Day, and they sometimes fasted in preparation for the sacraments of footwashing, the Lord's Supper, and ordination. Regular fasting that was not necessarily associated with the Christian calendar was also encouraged. For the most part, however, fasting did not follow a liturgical calendar, but was undertaken on the occasion of a crisis or an important event, or whenever they believed that their prayers needed additional strength. Fasting never appeared to be mandatory, but the choice to fast was left up to the individual.

It is clear that Pentecostals practiced fasting for varied lengths of time, depending upon the urgency of the situation. They often continued to fast either continuously or repeatedly until God sent the answer to their prayers.

C. The Function of Fasting in Early Pentecostalism

The literature suggests that fasting had at least ten functions in early Pentecostalism. Fasting functioned most often as an expression of urgent prayer.

1. Fasting as a Companion to Prayer

Early Pentecostals viewed fasting as a necessary accompaniment to any urgent prayer. In an article entitled 'Why You Can't Get Your

Prayers Answered', Sam C. Perry of the Church of God writes that sometimes prayers are not answered until we fast: '… there are blessings and decrees sometimes that seem to be out of our reach except through fasting and prayer'.[47] A reader of *Word and Witness* requested prayer for revival in San Antonio: 'It will take some real prayer and possibly fasting to break through in that sinful city'.[48] It is implied that prayer alone might not be sufficient – fasting must be added.[49] Pentecostals are in agreement with the biblical perspective that fasting moves God.[50]

Regarding fundraising toward the construction of a new assembly building for the Church of God, it is reported that the money was coming in very slowly: 'This is indeed a serious matter to those who feel the responsibility of this great Assembly. We have been thinking of calling for a special day of prayer and fasting. Something must be done and we feel at a loss to know just the proper action at this time.'[51] The urgency of the situation required desperate measures that included prayer and fasting.

R.L. Hatcher, in a piece entitled 'The Sure Word', encouraged Pentecostal believers to imitate Jesus Christ and the apostles, and one part of that imitation was prayer and fasting. He explained:

> If we pray fifteen minutes for faith we think that will do until dinner. Then we pray for more faith about five minutes then load the stomach with the good of the earthly table and deprive ourselves of the bread of life and fail to drink from the fountain. God help us to look and live. Jesus said we could cast out devils by fasting and prayer. Some of us fast but little and pray less.[52]

---

[47] *Church of God Evangel* 6.39 (Sept. 25, 1915), p. 3. Cf. independent Pentecostal evangelist Hall, *The Fasting Prayer*, who insists that fasting with prayer 'will overcome impossible obstacles' (p. 33).

[48] *Word and Witness* 8.10, p. 2.

[49] Fasting as a means of appealing to God in times of crisis, which is frequently observed in the Bible, in Wesley, and in early Pentecostalism, is often overlooked by Roman Catholic, Eastern Orthodox, and mainline Protestant writers. Cf., for example, Ryan, *The Sacred Art of Fasting*, p. 35.

[50] Cf. Lambert, 'Fasting as a Penitential Rite: A Biblical Phenomenon?', who writes, 'fasting in the Hebrew Bible is effective … because it produces an effect on the deity' (p. 511.)

[51] *Church of God Evangel* 6.27, p. 2.

[52] *The Christian Evangel* 87 (Apr. 24, 1915), p. 2.

Hatcher compares and contrasts the appetite for 'earthly' food with the appetite for 'the bread of life'. He argues that believers too often focus on the needs of the body while ignoring the needs of the spirit. He also points to the benefit of fasting and prayer as a means of obtaining spiritual power enough even to 'cast out devils'.

In early Pentecostalism, fasting was almost always joined with prayer. What follows includes many other types of prayer that were accompanied by fasting.

2. Fasting for Unity among Believers

'Believers in Sanctification' is the title of E.N. Bell's article in which he insists that the 'Finished Work' stream of Pentecostalism[53] believes in sanctification and holiness even though they do not accept the Wesleyan view that it is an 'instantaneous second-work [*sic*] of Grace'. He laments the divisions between the Pentecostal factions and writes, 'Is it not about time to mourn and call a solemn assembly of fasting, that God may take away these divisions which disgrace God and His people before an unbelieving world, instead of being puffed up with a spirit of superiority that kicks out a differing brother?'[54] Bell, therefore, calls for fasting as a vehicle for mourning over the divisions between the Finished Work and Wesleyan branches of the movement. The mourning and fasting would result in charity, tolerance, and unity among those who hold differing theological positions.[55] Bell points out that division in the Body of Christ is not a good witness to the gospel of Jesus, who prayed that his followers would be 'one'. His reference to a 'solemn assembly' alludes to Joel 1-2 and generates a mood of seriousness. For Bell, division among believers is a troubling matter that calls for fasting and repentance.

Alice Taylor writes, 'we began praying, and fasted ... and the Lord is bringing His saints together as Jesus prayed in the 17th of John'.[56]

---

[53] The Finished Work stream began in 1910 with William Durham, whose Baptistic roots caused him to reject the Wesleyan view of sanctification. Finished work theology is often identified with the Assemblies of God. See Alexander, *Pentecostal Healing*, p. 150.

[54] *The Christian Evangel* 59 (Sept. 19, 1914), p. 3.

[55] Cf. Hall, *The Fasting Prayer*, who asserted much later that 'Fasting prevents divisions' (p. 77).

[56] *Apostolic Faith* 1.10, p. 1.

3. Fasting for Personal Spiritual Renewal

Under the heading, 'He's Coming Soon', the W.F. Bryant encourages the readers to be prepared for the return of Jesus with times of fasting: 'Come! Awake! Be ready! You can be ready if you will. Stir up the gift that is in you, by prayer and fasting if needs be, and testimony, and praise, until you are all aglow and overflowing with His love again.'[57] The words 'fasting if needs be' suggest that fasting is able to bring about a depth of revival that could not be achieved by any other means.

A writer named only as 'A Worker' characterized his/her spiritual awakening with the title, 'Arrested for Jesus' Sake':

> I came from Frisco to Los Angeles five days after the earthquake and heard about these Pentecostal people. I visited their meetings and looked on rather critically. At first I opposed and openly fought them and said it was the devil. The result was I backslid altogether and had to go back and ask forgiveness and do my first works over again, even down to having the devils cast out of me. Afterward I received pardon and the cleansing blood again through fasting and prayer and much study of the word. Eight weeks ago, I received the baptism with the Holy Ghost and spoke with new tongues.[58]

This writer had criticized the Pentecostals and ended up in a backslidden state. After fasting, prayer, and reading the Bible, he/she received forgiveness and the same Spirit baptism that he/she had earlier criticized.

4. Fasting for Revival and Conversion of the Lost

Another important purpose of fasting was to plead with God for revival and the conversion of lost souls. In a testimony entitled 'Pentecost in Spokane, Wash', M.L. Ryan observes the benefits of fasting for revival:

> prayer had been going up to God for weeks and months there for a mighty revival ... The time came when a band of people from the Christian Alliance held a ten days' fast and prayer ... God began to work in Pentecostal power. Souls were saved and sanctified and baptized with the Holy Ghost, and healed in body

---

[57] *Church of God Evangel* 1.1, p. 8.
[58] *Apostolic Faith* 1.4, p. 3.

... Over one hundred souls have been saved, cleansed, and baptized with the Holy Ghost and fire, and the work has passed beyond all bounds or keeping track of same.[59]

Ryan indicates that the purpose of the fast was 'for a mighty revival'. His description of the resulting revival takes the form of elements from the Pentecostal Fivefold Gospel – people were saved, sanctified, baptized in the Holy Spirit, and healed in body.[60] The corporate fast was undertaken on behalf of others.

Philip Sidersky testifies that he sold all that he owned and went to North Carolina to serve as pastor of a 'little band of holiness people'. He writes that three of them had received their Spirit baptism, and he adds, 'The Lord laid the burden of the people on my heart. We fasted and prayed 'till God heard and answered. We now have a church, about 50 have received Pentecost.'[61] Sidersky's fasting was generated by a 'burden' that was given to him from the Lord. His flock was made up of 'holiness people', but only three had been baptized in the Holy Spirit. Sidersky prayed and fasted, not for himself, but for a revival that would produce an outpouring of the Holy Spirit upon his people and that would result in the founding of a church. He testifies that his prayers were answered.

In a report of activities at the Azusa Street Mission, we read, 'Three days of fasting and prayer were set apart at the Mission for more power in the meetings. The Lord answered and souls were slain all about the altar the second night. We have felt an increase of power every night.'[62] Apparently, Seymour and other leaders at the Mission perceived a decrease in the effectiveness of their meetings. Therefore, they added three days of fasting to their prayers. The visible sign of 'more power' was the large number of people who were 'slain all about the altar'.

Under the heading, 'Wednesday, June 3, a Preparatory Day of Prayer and Fasting', we learn that the church fasted in preparation for the Whitsuntide Conference at Sunderland, England:

---

[59] *Apostolic Faith* 1.7, p. 4.
[60] The Fivefold Gospel is the core theological narrative commitments of the Pentecostal movement: Jesus is Savior, Sanctifier, Spirit Baptizer, Healer, and Soon Coming King. See Land, *Pentecostal Spirituality*, p. 6.
[61] *Church of God Evangel* 1.19, p. 6.
[62] *Apostolic Faith* 1.8, p. 2.

A brother writes from Hertfordshire: – I am exceedingly pleased that you are having a conference; it is just the thing that is needed ... One thing ought to precede the conference, that is a week of fasting and prayer ... or if it was only part of a week it would be a great benefit if you suggested it to your followers and left it to the discretion of the individual. I believe all would fast at least one day, many two or three, and many a whole week. The great revival must break out, and is there any more likely place than a conference of true disciples.[63]

The writer from Hertfordshire makes a clear connection between corporate fasting and spiritual revival. When God's people fast and pray, a 'great revival must break out'. After that conference, we find this retrospective comment: 'Wednesday, June 3, we observed as a special day of Prayer and Fasting. We met in the Vicarage in the morning, and continued in earnest prayer and waiting till three, and then assembled in the evening ... The Lord wonderfully answered our prayers.'[64] Then a day of fasting was called for in preparation for another conference: 'The Day of Prayer for the International Conference, will be Thursday, May 20th (Ascension Day). We asked friends right round the world to join us in Fasting and Prayer on that day, both for the Conference and for His Pentecostal Work.'[65]

In a report entitled, 'Sister Etter to San Antonio', it is stated that Maria Woodworth-Etter would soon be conducting a special revival meeting in San Antonio, Texas; therefore, the readers are urged to offer special prayer 'that she might go in the power and unction of the mighty Spirit of God, and that God may grant a great outpouring of His Spirit there. It will take some real prayer and possibly fasting to break through in that sinful city.'[66] This writer calls for corporate fasting on behalf of a particular evangelist and with the goal of a 'great outpouring' of the Holy Spirit. Because San Antonio is perceived to be a 'sinful city', fasting is needed even more urgently.

A 'Report from Brewster, Fla.' by J.W. Buckalew includes his account of corporate prayer and fasting for revival. Buckalew writes, 'We arrived at Brewster, pitched the tents and prepared to take

---

[63] *Confidence* 1.2, p. 5.
[64] *Confidence* 1.3, p. 5.
[65] *Confidence* 2.3, p. 76.
[66] *Word and Witness* 8.10, p. 2.

meals with the saints. The Lord rolled the lost souls on our hearts and we began to cry, fast and pray for God to give us a revival.' Buckalew reports that many were converted, healed, and baptized with the Holy Spirit. On this occasion, he and his workers pray and fast for 'the lost souls' that the Lord had placed on their hearts.[67]

A.M. Flowers urges every reader to fast for the conversion of lost souls: 'Dear saints, I have felt for some time that we should fast and pray one day of every week for this sinful world, and for the nine gifts to be bestowed upon those that God can trust. I think it would be good to fast and pray every Thursday but not only pray on that day but every day until Jesus comes.'[68] Flowers pleads for regular fasting on behalf of 'this sinful world', which suggests a concern for those who have not received the gospel. The fasting also is aimed at the restoration of the gifts of the Spirit (1 Corinthians 12).

5. Fasting Resulting in Divine Guidance and/or Revelation

Fasting has resulted in revelations and divine guidance because Pentecostals have fasted whenever seeking God's will. Revelations have also attended fasting even when they were not the focus of the fasting. Mrs. G.W. Murphy was working as a street evangelist, and she writes, 'then I fasted and prayed, and went out to see how next God would lead in getting a place for services. I asked for churches but was refused.' Murphy fasted with the purpose of discerning the will of God for her ministry. Although, much like John Wesley, she was refused access to the official pulpits, she reports that after her fast, she was offered the opera house for free, and she began holding services there.[69]

Under the heading 'The Lord's Leading for the Camp Meeting', R.J. Scott, who had come from Winnipeg Canada to the Azusa Street revival, wrote to his people back in Canada:

> I expected to be back in Winnipeg, Canada, ere this, and would have been had not God spoken so plainly to me on the night of April 6, just after coming through three days of fasting and praying that God would show me what I was to do. About midnight I heard a rap at my door. I awoke and listened, and while listen-

---

[67] *Church of God Evangel* 5.38, p. 8.
[68] *Church of God Evangel* 6.9, p. 4.
[69] *Church of God Evangel* 6.35, p. 2.

ing Jesus appeared in a door about 6 feet wide and 8 feet high, standing, it seems, between me and heaven, with His arms stretched out and a most beautiful mantle covering Him to the tips of His fingers, and said to me: 'It is not my will that you should take your family back to Winnipeg just now'.

He reports that Jesus appeared again later in the night and said, 'Go, tell My people, behold I come quickly'.[70] Scott's vision was quite remarkable, but his original purpose for fasting was not to receive a vision. He fasted only as an aid in discerning God's will in his life. The Lord answered his prayer and more.

According to the testimony of Cora A. Nelson, she fasted in order to receive 'more power' from God. She writes, 'This was in 1904. I began to fast and pray for more power. On the fourth day of fasting and prayer at 9 o'clock in the morning, Aug. 27, Jesus appeared to me ... He said to me, I have chosen you to preach my Gospel.'[71] Nelson's fasting brought a response from God that exceeded her stated request. She asked for spiritual power, and the Lord used her time of fasting as an opportunity to call her into ministry. These kinds of call narratives are common in Pentecostalism.

6. Fasting Resulting in Various Worship Phenomena

Many of the early reports of fasting include various manifestations of the Holy Spirit, including healings, Spirit baptisms, glossolalia, and people falling onto the floor under the power of the Spirit. Other, less defined phenomena are also reported. In an article regarding ministry to orphans in India, Max Wood Moorhead reported that many of the children were confessing their sins and were receiving the gospel of Jesus Christ. At one point during a time of worship, the head of the school dismissed the children:

> but they would not be dismissed. Standing on their feet the power of God fell on them ... They shouted and praised God victoriously for an hour, for He had put a new song in their mouths. They had fasted all day, and instead of partaking of their evening meal at six o'clock, they danced and sang God's praises for some little time. This was not merely exuberance of spirits; in a score of instances boys and girls had prayed through to victory, and

---

[70] *Apostolic Faith* 1.8, p. 2.
[71] *Church of God Evangel* 5.39, p. 7.

for the first time in their lives and really tasted the joy of sins forgiven – for the first time had really received Jesus as personal Saviour in their hearts.[72]

The original purpose of their fast is not stated, but after fasting for about 12 hours, the children 'shouted and praised God'. They 'danced and sang God's praises' as an expression of the joy that had come to them through the Holy Spirit.

In 'Further News from Nyack, New York', A.W. Vian reports on the Annual Council of the Christian and Missionary Alliance and testifies to the following:

> [We witnessed] the marvelous workings of the Holy Ghost as never seen here ... Meetings ran on day and night for nearly a week without human leadership, no thought of time, trains, meals, sleep, etc. The Holy Ghost did wonderfully quicken and strengthen physically all those who thus fasted and waited upon him. Some men and women each fell under the power about the first night and came through speaking in tongues. I never heard such soul agony for sin, self-life, backsliding, etc., and soul travail for lost and perishing, mighty intercessions, visions of the cross, blood, throne, and deep whole souled shouts of glory and praise, all testifying 'Jesus is coming soon'.[73]

Vian describes meetings that were directed by the Holy Spirit in which the participants were so taken up into worship that they became oblivious to time. They were strengthened in body; they spoke in tongues; they agonized in prayer; they experienced visions; and they shouted God's praises with their whole hearts. The nature and purpose of their fasting is not stated, but the revival is quite extraordinary.

7. Fasting in Preparation for Receiving the Sacraments

Early Pentecostals were very loosely organized, and liturgical practices varied from one group to another. Although they had no formal liturgy, they practiced a number of sacraments/ordinances, and they often viewed fasting as a part of the preparation for receiving the sacraments. For example, in a report from Liberia, West Africa, missionary W.B. Williams writes, 'Deeply attentive audiences over-

---

[72] *Confidence* 3.5, p. 114.
[73] *The Household of God* 3.11, p. 6.

flowed the church and much feeling was manifested, culminating in Good Friday, when most of our women spent the entire day in the church, fasting and praying, preparatory to receiving the sacrament of the Lord's Supper'.[74] At least three significant points stand out in this report. First, the church observed Good Friday with a communion service, a practice that was not common to all Pentecostal churches. Second, the entire day was occupied with preparatory fasting and prayer. Third, it seems that only the women fasted and prayed. Perhaps the men were unable to find release from their work.

Many Pentecostals accepted footwashing as a sacrament, and W.R. Paul Ham testified, 'I fasted Tuesday in preparation for feet washing'.[75] Ham does not explain why the footwashing service was held on a Tuesday. Perhaps the church held a mid-week service on Tuesday evenings.

Like other Christian traditions, many Pentecostals practiced fasting in preparation for ordination. In a note entitled 'To the Ministers', all of the young ministers are urged to attend the State Convocation of the Church of God in Christ. It is added that those who 'are not ordained may come that we, after prayer and fasting, may lay hands on them, that they may be fully set apart for the work of the ministry'.[76] In regard to the ordaining of ministers, the Church of God (Cleveland, TN) decided 'It is also advised that the presbytery fast before laying hands on in ordination.'[77] In both of these cases, it appears that the elders were the ones who fasted, so that they might be prepared to lay hands upon those who were to be ordained.

8. Fasting for Sanctification

Pentecostalism emerged from the holiness movement, and after their conversion experiences, Pentecostals were expected to seek for entire sanctification. The process of self-examination and prayer that led to sanctification often included times of fasting. Relating the events that occurred a few years after his conversion, G.W. Batman testifies to his experience of sanctification:

---

[74] *The Latter Rain Evangel* 9.2, p. 23.
[75] *Church of God Evangel* 1.19, p. 6.
[76] *The Whole Truth* 4.4, p. 3.
[77] *Minutes of the Seventh Annual Assembly* (Cleveland, TN: Church of God Publishing House, 1912), p. 18.

I fasted and prayed for about three days and during that time I put off the old man Adam in the form of inbred sin and God came in and destroyed the devil's workshop by casting his tools on the outside. Praise God I got real evidence that I was sanctified and the Blood applied. After that, I received the baptism with the Holy Ghost and fire and now I feel the presence of the Holy Ghost, not only in my heart but in my lungs, my hands, my arms and all through my body and at times I am shaken like a locomotive steamed up and prepared for a long journey.[78]

An anonymous writer tells about a Christian brother who desired sincerely to be completely sanctified: 'At last, jaded from fasting and chastened in mind, his soul experienced an uplift which he called entire sanctification'.[79] In a third example, W.W. Rose writes, 'My wife received the Holy Ghost and this put me to praying for the carnal mind to be removed and for the Holy Ghost. I began to fast and pray and didn't want my wife nor anyone else to hear me pray until one night I told my wife that we would have prayers ... The Lord opened the windows of heaven and sanctified me ...'[80]

These descriptions suggest that fasting was an occasion for consecration, soul searching, and self-denial that intensified the seekers prayers and re-directed their affections toward God. After three days of fasting, Batman was able to 'put off the old man Adam' and cast the devil's 'tools on the outside'. Rose expressed his desire to be rid of 'the carnal mind', but he was so self-conscious and timid that he did not want even his wife to hear him pray. After fasting and after he invited his wife to pray with him, he received his sanctification. In none of these cases are we told how the seeker was able

---

[78] *Apostolic Faith* 1.4, p. 4.
[79] *The Christian Evangel* 51, p. 2.
[80] *Church of God Evangel* 6.30, p. 2. In her discussion of sanctification in the Church of God in Christ, Anthea D. Butler, 'Observing the Lives of the Saints: Sanctification as Practice in the Church of God in Christ', in Laurie F. Maffly-Kipp, Leigh Eric Schmidt, and Mark R. Valeri (eds.), *Practicing Protestants: Histories of Christian Life in America, 1630-1965* (Baltimore, MD: Johns Hopkins University Press, 2006), pp. 159-76, includes several references to fasting as a 'spiritual discipline' (p. 159) that helped to 'cleanse' believers (p. 162), ensuring that 'the flow of the Holy Spirit into the worshiper would not be hampered by substances in the body' (p. 162). She adds that fasting was used to 'free believers from sin and, at times, to intercede for healing' (p. 163).

to determine that sanctification had occurred, but they express assurance of having been sanctified.[81]

9. Fasting for the Baptism in the Holy Spirit

In early Pentecostal literature, fasting most commonly functioned as preparation for Spirit baptism. In some cases, the fast was carried out by the person who was seeking for the baptism in the Spirit; but at other times, people fasted on behalf of (or along with) other believers who were seeking the experience. In still other cases, a group of people might pray and fast for revival in general, and the resultant spiritual outpouring would include Spirit baptism for those who had not previously received the experience.

a. Corporate Fasting for the Holy Spirit

In a report of corporate fasting for the Holy Spirit, we read that after a ten-day fast in Spokane, Washington, 'Over one hundred souls have been saved, cleansed, and baptized with the Holy Ghost and fire'.[82] The fast resulted in multiple types of spiritual experiences, including conversions, sanctifications (those 'cleansed'), and Spirit baptism. Another testimony, entitled, 'Italians and Indians Receive the Holy Ghost', describes a trip in which A.H. Argue visited Toronto, Ottawa, Athens, and New York City. He states that while he was in New York City, 'twenty-five received the [Spirit] baptism in one week. Five of the Saints were fasting for ten days and, no doubt, God was there in a special way.'[83] Argue credits the ten day fast with generating the Holy Spirit's outpouring.

Alice Taylor reports on still another corporate fast in New Orleans, Louisiana:

> As soon as we received these *Apostolic Faith* papers, we began praying, and fasted and prayed, and Glory to His name, He made Himself known in our midst, and came and baptized four with the Holy Ghost and fire ... The fire is falling down here ... He is giving the gift of speaking with tongues and other gifts.[84]

Through the *Apostolic Faith* newspaper, this group of believers in New Orleans learned of the Azusa St. revival, in which numbers of

---

[81] See also Mary Bunkley's testimony in *Bridegroom's Messenger* 1.5, p. 4.
[82] *Apostolic Faith* 1.7, p. 4.
[83] *Apostolic Faith* 2.13, May, 1908, p. 4
[84] *Apostolic Faith* 1.10, p. 1.

people were being baptized with the Holy Spirit. They fasted and prayed for the same kind of revival; and, according to Taylor's testimony, their prayers were answered. Glossolalia and 'other gifts' were poured out by the Holy Spirit.

A minister by the name of A.H. Post recounted that he had ministered for more than 30 years in what he called a 'leading' denomination. For some time he had been seeking for a 'deeper fullness of God's love' and a 'greater anointing' for effective ministry: 'With this conscious need, a cry went up to God for a Pentecost'. He was aware of three people who had come from Texas to Los Angeles, in search of the Pentecostal experience, and he describes their experience:

> they unceasingly sought the Lord for the promise of the Father. So earnest became this little band that, with much fasting – they continued almost day and night for some days, till, indeed, their day had fully come, and as suddenly as on the day of Pentecost, the Spirit fell upon them and filled them, and all began to speak in other tongues as the Spirit gave utterance.

Post comments that Spirit baptism does not consist in the gift of tongues, but the gift of tongues 'was a sign and a powerful and a practical witnessing agency'. He reflects further upon the revival at Azusa St.:

> In these few months from the time the praying, fasting few received the long-sought-for rending of the heavens, and Jesus did baptize them with His Spirit, up until now, this work has spread to its influence has reached half round the world. Many of all ages and races, from varied conditions and abilities, from the very young to the octogenarian, those learned, and of no education, each alike has received a definite baptism of the Spirit.[85]

Post's testimony suggests that fasting was practiced when one became 'earnest' in seeking God. His further comments about the Holy Spirit's democratizing work apparently allude to Joel's prophecy that foretells the Spirit's outpouring:

> It will come about after this
> That I will pour out my Spirit on all flesh;

---

[85] *Apostolic Faith* 1.5 (Jan. 1907), p. 4

And your sons and daughters will prophesy,
Your old men will dream dreams,
Your young men will see visions.
Even on the male and female servants
I will pour out my Spirit in those days (Joel 2.28-29).

Agnes Ozman, in an article entitled, 'Where the Latter Rain First Fell: The First One to Speak in Tongues', describes going in the fall of 1900 to the Bible school run by Charles Parham in Topeka, Kansas where they engaged in the study of Scripture and spent much time in prayer. She writes, 'We were urged to seek for and to receive the promised baptism in the Holy Spirit. Our hearts became very hungry for this induement. We prayed earnestly and also fasted, as the Lord laid it upon us.' After a time of prayer and fasting, Agnes received her spirit baptism on January 1, 1901. She indicates that one man who was present was able to understand the foreign language in which she spoke. She describes her experience in these words: 'heaven's glory filled my soul,' and 'A continual feast is in my soul as I feed on the Word and pour out my soul in prayer ... My heart is burdened for the church.'[86] Ozman's testimony suggests that fasting was practiced corporately as the students sought God for the promise of the Holy Spirit. Agnes was the first to receive the experience there at Parham's Bible school.

b. Individual Fasting for the Holy Spirit

Anyone who was hungry for the Holy Spirit was encouraged to seek God with fasting, prayer, and waiting upon God (called 'tarrying'). The process of seeking involved a deep and passionate hunger for God. Mary Bunkley, for example, had visited prayer meetings that had aroused in her a desire to get closer to God, and she 'began praying to be saved and sanctified', which happened quite soon. Then, she states her hunger for the baptism in the Holy Spirit:

> I began to ask Jesus to baptize me with the Holy Ghost ... I was so hungry for the Holy Ghost that I could do nothing much but fast and pray. I began to feel that I cannot live in this world if I did not receive the blessed Comforter ... He did not leave me

---

[86] *Latter Rain Evangel* 1.4, p. 2.

waiting long before He gave me my heart's desire. On September 21st He baptized me with the blessed Holy Ghost. Glory![87]

Bunkley's passionate desire for God's Spirit is evident in her testimony and it moved her to fast and pray until her desire was fulfilled.

A similar passion is evident in the testimony of Cora A. Nelson. She states that she had a deep hunger and thirst for more of God. She writes, 'This was in 1904. I began to fast and pray for more power. On the fourth day of fasting and prayer at 9 o'clock in the morning, Aug. 27, Jesus appeared to me ... At this I opened my mouth and began to sing and speak in some unknown language.'[88] Nelson's fasting resulted in a supernatural vision of Jesus, which caused her to break out in song. The fact that she sang and spoke in an unknown language would have been a sign to her that she had received the baptism with the Holy Spirit.

F.L. Juillerat fasted and prayed for weeks, and he repeatedly attended meetings and sought for God in the altars with others praying for him. In his testimony entitled 'Durant, Fla.', he writes about his decision to fast:

> In 1895, the Holy Ghost put a hunger in my heart for Pentecost ... I fasted and prayed for the Holy Ghost, and as I was advised, took Him by faith, but ... the signs were not following ... I went on seeking off and on for years till the spring of 1906, ... In August, 1906, I came to Florida and soon received news and papers from Los Angeles of Pentecost. Then my hunger and need increased more and more until finally the Lord showed me to quit every kind of meeting which I did, unless it should be Pentecostal meeting.

With his hunger intensifying, he resorted to fasting. Finally, after some time, he reports that on a Tuesday morning he received the baptism in the Holy Spirit. The Holy Spirit 'came in and testified for Himself in songs of other tongues, glory to his name'.[89]

The hunger and thirst for God did not always produce an immediate experience of Spirit baptism. Sometimes the seekers would

---

[87] *Bridegroom's Messenger* 1.5, p. 4.
[88] *Church of God Evangel* 5.39, p. 7.
[89] *Bridegroom's Messenger* 1.3, p. 3.

wait before God for days, weeks, or months. M.D. Sellers, in 'Two classes of seekers', observes that not everyone receives their spirit baptism easily or quickly. He observes that for many it requires a time of 'prayer, restitution, confessions, fasting and waiting'.[90]

In a letter from Lake View, North Carolina, Anna Kelly writes that she had been a satisfied Christian for about 14 years, but then she began to seek God passionately:

> About three years ago, my heart began to hunger and thirst, and yet I had a witness clear to my sanctification. So I prayed and fasted. When I heard of the Holy Ghost being poured out in Los Angeles, Cal., and that they were 'speaking in tongues,' I realized they had an experience above me … [eventually,] I was so completely out of self that the blessed tender Holy Ghost could come in.

Kelly states that on January 30, 1907 she received her spirit baptism.[91] Apparently, her time of fasting enabled her to focus upon God more effectively, so that she became 'completely out of self'. At that point, the Holy Spirit came and filled her.

An architect from Berlin by the name of Beyerhaus had been influenced by a missionary from Scotland who stayed in his home in Germany and by leaders of the Salvation Army whom he had met when he visited London. He describes their impact upon his spiritual desires:

> by their very looks and living I knew that they had something I did not know anything about … After 14 days' fasting and longing to receive the Holy Ghost, I asked the Lord one evening so to purge me that I might not continue in sin. I asked the Lord to make it a reality, and a wonderful joy and purity streamed through my body and lit up things around me.[92]

Beyerhaus testifies that he eventually received the baptism in the Holy Spirit with the sign of speaking in tongues. He writes of a deep 'longing' for the Holy Spirit and a desire to be purged from

---

[90] *Bridegroom's Messenger* 1.8, p. 4.
[91] *Bridegroom's Messenger* 1.11, p. 3.
[92] *Confidence* 2.1, p. 6.

sin. Apparently, he experienced sanctification, which was soon followed by the experience of Spirit baptism.[93]

A man called 'Brother Mead', who was a missionary to Africa, testified of his experience of receiving Spirit baptism. He states that while in Africa he had sensed that God was moving, and the Holy Spirit had come to him in a deeper way. He heard of the meetings at Azusa St. and he came to Los Angeles in search of spiritual fullness. He explains that fasting was valuable as preparation for receiving the Spirit:

> The first night at the meetings, my heart went out for the baptism. I went forward to be prayed for, and hands were laid on me, and prayer was made, that I might receive the baptism of the Holy Spirit. I continued praying and fasting, in hope and much comfort. One evening, in complete abnegation of self … my soul was flooded with Divine love; and I commenced to speak as I would sing a new song.[94]

Although Bro. Mead was hungry for the Spirit, he did not receive his baptism on the first night when they laid hands on him and prayed for him. It was only after he 'continued praying and fasting', which led to his 'complete abnegation of self', that he was baptized in the Holy Spirit.

G.B. Cashwell of Dunn North Carolina traveled to Los Angeles to become part of the Azusa St. revival. He writes of fasting during his six day journey:

> [I] started for Los Angeles. Glory to God. I was six days on the road, was fasting and praying to the Lord continually. As soon as I reached Azusa Mission, a new crucifixion began in my life and I had to die to many things, but God gave me the victory. The first altar call I went forward in earnest for my Pentecost. I struggled from Sunday till Thursday. While seeking in an upstairs room in the Mission, the Lord opened up the windows of heaven in the light of God began to flow over me in such a power as never before.[95]

---

[93] *Confidence* 2.1, p. 6.
[94] *Apostolic Faith* 1.3, p. 3.
[95] *Apostolic Faith* 1.4, p. 2.

He then went to the room where worship was ongoing, and he writes, '[I began to] speak in tongues and praise God ... He filled me with His spirit and love ... The Lord also healed my body [of arthritis]'.[96] Cashwell's earnest desire for spiritual fullness caused him to fast and pray during his six day trip to the west coast. The fasting was part of the 'crucifixion' that prepared him to overcome his racism and submit to the leadership of William Seymour, an African-American. Cashwell's visit to the Azusa revival transformed his life and filled him with love for all people. Cashwell left California and went back east and brought the Pentecostal revival to North Carolina and Georgia, where he became a leading voice in the early Pentecostal movement. He founded *The Bridegroom's Messenger*.

In an article entitled, 'Have Ye Received the Holy Ghost Since Ye Believed?', A.F. Lee begins with Acts 19 and deduces that the gift of the Holy Spirit is incumbent upon every believer. He sees the outpouring of the Holy Spirit at the home of Cornelius as a paradigm for today's believers:

> the consecration must be so sincere and complete that there shall be a willingness of heart to comply with every requirement of the Divine will ... This may be seen by what occurred at Caesarea in the household of Cornelius where the company had been prepared for the reception of the truth through fasting and prayer – Acts 10:30, 31.[97]

He infers, therefore 'that where the consecration is complete and the heart fully yielded, God condescends to bestow His blessing upon His children'.[98] Apparently, fasting was considered by him to be a part of the full consecration and yielded heart that are necessary for the reception of the Spirit.

Julia McCallie Divine, in 'My Inheritance', recounts that her baptism in the Holy Spirit did not come quickly or easily. Her time of waiting and fasting was sustained by a deep passion for God. She writes, 'I fasted and prayed many days. Now my family began to notice my distress, and I saw I must get through quickly or I might be overruled. I must have the conscious presence of God. All the world, its glitter and pride, sank out of my view; and my heart pant-

---

[96] *Apostolic Faith* 1.4, p. 2.
[97] *Latter Rain Evangel* 1.6, p. 23.
[98] *Latter Rain Evangel* 1.6, p. 23.

ed after God.' She fasted so much that she grew weak. She writes, 'I was so weak from the awful spiritual conflict that toward evening I lay down on a cot, nigh unto death ...' Soon afterwards, while praying at the home of a friend, she received her spirit baptism.[99] Divine's testimony suggests that her fasting was helpful in shifting her gaze away from the 'glitter and pride' of the world until her 'heart panted after God'. Fasting was a sign of her desperation to attain the 'conscious presence of God'.

Other examples of fasting as a part of the seeking process for Spirit baptism include G.W. Batman and C.B. Herron. Batman writes that he 'fasted and prayed for about three days' for the experience of sanctification. Afterwards, he 'received the baptism with the Holy Ghost and fire'.[100] In a report from India, missionary C.B. Herron states, 'One native Christian has been immersed and is waiting daily before the Lord for his [Spirit] baptism ... He is here fasting three days before the Lord and praying.'[101] Finally, in a historical review entitled, 'History of Tongues', V.P. Simmons listed the groups throughout history who spoke in tongues. In the case of the seventeenth-century Camisards, he found a connection between fasting and their reported experiences of Spirit baptism.[102]

10. Fasting for Divine Healing

The Pentecostal Fivefold Gospel declares that Jesus is savior, sanctifier, Spirit baptizer, healer, and coming king. This survey has already shown that fasting often produced reports of healing. The following testimonies are further examples of fasting by early Pentecostals when they were praying for divine healing for themselves and for others.[103]

a. Fasting for the Healing of Others

Anna Bauers offers an impassioned narrative regarding her baby's illness. The child grew sick with very bad sore throat, which Bauers diagnosed as diphtheria:

---

[99] *Church of God Evangel* 1.5, pp. 5-6.
[100] *Apostolic Faith* 1.4, p. 4.
[101] *Christian Evangel* 62 (Oct. 10, 1914), p. 4.
[102] *Bridegroom's Messenger* 1.3, p. 2.
[103] Early Pentecostals' reliance upon fasting as a pathway to healing is discussed by Williams, *Spirit Cure*. See especially pp. 27-30, and 65-69.

> He gradually grew worse, until it seemed that mortification had commenced ... I vowed before God I would not eat until He healed my child. I fasted three days and nights ... At last I went to the bed where lay my baby, threw myself over the child, and cried, 'Oh, God! Oh God! How much longer can I stand this?' Almost instantly a bright light shone over my head. I closed my eyes, the brightness was so intense, but I saw it just as plainly. I soon raised up, took my baby up, went to the kitchen to my husband, and said, 'My baby is healed!' ... In a few minutes my darling was playing on the floor as well as ever.[104]

Bauers' experience is quite striking and moving. Her intention to fast until the child was healed demonstrates that, to her, fasting was more than a liturgical ceremony or means of spiritual discipline.

To Bauers and to other early Pentecostals, fasting was a means of access to the throne of God, a way of deepening and strengthening one's prayers. A briefer but similar account is given by Lillie Tilghman in a letter to the *Evangel*. She writes, 'I had been fasting and praying for God to heal two of our children that were having chills.' She goes on to report that all of her children were healed.[105]

The Church of God in Christ was led by C.H. Mason, who was known to fast often. Under his influence, the church practiced frequent fasting.[106] The 'Report of the Annual Convocation Held at Lexington, Miss., July 23-August 20, 1911' describes a fast day:

> July 28 (Sixth Day) – The Lord gave us today to fast and pray for the healing of the sick. With the full guidance of the Spirit, the Scripture lesson was the 21st chapter of Luke and other Scriptures. Sermon by Elder Driver. As he preached to those that were traveling the downward road, the Holy Ghost fell and many were baptized and sinners were saved.[107]

During the convention, a fast day was devoted explicitly to the healing of the sick. It was reported, however, that the Holy Spirit moved upon the congregation and many were converted and baptized in the Spirit.

---

[104] *The Household of God* 4.12, pp. 14-15.
[105] *Church of God Evangel* 6.37 (Sept. 11, 1915), p. 2.
[106] Cf. Butler, 'Observing the Lives of the Saints', pp. 162-63.
[107] *The Whole Truth* 4.4, p. 1.

Finally, missionaries Edmund S. Barr and his wife speak of fasting as a part of spiritual 'battle'. Residing temporarily in St. Petersburg, Florida, they write about the power of fasting:

> After finding a few of God's dear Saints we began the battle, preaching, praying, fasting, asking God to move the dark clouds and give victory. The people at times seemed to make light of us and our God ... So we continued our little meeting, preaching and telling the people that our God will heal both soul and body. The number applied to the great Physician and he healed them every time. Praise God.[108]

The Barrs located a small group of believers with whom they could share fellowship, worship, and ministry. Their attempts at evangelism were not met with approval, but they continued steadfast, and declared that those who sought God for healing were healed 'every time'.

Like the Barrs, Carrie Judd Montgomery viewed fasting as one of the weapons of spiritual warfare that could be employed against disease. According to Montgomery, it was fasting that brought an end to influenza in Oakland, CA during the epidemic of 1918:

> Let us trust God to use these weapons today as we come to Him in prayer and fasting, so that we may have the assurance of victory, as we did when the influenza was at its height in Oakland; we called a day of prayer and fasting and immediately God raised His hand to show that He was God, and gave deliverance. At once there was a marked decrease in the disease, and in a few days the daily papers declared that it was stamped out of Oakland.[109]

Other testimonies of fasting on behalf of the sick include Anna E. Kirby, who writes in 'A letter from China', 'Sisters Law and Pittman both have the smallpox and are in a boat on the water, quarantined. Oh, it was so sad to us when we heard it, but the little church went to fasting and prayer for their deliverance, and felt God had heard our prayers.'[110] Apparently, the entire church fasted and

---

[108] *Church of God Evangel* 5.7, p. 7.
[109] Carrie Judd Montgomery, *Secrets of Victory* (ed. Sadie A. Cody; Oakland, CA: Office of Triumphs of Faith, 1921), pp. 130-31.
[110] *Bridegroom's Messenger* 1.14, p. 1.

prayed for the two sick women. Also, in a report of the camp meeting at Pleasant Grove, Florida, we read, 'after considerable fasting and prayer, the sick were healed and were able to attend the services'.[111] In another report from Indianapolis, Indiana, it was reported that fasting led to many healings:

> recently the saints went down before God in a fast of three days, and the result was that many were healed. There was a general time of heart-searching and giving up of the self life and pride, and wonderful manifestations of the Spirit were seen in the meetings.[112]

The fasting resulted not only in healings but also in self examination, repentance, and other spiritual phenomena.

b. Fasting for the Healing of Oneself

Given the role of fasting in the nineteenth-century healing movement as an aid to personal faith,[113] we would expect to find many narratives of fasting for one's own healing. However, stories of fasting on behalf of others who are sick far outnumber the cases where people fasted for their own healing. The following example, therefore, is notable. Among a series of testimonies about healing, we find one submitted by Margaret Gill:

> I want all of you to know how the Lord has cured me of an incurable disease of about eight years' standing, and made me perfectly whole … The Lord sent Sister Kennison from Redlands over to pray for me, and she came and we fasted and prayed for about four days. We had a hard fight with the devil, but thank the Lord, we at last got glorious victory.[114]

The sick woman fasted, but she states clearly that she was not alone. Sister Kennison prayed and fasted with her and for her. The two of them fought side by side until the victory was won.

---

[111] *Church of God Evangel* 1.18, p. 1.
[112] *Apostolic Faith* 18 (Portland, OR), p. 1.
[113] See, for example, Judd, *The Prayer of Faith*, pp. 126-42.
[114] *Apostolic Faith* 1.6, p. 6.

11. A Summary of the Function of Fasting among Early Pentecostals

This overview of early Pentecostal fasting leads to several observations regarding its function and meaning. Despite the well-known theological distinctions between the Finished Work and Wesleyan–Holiness streams of the tradition, the early literature regarding fasting does not betray those differences. In the Finished Work stream, where all the benefits of the Cross are already accomplished and available to believers simply by the confession of faith, we would expect fasting to be superfluous; but that is not the case. Fasting (at least until 1915) continued to serve a crucial role in the reception of spiritual blessings such as Spirit baptism and divine healing, just as it did among Wesleyan Pentecostals. Apparently, fasting had been such an essential part of pre-Pentecostal spirituality, that both streams continued to value it as companion to prayer.

In early Pentecostalism, fasting was utilized as an aid to any kind of urgent prayer, especially when pleading for revival and the salvation of lost souls. Pearl Page Brown of the Church of God in Christ asserts the power of fasting:

> Prayer and fasting go together to penetrate and to break through every resistance that the enemy has built. Fasting strengthens and intensifies our prayers. As you begin to use your spiritual weapon of fasting, as you humble yourself through fasting and prayer before God, you will break through enemies and territories and claim victory in every circumstance.[115]

Pentecostals also resorted to fasting when in need of divine guidance and when specific needs were evident in the life of an individual, in the society, or in the church.

In addition to their view of fasting as an aid to prayer and as a spiritual discipline, which they inherited from the Wesleyan–Holiness movement, early Pentecostals saw fasting through the theological lens of the Fivefold Gospel, which was the core belief system of the movement. Therefore, fasting was valuable particularly in preparing seekers for the experiences of sanctification, Spirit baptism, and divine healing (for themselves and for others). Most

---

[115] Pearl Page Brown, *Sewing Circle Artistic Fingers* (n.p.: Church of God in Christ, Women's International Conventions, n.d.), p. 15. Cited by Butler, 'Observing the Lives of the Saints', p. 162.

of the testimonies suggest that fasting was generated by affectivity – the seeker's passionate pursuit of God and deep-seated love for others, whether the other be sinner or believer. Thus, fasting was a part of relationality, and those who fasted approached God not with an attitude of entitlement but with humility, consecration, obedience, and supplication – as a needy child would approach a parent.

Pentecostals did not practice fasting as penance, punishment, or to suppress the desires of the physical body; but fasting could be an aid to repentance and sanctification as the desires of the body were transformed and directed toward heaven. Unlike other traditions, Pentecostals did not practice fasting as a memorial of past events such as the crucifixion; instead, they always looked forward.[116] Fasting was seen as an important part of the preparation for the sacraments and ordinances of the Church (including footwashing and ordination). Furthermore, fasting on a regular basis was encouraged as a means of self-examination and deeper spiritual formation, especially in light of the soon return of Jesus.

Eastern theology distinguishes between two kinds of fasting, liturgical and ascetic, and early Pentecostals practiced both; but more often, they practiced a third kind of fasting that might be described as crisis oriented fasting. Their practice was similar to the early Protestant fasts; but unlike the Protestant fasts, Pentecostal fasts were not always communal. The wide range of purposes for fasting corresponds to the purposes that we found in the Bible and in the practice of John Wesley. Most often early Pentecostal fasting was joined with prayer as a means of appealing to God for the outpouring of God's grace in identifiable acts of revival, salvation, sanctification, healing, and Spirit baptism either for oneself or for others.

---

[116] Cf. also the Jewish fast days, which (in contrast to the Pentecostal practice) are memorials to past events in Jewish history. The exception is the Day of Atonement, which a day of repentance. The Day of Atonement, as mentioned earlier, is the only fast day that is stipulated in Scripture.

Illustration from Franklin Hall's
The Fasting Prayer

7

TOWARD A PENTECOSTAL THEOLOGY OF FASTING

> *Fasting in this age of the absent Bridegroom is in expectation of His return. Soon there will be the midnight cry, 'Behold, the Bridegroom! Come out to meet Him.' It will be too late then to fast and pray. The time is* now. – Arthur Wallis[1]

The purpose of this chapter is to construct an approach to fasting that is consistent with Pentecostal theology and spirituality. Taking into consideration the chapters that have preceded this one but without repeating the conclusions already stated there, I will address the significance of fasting for the Pentecostal spirituality, and I will explore the theological function of fasting. Then, I will suggest how contemporary Pentecostals might appropriate fasting into their spiritual lives and into the corporate life of their churches.[2]

A. Fasting as a Component of Pentecostal Spirituality

If Pentecostalism is to continue as a vibrant movement of the Holy Spirit, it must identify and retain the heart of the movement, which then must be transmitted to the next generation. When I speak of the heart of the movement, I mean more than doctrinal commit-

---

[1] Wallis, *God's Chosen Fast*, p. 135. Wallis was a Pentecostal leader in what has been called the British New Church Movement.

[2] This book offers only a short introduction to the subject of fasting. My research suggests that a doctoral thesis or full-length scholarly study of Pentecostal fasting is in order.

ments; because Pentecostalism, like other Christian traditions, consists of a combination of beliefs and practices that work to together to shape a distinct spirituality. For example, the theological core of Pentecostalism is the Fivefold Gospel – Jesus is savior, sanctifier, Spirit baptizer, healer, and soon-coming king. However, the Fivefold Gospel is not only a statement of belief; it is way of being in the world; it is a spirituality. Pentecostal spirituality/theology is an expression of the Spirit-transformed affections which are centered and integrated in the affection of love.[3] Spirituality, however, is not a static attainment. It must be nurtured, developed, instilled, and made steadfast by means of spiritual practices, what John Wesley called 'the means of grace'. For Pentecostalism, these means of grace include uninhibited worship, tarrying in prayer,[4] seasons of fasting, caring for one another, bearing witness to the world, self-sacrifice, preaching the whole Gospel, healing the sick, immersion in God's Word, and seeking for the Spirit's gifts. All of these are done with a sense of urgency and longing in light of the soon return of Jesus. 'Fasting is calculated to bring a note of urgency and importunity into our praying'.[5] Fasting, like other spiritual practices, represents the Pentecostal 'yearning for direct contact with God'.[6] Therefore, fasting often accompanies tarrying prayer, which is explained by Daniel Castelo:

---

[3] See John Christopher Thomas, '"What the Spirit Is Saying to the Church": The Testimony of a Pentecostal in New Testament Studies', in Kevin L. Spawn and Archie T. Wright (eds.), *Spirit and Scripture: Exploring a Pneumatic Hermeneutic* (New York: T & T Clark, 2012), p. 117, who suggests five affections that correspond broadly to the elements of the Fivefold Gospel: Salvation/Gratitude, Sanctification/Compassion, Spirit Baptism/Courage, Healing/Joy, Return of Jesus/Hope. Thomas' list is an expansion based on the earlier work of Land, *Pentecostal Spirituality*, who argued that the affections of 'gratitude as praise-thanksgiving, compassion as love-longing, and courage as confidence-hope' (p. 47) form the 'integrating center' of Pentecostal spirituality (pp. 50, 52, 63).

[4] Our study of the biblical texts revealed that fasting is connected closely to prayers of lament, which are a form of what Pentecostals call 'tarrying'. See McQueen, *Joel and the Spirit*, pp. 68-103. Tarrying is, in some respects, similar to the contemporary 'soaking prayer' movement, though tarrying is traditionally more active than soaking prayer. For a scholarly study of soaking prayer, see Michael Wilkinson and Peter F. Althouse, *Catch the Fire: Soaking Prayer and Charismatic Renewal* (DeKalb, IL: Northern Illinois University Press, 2014).

[5] Wallis, *God's Chosen Fast*, pp. 51-52.

[6] Wacker, *Heaven Below*, p. 123.

In Pentecostal worship, tarrying implies travailing, waiting, prostrating, and submitting oneself before the presence of God in hopes that God's presence might break forth in the mundane and profane circumstances of life. Tarrying is an embodiment and demonstration of human desire in search of being ordered by God's very presence.[7]

Fasting has been an important constituent of Pentecostal identity, and if we discontinue the practice of fasting, we become something other than Pentecostal.[8] Whether we fast or not affects our way of life, our desires, our goals, and our beliefs.

Furthermore, the Fivefold Gospel is a testimony of one's experience of God's grace, of which the believer affirms, 'I thank God that I am saved, sanctified, filled with the Holy Ghost, trusting God with my body, and looking for Jesus to come'. Consequently, the churches can continue to affirm the core beliefs of Pentecostalism; but if they fail to transmit the spirituality of Pentecostalism experientially, they will have only 'a form of godliness, but denying its power' (2 Tim. 3.5). Pastors and other leaders, therefore, must be more than administrators and 'coaches', they must be 'examples to the flock' (1 Pet. 5.3).[9] They must be active participants in the pursuit of God, models of Pentecostal spirituality. Furthermore, the churches must provide continuing opportunities for people to experience salvation, sanctification, healing, and Spirit baptism. According to Daniel Castelo, worship (which, I would argue, includes fasting) is the optimal location for spiritual formation:

> The inculcation and formation of the affections arise from a context of worship, for this activity is the one in which God is the principle object ... Only in the particular context of prayer and adoration can belief be formed and sustained ... One learns to love God by beholding Him and communing with Him.[10]

---

[7] Daniel Castelo, 'Tarrying on the Lord: Affections, Virtues and Theological Ethics in Pentecostal Perspective', *Journal of Pentecostal Theology* 13.1 (2004), p. 50.

[8] See Castelo, 'Tarrying on the Lord', pp. 31-56. Castelo wants Pentecostals to consider 'what attitudes and actions can facilitate the approximation of their purpose or *telos* as a group' (p. 49). I would argue that fasting is one of those actions.

[9] A multitude of 'church programs' do not replace the spiritual role of fasting (Franklin, *Fasting*, pp. 79-80).

[10] Castelo, 'Tarrying on the Lord', pp. 37, 38.

Many Pentecostal churches have eliminated week-long revival services, and they have limited themselves to only one worship service per week, making it very difficult for seekers to find a time, a place, and communal support for extended prayer. Therefore, creative solutions that are appropriate to each context must be invented in order to provide the opportunities necessary for spiritual growth.

My concern is not for the continuation of Pentecostalism as an end in itself, but, rather, as a continuation of the Spirit's work in redeeming the world. Those who have lost their way and are bound by sin need Jesus the savior. Those who are fighting hopelessly against addictions and are harboring deep struggles need Jesus the sanctifier. Those who desire to serve God in fullness need Jesus the Spirit baptizer. Those who suffer from illnesses, whether small or great, need Jesus the healer. Those who find themselves acclimating to this world order and those who find themselves as aliens in this world need Jesus the soon-coming King. God is at work, redeeming the world unto himself, and God has used the Pentecostal movement in that redemptive process.

While fasting is but one component of traditional Pentecostal spiritual life, our study of the early literature demonstrates that it is a vital component. If Pentecostalism abandons the practice of waiting upon God in fasting and prayer, its overall spiritual matrix is in danger of collapsing. Pentecostals should consider the words of Symeon, an ancient Eastern writer, who argued that 'fasting is the beginning and foundation of every spiritual activity'.[11] Similarly, John Wesley insisted that without fasting, 'it is impossible to grow in grace'.[12]

B. Fasting and the Fivefold Gospel

Scripture indicates that fasting is a natural bodily response to an intense affective experience, such as the experience of fear, danger, grief, suffering, humility, or awe. The function of fasting as a spiritual discipline is to produce humility and single-mindedness in the person fasting, which will result in added effectiveness in spiritual pursuits.[13] The biblical characteristics of fasting are evident in Pen-

---

[11] Symeon, *Symeon the New Theologian*, p. 169.
[12] Wesley, *The Works of the Rev. John Wesley*, VI, p. 333, cf. p. 510.
[13] Cf. Prince, *Fasting*, pp. 6-8; Ryan, *The Sacred Art of Fasting*, pp. 141-42.

tecostal practice as well. For example, Franklin Hall affirms the benefit of fasting as an aid to prayer:

> The Fasting-Prayer is far more effective than usual prayers. The Fasting-Prayer will operate the Holy Spirit in our behalf, and will overcome impossible obstacles ... It transcends the natural laws and causes God to move behind the scenes with Divine Power.[14]

Additionally, however, early Pentecostals often viewed fasting through the lens of the Fivefold Gospel – Jesus is savior, sanctifier, Spirit baptizer, healer, and soon coming king. Therefore, in this section, we will suggest briefly how a theology of fasting may be informed by the Fivefold Gospel.

1. Fasting and Jesus the Savior

The first and most obvious area of correspondence between fasting and salvation is in fasting's relationship to repentance. The biblical, Wesleyan, and early Pentecostal approaches to fasting are in agreement that fasting facilitates repentance. In Pentecostal soteriology, salvation is a gift of God that is received entirely by grace through faith. Repentance, however, is a necessary human response to God's offer of salvation in Christ. Repentance includes confession of sin, turning away from sin, and turning to God.

While it facilitates repentance, fasting is not meritorious, and it does not contribute to satisfaction for sin.[15] When we fast, we must keep in mind that we cannot earn God's favor or blessings by fasting or by any other means. No matter how devout or disciplined we may become, we never deserve the favor of God. According to Isaiah, even 'all our righteousnesses are as filthy rags' (Isa. 64.6). Similarly, the psalmist declares, 'Everyone at their best state is altogether vanity' (Ps. 39.5). Everything that we have is a gracious gift from God, and fasting is not a way of working for salvation or any other blessing.

As an aid to repentance, fasting is valuable in the Christian's ongoing process of self-evaluation and confession of sin.[16] Wynand de

---

[14] Hall, *The Fasting Prayer*, p. 33.
[15] Cf. Franklin, *Fasting*, pp. 111, 182. Contra the Roman Catholic view that continues to be represented, for example, by Murphy, *The Spirituality of Fasting*, pp. 83-84.
[16] Cf. Hickey, *The Power of Prayer and Fasting*, p. 196; and Franklin, *Fasting*, pp. 164-65.

Kock points out that, although we are saved, we continue to need Christ's saving grace and presence. The Pentecostal church, therefore, is 'a community that is redeemed, needs redemption and has a redeeming presence in this world'.[17] Redeemed believers and the redeemed community continue to stand in need of redemption regarding certain failings. We need to repent of our desire for power, our pride, our greed, and our self-justification.[18] The Church is called to be different from the world, but insofar as we are like the world, we must repent. The Holy Spirit calls both men and women of every ethnic group to ministry (Joel 2.29); therefore we must repent of our resistance to women and to ethnic leaders. Pentecostal pastor Jentezen Franklin states, 'The discipline of fasting will humble you, remind you of your dependence upon God, and bring you back to your first love'.[19] Repentance is needed on both the individual and corporate levels; and fasting, which generates humility, can assist our repentance in all of these areas.

Moses, Ezra, Nehemiah, Daniel, John Wesley, and early Pentecostals fasted as a means of communal repentance for the sins of the Church and sins of society. Our repentance never ends because humans are skilled at finding new ways to rebel against God and to abuse one another. However, Pentecostals believe optimistically that 'Salvation in Christ, then, breaks all oppressions and liberates us to liberate others from structural violence which completely disfigures the purpose of God: that they may live the full and abundant life which He offers them'.[20]

Because Jesus is savior, Pentecostals desire to participate in his mission of reconciling the world unto himself. Jesus' role as savior carried him to the cross, where he suffered and died willingly for

---

[17] Wynand J. de Kock, 'The Church as a Redeemed, Un-Redeemed, and Redeeming Community', in John Christopher Thomas (ed.) *Toward a Pentecostal Ecclesiology: The Church and the Fivefold Gospel* (Cleveland, TN: CPT Press, 2010), pp. 47-68 (p. 51). Cf. Darío Andres López Rodríguez, 'The Redeeming Community: The God of Life and the Community of Life', in Thomas (ed.) *Toward a Pentecostal Ecclesiology*, pp. 69-86.

[18] de Kock, 'The Church as a Redeemed, Un-Redeemed, and Redeeming Community', pp. 56-57.

[19] Franklin, *Fasting*, p. 71.

[20] López Rodríguez, 'The Redeeming Community', pp. 82-83. Cf. Veli-Matti Kärkkäinen, 'Spirit, Reconciliation and Healing in the Community: Missiological Insights from Pentecostals', *International Review of Missions* 94.372 (2005), who writes that redemption in Christ is the 'key to social transformation' (p. 44).

others. God's love for the world was manifested in the cross, and as a saved people, we are called to take up our crosses and follow Jesus. The Holy Spirit urges us to join with God in his mission of salvation through fasting on behalf of others, even on behalf of our enemies. Therefore, fasting is beneficial not only in relation to repentance but also in relation to intercessory prayer.[21] Just as Moses, Ezra, and Daniel fasted while interceding for others, so did Wesley and the early Pentecostals. 'The person filled by the Spirit of God is impelled by that same Spirit to cooperate with God in the work of evangelism and social action in the anticipation of the new creation'.[22] Wade H. Horton writes, 'If we are not concerned enough about lost souls to fast, we are not concerned enough'.[23] Fasting contributes to the effectiveness of our intercessory prayers as we seek God for revival, for renewal, for justice, for righteousness, and for peace. In its redemptive actions (which includes fasting), the 'redeemed community is also a sacrament, since the Spirit enables the Church to transmit the grace of God, in Christ, throughout the world'.[24]

Viewed through the lens of Jesus as savior, fasting becomes an aid to personal and corporate repentance and it strengthens and deepens our intercessory prayers for others who stand in need of salvation. However, there remains another reason for fasting that relates to Jesus as savior, and that is liturgical fasting. Liturgical fasting has been important throughout church history; and even though it has not been prominent in Pentecostalism, it has been present there to some degree. The Christian calendar is organized along the lines of salvation history and the life of Jesus, the savior. Fasting has been placed on the calendar at significant times of the year as reminders that help us to re-imagine the events of the gospel and to order our lives in accord with the life of Jesus.

2. Fasting and Jesus the Sanctifier

Throughout history, fasting has been closely associated with sanctification. Early Pentecostals often fasted as means of facilitating the

---

[21] Cf. Franklin, *Fasting*, p. 96.
[22] Kärkkäinen, 'Spirit, Reconciliation and Healing in the Community', p. 45.
[23] Wade H. Horton, *Pentecost Yesterday and Today* (Cleveland, TN: Pathway Press, 1964), p. 125.
[24] de Kock, 'The Church as a Redeemed, Un-Redeemed, and Redeeming Community', p. 55.

total consecration that was necessary for experiencing sanctification. For Pentecostals, sanctification is purification and separation unto God. It is the transforming of the affections so that we love God with all of our hearts, and we love our neighbor as ourselves. Fasting produces the humility required for complete surrender to God, and it is an expression of the relational longing for God and the desire for righteousness and holiness.[25] Fasting is a means of redirecting the affections away from selfish desires and toward the desire for God alone. Therefore, fasting is generated by affectivity – the seeker's passionate pursuit of God and deep-seated love for others, whether the other be sinner or believer. Thus, fasting is a part of relationality, and those who fast approach God not with an attitude of entitlement but with humility, consecration, obedience, and supplication – as a needy child would approach a parent.

If compassion for our neighbor is an affective result of sanctification, then fasting for others should awaken and deepen our concern for those neighbors who are poor and hungry. The pangs of hunger that come during fasting should cause us to 'remember that one-third of the people in this world go to bed with that same feeling every night because they have no food'.[26] The injunctions of Isaiah 58 and the early Christian practice of fasting for the poor should compel us to set aside certain fast days that are devoted especially to prayer for the poor and for giving to the poor. 'Fasting for a day might be what we most need to change our own pathetic passivity in the face of famine'.[27]

Jesus sanctifies the entire human being, including the body,[28] and the Pentecostal believer can say with David, 'my body longs' for God (Ps. 63.2). 'Fasting is the body talking what the spirit yearns, what the soul longs for'.[29] Because there is no dualism between the body and the spirit, the function of fasting is not to suppress or punish the physical body; but, as Pentecostal evangelist Franklin Hall writes, fasting incorporates the body into the experience of salvation:

---

[25] Wallis, *God's Chosen Fast*, pp. 44-48.
[26] Franklin, *Fasting*, p. 112.
[27] McKnight, *Fasting*, p. 33.
[28] López Rodríguez, 'The Redeeming Community', pp. 69-70.
[29] McKnight, *Fasting*, p. 11. McKnight provides a very helpful theology of the body (pp. 1-12)

> This is the most important teaching in this volume ... Fasting properly unto our Lord brings forth the glory of the cross, enabling God's people to come into full realization that we may also obtain a fundamental Bodyfelt as well as the fundamental Heartfelt salvation experience.[30]

When the apostle Paul speaks of the negative influence of the 'flesh' (Rom. 7.25), the 'works of the flesh' (Gal. 5.19), and the opposition of the flesh to the Spirit (Gal. 5.17), he is referring not to the physical body but to the sinful nature, the fallenness of humanity that consists of misdirected affections and desires. For Paul, the body itself is not evil. Likewise, Pentecostals believe that the body is good – it is the temple of the Holy Spirit.[31] Steven Land explains:

> The body was for the Lord, therefore periods of fasting were to draw nigh to God with one's whole being. This bodily dedication was necessary, because spirituality involved the whole person and all of his or her life. Fasting was not a punishment; it was a feeding on the Lord and drinking of the Spirit.[32]

Similarly, Grant Wacker characterizes Pentecostalism's utilization of the body as a sacramental appropriation:

> The Holy Spirit occasionally flowed out beyond the tongue, transforming the entire human body into a living sacrament ... Little realizing what they were doing, perhaps, believers effectively sacramentalized the divine power by locating it within their own bodies, within time and space.[33]

A holistic view of the human person suggests mutual interaction between the body and the spirit, but the ascetics have insisted that the body's influence is consistently negative. John Wesley would agree in part, teaching that a full stomach is not conducive to spiritual hunger. However, Wesley's semi-ascetic perspective must be

---

[30] Hall, *Atomic Power with God through Fasting and Prayer*, p. 5. See also p. 43, where he explains that the whole person, including the body, must be 'yielded to the Lord for service'.

[31] See Wallis, *God's Chosen Fast*, pp. 88-93. Baab, *Fasting*, provides sound teaching regarding a healthy body image, particularly as it relates to women (pp. 21-27, 93-118).

[32] Land, *Pentecostal Spirituality*, p. 109.

[33] Wacker, *Heaven Below*, p. 108. Cf. Butler, 'Observing the Lives of the Saints', pp. 159-76.

modified to some degree. I would argue that the state of fullness and the state of hunger each presents its own temptations and its own benefits, and the apostle Paul testified to his ability to face the challenges of each state: 'I have learned the secret of being filled and going hungry, both of having abundance and suffering need' (Phil. 4.12). Asceticism, however, recognizes the benefits only of emptiness, while ignoring the blessings and benefits that can result from fullness.[34]

Fullness should generate worship, gratitude, and thanksgiving to God, who is the source of every good gift. Jewish theology, for example, views

> the joys of earth as God-given and therefore to be cherished with gratitude toward the divine giver ... the Jew partook with genuine zest of the good cheer of life, without, however, lapsing into frivolity, gluttony, or intemperance ... he sought and found true joy in the consecration of his life and all of its powers and opportunities to the service of his God, a God who had caused the fruit of the vine to grow and the earth to give forth the bread.[35]

The Old Testament calendar included only one fast day, but twenty feast days. Throughout Scripture, God's people are encouraged to give thanks for every material blessing, including food. This does not mean, however, that we should seek a constant state of fullness. Moderation and self-control are marks of maturity.[36] Nevertheless, our study of Scripture has shown that fasting is not the appropriate response to every situation. For example, Jesus' disciples did not fast while he was with them. However, just as there are times when fasting is inappropriate, there are times when fullness is inappropriate: there is 'a time to weep and a time to laugh; a time to mourn and a time to dance' (Eccl. 3.4). A sanctified spirituality includes the ability to discern the time for eating and the time for fasting.[37]

---

[34] Cf. Murphy, *The Spirituality of Fasting*, pp. 103-105.
[35] Hirsch, 'Asceticism', p. 167.
[36] See Baab, *Fasting*, pp. 138-41.
[37] The ancient rabbinic sage Eliezer ha-Kappar wrote, 'Whosoever undergoes fasting and other penances for no special reason commits a wrong' ('Hirsch, 'Asceticism', p. 167).

3. Fasting and Jesus the Spirit Baptizer

In the book of Joel, the Lord calls upon the people of Israel to fast and repent. He declares, 'Return to me with all your heart, and with fasting, weeping, and mourning' (Joel 2.12). The culmination of God's bountiful response to their fasting is his gift of the Holy Spirit. The Lord says, 'and it will happen after this that I will pour out my Spirit upon everyone' (Joel 2.28). The words, 'after this', refer to all that had occurred earlier in the book, which includes Israel's fasting and repentance.[38]

In light of Joel's prophecy, the Pentecostal practice of fasting in preparation for Spirit baptism is not surprising. In some cases, the fast was carried out by the person who was seeking for the baptism in the Spirit. Anyone who was hungry for the Holy Spirit was encouraged to seek God with fasting, prayer, and waiting upon God. The process of seeking involved a deep and passionate hunger for God. At other times, people fasted on behalf of (or along with) other believers who were seeking the experience. In still other cases, a group of people might pray and fast for revival in general, and the resultant spiritual outpouring would include Spirit baptism for those who had not previously received the experience.

Our study of the biblical texts also revealed that the three-day fast of Saul had the effect of preparing him to be filled with the Holy Spirit. Although Saul had seen a vision of his healing only, Ananias knew that Saul's greater need was the endowment of the Holy Spirit. Therefore, when he prayed for Saul, he said, 'the LORD Jesus ... has sent me so that you may regain your sight, and *be filled with the Holy Spirit*' (Acts 9.17, emphasis added).

Jesus taught that those who hunger and thirst for righteousness will be filled (Mt. 5.6); and, for Pentecostals, fasting is an expression of intense hunger for God. Fasting transforms our desires, generates humility, builds faith, and makes us receptive to the working of the Holy Spirit. Jentezen Franklin writes that fasting helps us 'to stay sharp and sensitive to the Holy Spirit'.[39] God pours out his Spirit on all who are eager to receive, and fasting is evidence of that eagerness. The early Pentecostal testimonies show that fasting often

---

[38] Cf. Prince, *Fasting*, pp. 50-59; Wallis, *God's Chosen Fast*, p. 132.
[39] Franklin, *Fasting*, p. 69.

results in an outpouring of the Spirit and the manifestations of Spirit's gifts.

The experience of Jesus suggests that fasting relates to the Spirit in another way. At the time of Jesus' baptism in water, the Holy Spirit descended upon him. Then the Spirit led Jesus into the wilderness to be tested, where he fasted for forty days and nights. Pentecostals have discovered that the Holy Spirit leads us to fast and pray that we might be prepared for effective ministry.

4. Fasting and Jesus the Healer

Many of the urgent prayers recorded in the Bible are pleas for healing. King David recalls that when his enemies were sick he had fasted and prayed for their healing (Ps. 35.13). When David's baby grew sick, he 'prayed to God for the child, and he fasted, and he went in and lay all night upon the ground' (2 Sam. 12.16). He fasted and prayed for seven days, pleading with God for the life of the child. It is evident that David considered fasting to be an important companion to his prayers for the healing of his child. He said, 'While the child was alive, I fasted and wept; for I said, "Who knows, the LORD may be gracious to me, that the child may live"' (2 Sam. 12.22). He believed that fasting would verify his repentance, his humility, his sincerity, his pain, and his urgency.

Pentecostals have testified that fasting often leads to healing. To Pentecostals, fasting is a means of access to the throne of God, a way of deepening and strengthening one's prayers. Early Pentecostals fasted frequently on behalf of others who are sick, and they fasted occasionally for their own healing.[40] However, they have always understood that fasting does not guarantee healing. A.J. Tomlinson, who routinely fasted,[41] relates the story of a child named Jessica, who became gravely ill, and Tomlinson called a fast on her behalf. He stated that they would fast until she was healed or until the Lord took her. After several days of fasting and prayer, Jessica died.[42]

The fact that fasting can lead to healing may be related to the Lord's role as sustainer of all life. Like the Israelites, we are tempted

---

[40] I find it interesting that Lynne Baab, a Presbyterian minister, encourages fasting for healing (Baab, *Fasting*, pp. 39-41).

[41] R.G. Robins, *A.J. Tomlinson: Plainfolk Modernist* (Religion in America Series; New York: Oxford University Press, 2004), p. 139.

[42] Robins, *A.J. Tomlinson: Plainfolk Modernist*, pp. 140-41.

to believe that food is our source of life and strength and that we obtained it by our own ingenuity. 'When we give up eating, we are deliberately turning away from the natural by turning to God and to the supernatural'.[43] Fasting humbles us and tests our commitment to the word of life. Fasting reveals what is in our hearts. When Jesus was tempted, he cited Deut. 8.3, 'A person does not live by bread alone but by every word that comes forth from the mouth of God'. Rather than turn the stones into bread in order to satisfy his physical hunger, Jesus affirmed the life-giving power of the word of God. Jesus knew that even as all living things came into existence by God's word, they continue to be sustained by that same living word.

Fasting can be an effective means not only to physical healing but also to emotional healing. The universal human desire for comfort and the aversion to pain causes us to medicate all pain, whether it be physical or emotional pain.[44] Addictions to drugs, alcohol, pleasure, power, and food are often attempts to alleviate guilt, emotional injuries, dysfunction, grief, regret, and other psychological suffering.[45] However, the hiding and avoiding of pain does not heal it; it remains under the surface, throbbing, stinging, torturing. 'We inhabit a culture obsessed with liberty, but we habituate ourselves into bondage'.[46] Fasting eliminates the food drug that anesthetizes and conceals suffering. Consequently, rather than suppressing and burying the pain, fasting brings it to the surface and facilitates its presentation to God in prayer so that it can be healed.[47]

5. Fasting and Jesus the Coming King

Fasting in the Bible and in early Pentecostalism was, for the most part, anticipatory of future blessings. When asked why his disciples did not fast, Jesus explained that the bridegroom's attendants do not fast while the bridegroom is with them because it is a time of joy and celebration, and mourning would not be appropriate. When the bridegroom departs, the celebration will be ended, and then will be the proper time for sorrow. In the same way, Jesus (the bridegroom)

---

[43] Prince, *Fasting*, p. 16.
[44] See Franklin, *Fasting*, pp. 91-96, 135-36, 207.
[45] Cf. Amy Johnson Frykholm, 'Soul Food: Why Fasting Makes Sense', *Christian Century* 122.5 (2005), pp. 24-25.
[46] Baab, *Fasting*, p. 10.
[47] Cf. Hickey, *The Power of Prayer and Fasting*, p. 37. Cf. Wallis, *God's Chosen Fast*, pp. 60-65.

is with his disciples, and it is a time of joy. When Jesus departs from them, then it will be appropriate for them to fast.

We find eschatological connections in Jesus' words here. We are now in a period in which Jesus is absent from us (though he is present through the Holy Spirit). Jesus went away, and he promised to return, but he has not returned yet. While the bridegroom is away, we fast, just as he said the disciples would fast after the bridegroom departed. During this time of waiting, Jesus fasts along with us.[48] At the Last Supper, he declared as much:

> And he said to them, 'I have earnestly desired to eat this Passover with you before I suffer; for I say to you, I shall never again eat it until it is fulfilled in the kingdom of God'. And having taken a cup and given thanks, he said, 'Take this and share it among yourselves; for I say to you, I will not drink of the fruit of the vine from now on until the kingdom of God comes' (Lk. 22.15-18).

We are living in a time of anticipation, awaiting the return of Jesus, at which time we will be invited to the Marriage Supper of the Lamb. Therefore, in some ways, we are grieving over his absence and long to see him face to face when we will receive the fullness of his presence.

Fasting anticipates a divine encounter; therefore, it is a deeply eschatological act that seeks and hopes for the 'already' of the already-not-yet paradigm of God's inbreaking kingdom. When Christ returns, fasting will be unnecessary, but until then, fasting is a part of tarrying on the Lord, waiting patiently for his coming. Those who wait on the Lord in fasting and prayer are transformed, formed, and sanctified by his presence. As we await the return of Jesus, we fast as means of self-examination and deeper spiritual formation, in order to ensure that we are ready for his coming.[49] Fasting tests the affections to see if they are pure and genuine; then, as the waiting in faith continues, fasting deepens and stabilizes those same affections so that one is enabled to obey Paul's admonition: 'Set your affections on things above, not on things on the earth' (Col. 3.2). Through fasting, the believer encounters God's presence, which produces humility and a longing to be like God.

---

[48] Cf. Franklin, *Fasting*, p. 105.
[49] Cf. Tomlinson, *Church of God Evangel* 1.1, p. 8., mentioned earlier.

C. A Contemporary Pentecostal Approach to Fasting

Given the conclusions of the previous chapters, there are a number of ways that contemporary Pentecostals might appropriate fasting into their spiritual lives and into the corporate life of their churches. Fasting should be practiced both privately and corporately as an aid to any kind of urgent prayer, especially when seeking God for revival and the salvation of lost souls. Fasting should be observed when individuals or churches are in need of divine guidance and when specific needs are evident in the life of an individual, in the society, or in the church. Fasting is valuable particularly in preparing seekers for the experiences of sanctification, Spirit baptism, and divine healing. Our fasting should be joined with prayer as a means of appealing to God for the outpouring of God's grace in our lives, in our churches, and in the world.

Pastors and other leaders should practice fasting and teach its meaning and its benefits. Ministerial candidates in the Church of God in Christ are required to affirm that, with God's help, they will be 'diligent in prayer and fasting'.[50] In times of crisis, parishioners should be encouraged to fast and pray, and they should be assembled together so that they may seek God with and for one another. 'If there is a local church threatened with discord and division, if spiritual life is waning and worldliness abounding, if conversions are few and backslidings frequent, would not this be a time when leaders should call that church to prayer and fasting?'[51] Through annual, monthly, and weekly planning, church leaders should be prepared to make recommendations to the congregation regarding fast days. At least one Pentecostal denomination includes fasting as a regular practice. As mentioned above, Tuesday and Friday of every week are fast days in the Church of God in Christ.[52]

However, inasmuch as fasting is a voluntary observance, care should be taken not to imply that those who fast are more spiritual than those who do not fast. The Pharisee fasted twice a week, but Jesus was not impressed with his spirituality (Lk. 18.12).

---

[50] Church of God in Christ Editorial Commission (ed.), *Official Manual with the Doctrines and Discipline of the Church of God in Christ* (Memphis, TN: Church of God in Christ, Inc., 1991), p. 209.

[51] Wallis, *God's Chosen Fast* p. 37.

[52] Church of God in Christ, *Church of God in Christ 105th Annual Holy Convocation*, p. 4.

Fasting can be an important part of the preparation for important events such as special services, conventions, meetings, and election of leaders. Throughout history, Christians have fasted prior to the celebration of the sacraments and ordinances of the Church. Congregations should be reminded to fast in anticipation of these events.

Regular fasting can be beneficial, but decisions regarding fast days must not turn into a legalistic requirement. For example, rather than deciding to fast every Friday, we should plan to fast every Friday for one month. At the end of the month, we can then make adjustments to our plans, depending upon our schedule, our family's wishes, and the effect of fasting upon our bodies.

Fasting also must not become a private enterprise only. If Christians are to be formed into the image of Christ, they will do so only within the context of the believing community – the Church. For this reason, fasting must be encouraged as an ongoing communal activity; and believers must gather to pray and fast together.

The Roman Catholic and Eastern Orthodox concern to establish universally binding fast days, along with their attendant detailed stipulations, has both advantages and disadvantages. The disadvantage of making fasting obligatory is that it can easily become a work of merit. Furthermore, as the Church multiplies its regulations regarding ritualized fasting, the voluntary nature of fasting becomes obscured, and the rules of fasting overshadow the reason for fasting.[53] Despite the disadvantages, liturgical fasting has its benefits. 'Regular fasting need not become ritualistic, any more than regular praying.[54] Communal fasting in accord with the Christian calendar provides seasonal reminders of the story of the gospel and should evoke anticipation for the return of the bridegroom.[55] It also serves as an antidote to individualism by keeping Christians in touch with their historical roots and with the Church universal. Finally, for those who are not normally inclined toward self-examination and

---

[53] This point is reflected in the nature of contemporary Roman Catholic resources on fasting. Most of them are devoted to the details of Canon Law and include very little theology.

[54] Wallis, *God's Chosen Fast*, p. 34.

[55] See especially Berghuis, *Christian Fasting: A Theological Approach*, p. 118.

confession, liturgical fasting provides regular opportunities for those important spiritual exercises.[56]

Considering the benefits of liturgical fasting and in light of its historic importance in the Church, I would encourage pastors to include specific fast days on the annual church calendar. The significance of Lent, Advent, Good Friday, and other holy days should be explained to the congregation.

Many Pentecostal churches have observed an annual fast during the first twenty-one or forty days of the new year, in order to set the church on the right course.[57] This practice is commendable, but it coincides with the secular year, not the Christian year. I would suggest, instead, that the New Year fast be shortened to a single day or week, and a fast of twenty-one or forty days be instituted leading up to the Day of Pentecost, which is a day of new beginnings in the New Testament story. A Pentecost fast would have much deeper theological significance and might result in a resurgence of Pentecostal revival in our churches.

---

[56] Cf. McKnight, *Fasting*, pp. 81-98.
[57] See Franklin, *Fasting*, pp. 27-28.

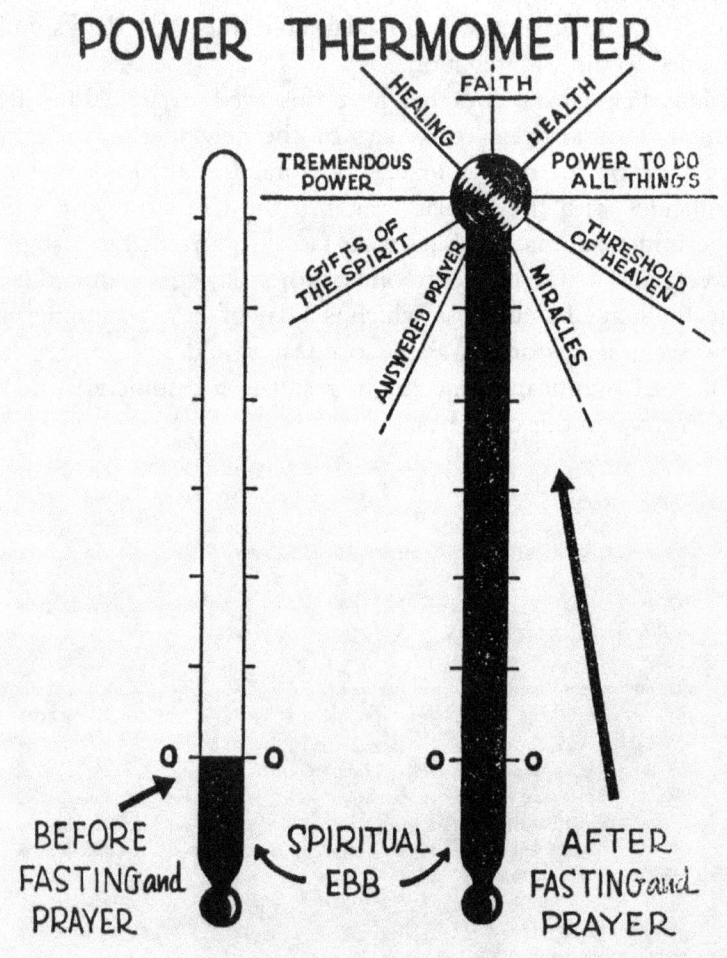

Illustration from Franklin Hall's
Atomic Power with God through Fasting and Prayer

8

PRACTICAL GUIDELINES FOR FASTING

> *Denying material food, which nourishes our body, nurtures an interior disposition to listen to Christ and be fed by His saving word.*
> – Pope Benedict XVI[1]

Fasting is not a badge of spirituality, and fasting is not a practice to be checked off from a list of spiritual duties.[2] In order to be effective, fasting must be generated by an urgent need or by the desires placed in the heart by the Holy Spirit for growth, maturity, and intimacy with God. Therefore, whenever we decide to fast, we should identify very clearly the reasons for our fasting. Then, while fasting, we should devote a significant amount of time in prayer, Bible reading, meditation, and worship aimed toward the purpose for which we are fasting.

Inasmuch as the human body tends to prefer a regular routine, fasting, which is a break in that routine, will cause bodily discomfort. The amount of discomfort will vary from person to person, and may include headaches, weakness, nausea, and insomnia. Side effects can be more noticeable in people who normally consume significant quantities of caffeine and/or sugar products. For most people, therefore, it is advisable to begin with a fast of only a few hours. One way to begin fasting is to skip breakfast or lunch a few times. Once the body becomes accustomed to surviving a few hours without food, a fast of two meals would be an appropriate

---

[1] http://www.vatican.va/holy_father/benedict_xvi/messages/lent/documents/hf_ben-xvi_mes_20081211_lent-2009_en.html.
[2] Franklin, *Fasting*, p. 203.

next step. If the level of discomfort is bearable and if there is no sign of health risks, a fast of 24 hours or longer may be attempted. Whatever the length of the fast, plenty of water should be consumed, and light exercise should be a part of daily activities (walking, biking, or swimming). It is not wise to overeat before beginning a fast or when breaking a fast.

Before fasting, a doctor should be consulted to confirm that one is healthy enough to endure the experience. People with certain illnesses and health conditions should not fast without medical supervision. These include persons with diabetes or hypoglycemia, women who are pregnant, or persons who have suffered from an eating disorder, among others. Anyone whose body is unable to withstand the rigors of fasting all food can consider a juice fast or a partial fast in which the diet is restricted in a significant way. Those who cannot fast at all should seek for an alternative method of expressing devotion and consecration.[3]

The length of the fast depends upon the purposes for fasting and upon the individual's ability to survive without food. The human body will seldom last more than seven days without water, but most people could live at least forty days without food. On the day of Atonement the Jews fast for twenty-four hours (Lev. 23.32). Saul of Tarsus fasted for three days (Acts 9.9); David fasted for seven days (2 Sam. 12.16-18); and Jesus fasted for forty days (Mt. 4.2). As you can see from the above examples the length of the fast depends on the need and the circumstances. The matter is between the individual and the Lord.

The frequency of your fasting is also up to the individual and the Lord. The Lord commanded Israel to fast one day per year (Lev. 23.27). After the Babylonian Captivity the Jews added four more annual fasts (Zech. 8.19); and in the New Testament, the Pharisees fasted two days each week (Lk. 18.12); but these additional fasts were not divine mandates.

Many Christians fast during times of urgent prayer and others fast in conjunction with the Christian calendar, especially during Lent. Churches sometimes schedule a season of fasting at the be-

---

[3] Although devotional practices such as giving up television or social media cannot properly be called fasting, they may be the next best thing for people who are unable to fast. Cf. McKnight, *Fasting*, p. 19. On the value of substitutes for fasting, see Baab, *Fasting*, pp. 105-18, especially p. 109.

ginning of each year. Fasting on a regular basis can be very beneficial, but God does not require a specified amount of fasting. Instead, he expects believers to fast when the need arises and when he leads them to fast.

When fasting is an expression of suffering and humility, it touches the heart of God and moves God to act. However, when used as leverage or as an attempt to force God to act against his will, fasting offends God and incurs God's judgment. Fasting does not make God more available, rather it makes the Christian more open to God. James insists that many prayers are not answered because of wrong motives: 'You ask, and receive not, because you ask amiss, that you may consume it upon your lusts' (Jas 4.3). Fasting helps to weed out our wrong motives and attitudes, thus placing us in a position to receive the blessings of God, blessings that God is eager to bestow.

The Temptation of Christ in the Wilderness
Juan de Flandes (16th Century).

9

CONCLUSION

Who should fast? Anyone who wants to draw near to God.
– Lynne M. Baab[1]

I will conclude with a word of personal testimony. I was eager to write this book because of the important role of fasting in my own life. At the age of seventeen, I was introduced to fasting by Rev. Mae Terry, the woman evangelist who founded my home church. She affirmed that her practice of fasting every Friday had a significant impact on her spiritual life and on her effectiveness as a minister.

Early in my own ministry, I gave myself to prayer, Bible reading, and worship; and these practices had a strong impact upon my spiritual formation. However, it was only when I added the practice of fasting on a regular basis, that my spiritual life and my ministry were completely transformed.

Over and over, my life has been affected in significant ways through fasting and prayer. It was during a time of fasting and prayer that I met Karen Luke, who would become my wife. Later, while fasting and praying about my future, the Lord miraculously opened the door for me to enter a doctoral program. Recently, I fasted in anticipation of the Day of Pentecost, and God poured out the Holy Spirit upon our church. Gifts of the Spirit were evident, and fervent prayers ascended to heaven. At the end of the service I was led by the Spirit to pray for a young man. After we prayed, he told me that

---

[1] Baab, *Fasting*, p. 33.

his doctor suspected he had cancer. Two weeks later, he tested free of cancer.

Furthermore, I have experienced the benefits of fasting in times of crisis. On many occasions, I have witnessed revivals, healings, miracles, the working of spiritual gifts, the resolution of church conflicts, and divine guidance in response to fasting and prayer.

There have been times when I saw no immediate results from fasting, and I wondered if my fasting was in vain. However, I have learned that the benefits of fasting are often delayed. More than once, I did not become aware of the effect of my fasting until months or years later.

While writing this book, I fasted frequently, and the experience has only confirmed once again the value of fasting for spiritual health. Fasting is one of the many means of grace that enable to us to draw near to God; and, along with James, I encourage you: 'Draw near to God, and he will draw near to you' (Jas 4.8).

BIBLIOGRAPHY

Monographs on Fasting

Baab, Lynne M., *Fasting: Spiritual Freedom Beyond Our Appetites* (Downers Grove, IL: IVP Books, 2006). Baab is a Presbyterian minister who has practiced fasting. A well-written and complete study of the topic, its uniqueness lies in its specific advice to women, especially to women who have experienced eating disorders. Baab's work is helpful for everyone, but it will be especially helpful for those who, for whatever reason, need an alternative to fasting from food.

Berghuis, Kent D., *Christian Fasting: A Theological Approach* (Richardson, TX: Biblical Studies Press, 2007). This study was Berghuis' doctoral dissertation at Trinity International University. As dissertations go, however, it is quite readable. His analysis of the biblical material is helpful, and his overview of fasting in Church history is quite detailed. Berghuis' work is recommended for anyone who is interested in a serious study of fasting. Berghuis is a minister with the American Baptist Church.

Foster, Richard J., *Celebration of Discipline: The Path to Spiritual Growth* (San Francisco: HarperOne, 3rd edn, 1998). The classic work on spiritual disciplines, the chapter on fasting emphasizes the benefits of fasting for spiritual discipline and formation.

Franklin, Jentezen, *Fasting* (Lake Mary, FL: Charisma House, 2008). Franklin is a Pentecostal megachurch pastor who has practiced fasting privately and who has led his church to practice fasting corporately. A very helpful work on the popular level. He refers to many of the biblical examples of fasting.

Hall, Franklin, *Atomic Power with God through Fasting and Prayer* (Phoenix, AZ: s.n., new edn, 1973).

—*The Fasting Prayer* (San Diego, CA: Franklin Hall, 1947). Hall was a Pentecostal evangelist who ministered from the 1930's to the 1970's. His books on fasting were quite popular and influenced many of the healing evangelists of his day. In 1956, Hall founded the Deliverance Foundation, which in 1970 reported thirty-two affiliated churches and two thousand members.

Hickey, Marilyn, *The Power of Prayer and Fasting* (New York: Warner Faith, 2006). A Pentecostal pastor whose book is helpful but sometimes wanders outside the bounds of good exegesis. Hickey's unique contribution is her emphasis on fasting's deep connection to prayer. She devotes an entire chapter to prayer.

McKnight, Scot, *Fasting* (The Ancient Practices Series; Nashville, TN: Thomas Nelson, 2009). A well-written study that provides perhaps the best exposition of fasting's connection to a healthy theology of the human body as God's temple. An Anabaptist, McKnight views the essence of fasting as 'the natural response to a sacred moment', a point that is urgently needed but tends to be reductionistic. Some of the biblical texts do not conform to his paradigm, but he tries to squeeze them into it.

Miles, Margaret R., *Fullness of Life: Historical Foundations for a New Asceticism* (Philadelphia, PA: Westminster Press, 1981). A reappropriation of the ascetic practice of fasting.

Montgomery, Carrie Judd, *Secrets of Victory* (ed. Sadie A. Cody; Oakland, CA: Triumphs of Faith, 1921). Montgomery was a leader in the healing movement before becoming a Pentecostal. Her book includes a chapter on fasting.

Murphy, Charles M., *The Spirituality of Fasting: Rediscovering a Christian Practice* (Notre Dame, IN: Ave Maria Press, 2010). One of the best books on the Roman Catholic theology and practice of fasting.

Murray, Andrew, *With Christ in the School of Prayer* (Christian Classics; Virginia Beach, VA: CBN University Press, 700 Club edn, 1978). Born in 1828, Murray served as pastor in South Africa and led in a revival there. He wrote many popular books on the spiritual life. This and his other works are available freely on the internet.

Piper, John, *A Hunger for God: Desiring God through Fasting and Prayer* (Wheaton, IL: Crossway Books, 1997). Piper is a leading Evangelical writer, and his study of fasting emphasizes fasting as a key to spiritual growth and discipleship. A good Calvinist, he argues that fasting changes the person who fasts, but he strongly opposes the view that fasting moves God.

Prince, Derek, *Fasting* (New Kensington, PA: Whitaker House, 1993). A very brief (61 pages) but helpful study of fasting from a Pentecostal perspective. He connects fasting to the outpouring of the Holy Spirit, both in the book of Joel and today.

Ryan, Thomas, *The Sacred Art of Fasting: Preparing to Practice* (Preparing to Practice; Woodstock, VT: SkyLight Paths Pub., 2005). A Roman Catholic, Ryan discusses fasting as a spiritual practice in Judaism, Christianity, Islam, Hinduism, Buddhism, and Mormonism.

Schmemann, Alexander, *Great Lent* (Crestwood, NY: St. Vladimir's Seminary Press, rev. edn, 1974). This well-known Eastern Orthodox scholar explains the place of fasting in the Orthodox liturgical calendar. The strength of the book for non-Orthodox readers is his profoundly spiritual theology of fasting. A must read, particularly for anyone interested in theology.

–*Introduction to Liturgical Theology* (trans. Asheleigh E. Moorhouse; Library of Orthodox Theology; Portland, ME: American Orthodox Press, 1966). This work offers a helpful overview of the history of liturgical theology, including the twofold history of the development of fasting: liturgical fasting and monastic (ascetical) fasting.

Towns, Elmer L., *Fasting for Spiritual Breakthrough* (Ventura, CA: Regal Books, 1996).

Wallis, Arthur, *God's Chosen Fast* (Ft. Washington, PA: Christian Literature Crusade, 1968). Wallis was a Pentecostal leader in what has been called the British New Church Movement. His popular-level work on fasting was the standard work for Pentecostals for many years.

Willard, Dallas, *The Spirit of the Disciplines: Understanding How God Changes Lives* (San Francisco: Harper & Row, 1988). Willard has been a leading advocate among Evangelicals for the practice of fasting. Like Piper, Willard stresses fasting as a means of self-transformation and as an expression of discipline and obedience.

Journal Articles on Fasting

Anderson, Edgar R., 'The Holy Spirit's Role in Prayer and Fasting', in *Conference on the Holy Spirit Digest, Vol 2* (Springfield, Mo: Gospel Publ House, 1983), pp. 225-29.

Bainbridge, Gregory, 'Is Fasting Obsolete?', *Worship* 34.9 (1960), pp. 573-78.

Baker, Aelred, 'Fasting to the World', *Journal of Biblical Literature* 84.3 (1965), pp. 291-94.

Brattston, David W. T., 'Fasting in the Earliest Church', *Restoration Quarterly* 53.4 (2011), pp. 235-45.

Buchanan, Mark, 'Go Fast and Live: Hunger as Spiritual Discipline', *Christian Century* 118.7 (2001), pp. 16-20. A popular level article that encourages fasting as a means of interrupting the fast-paced lifestyle of contemporary Christians. Buchanan insists that Christians must slow down and make time for engaging God.

Carter, Ginger, 'Fasting: Spiritual Freedom Beyond Our Appetites', *Congregations* 33.3 (2007), pp. 38-38.

Castelli, Jim, 'Catholic Bishops Call for Fasting', *Christian Century* 91.43 (1974).

Courneen, Francis V., 'Notes: Recent Trends with Regard to Fasting', *Theological Studies* 7.3 (1946), pp. 464-70.

Derby, Josiah, 'Fasting and Atonement', *Jewish Bible Quarterly* 23.4 (1995), pp. 238-41.

Duffy, Eamon, 'To Fast Again', *First Things* 151 (2005), pp. 4-6.

Dugan, Kathleen M., 'Fasting for Life: The Place of Fasting in the Christian Tradition', *Journal of the American Academy of Religion* 63.3 (1995), pp. 539-48.

Dura, Ioan, 'The Canons of the Sixth Ecumenical Synod Concerning Fasting and Their Application to the Present Needs of the Orthodox Faithful', *Greek Orthodox Theological Review* 40.1-2 (1995), pp. 149-64.

Fischer, Walter F., 'Fasting and Bodily Preparation: A Fine Outward Training', *Concordia Theological Monthly* 30.12 (1959), pp. 887-901.

Frykholm, Amy Johnson, 'Soul Food: Why Fasting Makes Sense', *Christian Century* 122.5 (2005), pp. 24-25.

Gardner, Christine J., 'Hungry for God: Why More and More Christians Are Fasting for Revival', *Christianity Today* 43.4 (1999), pp. 32-38.

Goetz, Ronald G., 'Modest Proposal for Fasting and Meatless Days', *Christian Century* 91.41 (1974), pp. 116-17.

Hintz, Marcy, 'Fasting', *Christianity Today* 53.4 (2009), pp. 61-62.

Johnson, Pierce, 'Fasting as a Modern Discipline', *Religion in Life* 44.3 (1975), pp. 331-37.

Kee, Alistair, 'Question About Fasting', *Novum Testamentum* 11.3 (1969), pp. 161-73.

Lambert, David, 'Fasting as a Penitential Rite: A Biblical Phenomenon?', *Harvard Theological Review* 96.4 (2003), pp. 477-512. Lambert argues convincingly that the essence of fasting in the biblical text was not penance. He singles out the phrase 'to afflict oneself' as the core meaning of fasting. Fasting, therefore, is a means of involving the human body in the process of prayer, particularly the prayer of lament.

Larin, Vassa, 'Feasting and Fasting According to the Byzantine Typikon', *Worship* 83.2 (2009), pp. 133-48.

Loughlin, Stephen, 'Thomas Aquinas and the Importance of Fasting to the Christian Life', *Pro Ecclesia* 17.3 (2008), pp. 343-61.

Lowy, S., 'The Motivation of Fasting in Talmudic Literature', *Journal of Jewish Studies* 9.1-2 (1958), pp. 19-38.

MacDonald, G. Jeffrey, 'Fasting Like Daniel Gains a Following During Lenten Season', *Christian Century* 130.6 (2013), pp. 18-19.

Martin, Paul, 'Benefits of Fasting', *Christian Century* 94.11 (1977), pp. 298-301.

Maximus of Turin, 'The Fasting of Christ', *Orate Fratres* 24.4 (1950), pp. 145-46.

McGuckin, John A., 'Fasting in the Ancient World', *Living Pulpit* 9.1 (2000), p. 9.

Mentzer, Raymond A., 'Fasting, Piety, and Political Anxiety among French Reformed Protestants', *Church History* 76.2 (2007), pp. 330-62. Mentzer supplies detailed accounts of the French Protestant practice of corporate fasting.

Mercurio, Roger, 'And Then They Will Fast', *Worship* 35.3 (1961), pp. 150-54.

Mitchell, Curtis C., 'The Practice of Fasting in the New Testament', *Bibliotheca Sacra* 147.588 (1990), pp. 455-69.

Moore, Julie L., 'Spirit of Food: Thirty-Four Writers on Feasting and Fasting toward God', *Christianity and Literature* 61.3 (2012), pp. 522-25.

Nolan, Joseph T., 'The Joyous Season of Lent', *Orate Fratres* 24.4 (1950), pp. 177-81.

Norwood, Percy Varney, 'The Truth About Fasting: With Special Reference to Fasting-Communion', *Anglican Theological Review* 11.3 (1929), pp. 271-72.

O'Loughlin, Thomas, 'The Didache as a Source for Picturing the Earliest Christian Communities: The Case of the Practice of Fasting', in *Christian Origins* (London: Sheffield Academic Press, 2003), pp. 83-112.

'PCUSA Fasting Monthly to Identify with Poor', *Christian Century* 125.21 (2008), pp. 18-18.

Rexine, John E., 'Fasting in the Orthodox Church: Its Theological, Pastoral, and Social Implications', *Greek Orthodox Theological Review* 36.1 (1991), pp. 99-101.

Segal, Eliezer, 'Holy Men and Hunger Artists: Fasting and Asceticism in Rabbinic Culture', *Journal of the American Academy of Religion* 73.3 (2005), pp. 911-13.

Shepherd, Massey Hamilton, 'Fasting among Churchmen', *Anglican Theological Review* 40.2 (1958), pp. 81-94.

Taft, Robert F., 'Lent: A Meditation', *Worship* 57.2 (1983), pp. 123-34.

Tamney, Joseph B., 'Fasting and Modernization', *Journal for the Scientific Study of Religion* 19.2 (1980), pp. 129-37.

Vincie, Catherine, 'A History of Holy Week', *Liturgical Ministry* 13 (2004), pp. 105-18.

Webster, Robert, 'The Value of Self-Denial: John Wesley's Multidimensional View of Fasting', *Toronto Journal of Theology* 19.1 (2003), pp. 25-40.

Wilson-Hartgrove, Jonathan, Anne Graham Lotz, and Dallas Willard, 'Growing in Christ: What Classic Spiritual Discipline Needs the Most Renewal among American Christians?', *Christianity Today* 57.2 (2013), pp. 46-47.

Witetschek, Stephan, 'Going Hungry for a Purpose: On Gos. Thom. 69.2 and a Neglected Parallel in Origen', *Journal for the Study of the New Testament* 32.4 (2010), pp. 379-93.

Zimmerman, Joyce Ann, 'Fasting as Feasting', *Liturgical Ministry* 19.2 (2010), pp. 72-77.

Miscellaneous Works on Fasting

Baab, Lynne M., 'Fasting', in G.G. Scorgie, *et al* (eds.), *Zondervan Dictionary of Christian Spirituality* (Grand Rapids, MI: Zondervan, 2011), pp. 442-43.

Behm, J., 'νῆστις, νηστεύω, νηστεία', in G. Kittel, G.W. Bromiley, and G. Friedrich (eds.), *Theological Dictionary of the New Testament* (trans. G. Bromiley; 10 vols.; Grand Rapids, MI: Eerdmans, 1967), IV, pp. 924-35.

Conn, C.W., 'Fasting', in Stanley M. Burgess, Gary B. McGee, and Patrick H. Alexander (eds.), *Dictionary of Pentecostal and Charismatic Movements* (Grand Rapids, MI: Regency Reference Library, 1988), pp. 303-304.

Hartley, J.E., 'צוּם' in R.L. Harris, G.L. Archer, and B.K. Waltke (eds.), *Theological Wordbook of the Old Testament* (2 vols.; Chicago: Moody Press, 1980), II, pp. 758-59.

Hirsch, Emil G., 'Asceticism', in Isidore Singer and Cyrus Adler (eds.), *The Jewish Encyclopedia* (12 vols.; New York: Ktav Pub. House, 1964), II, pp. 165-67.

Mendenhall, G.E., 'Fast, Fasting', in George Arthur Buttrick (ed.), *The Interpreter's Dictionary of the Bible* (4 vols.; New York: Abingdon Press, 1962), II, pp. 241-44.

Muddiman, John, 'Fast, Fasting', in D.N. Freedman (ed.), *Anchor Bible Dictionary* (6 vols.; New York: Doubleday, 1992), II, pp. 773-76.

Rahner, Karl, 'Penance', in Karl Rahner (ed.), *Encyclopedia of Theology: The Concise Sacramentum Mundi* (New York: Seabury Press, 1975), pp. 1189-1204. Rahner's article includes an explanation of the Roman Catholic teaching regarding the meritorious nature of fasting. Through repentance, the believer is forgiven from the spiritual penalty of sin; but it is through fasting that the believer offers 'satisfaction' for the temporal penalties of sin.

Rothenberg, F.S., 'Fast', in Colin Brown (ed.), *New International Dictionary of New Testament Theology* (Grand Rapids, MI: Zondervan, 1975), I, pp. 611-13.

Stolz, F., 'צוּם', in Ernst Jenni and Claus Westermann (eds.), *Theological Lexicon of the Old Testament* (trans. Mark E. Biddle; 3 vols.; Peabody, MA: Hendrickson Publishers, 1997), III, Logos Version, no page nos.

Way, R.J., 'צוּם', in Willem Van Gemeren (ed.), *New International Dictionary of Old Testament Theology and Exegesis* (5 vols.; Grand Rapids, MI: Zondervan, 1997), Logos Version, no page nos.

Wesley, John, 'Upon Our Lord's Sermon on the Mount: Discourse Seven', in *Sermons on Several Occasions* (2 vols.; London: Caxton Press, by Henry Fisher, 9th edn, 1829), I, 304-18. Wesley addresses a broad range of issues on fasting in general, from its history to its theological significance. The sermon expresses Wesley's views on the subject very well. Available freely online.

Other Works Cited

Alexander, Kimberly E., *Pentecostal Healing: Models in Theology and Practice* (JPTSup 29; Blandford Forum, UK: Deo Publishing, 2006).

Archer, Melissa L., *'I was in the Spirit on the Lord's day': A Pentecostal Engagement with Worship in the Apocalypse* (Cleveland, TN: CPT Press, 2014).

Augustine, Daniela C., *Pentecost, Hospitality, and Transfiguration: Toward a Spirit-Inspired Vision of Social Transformation* (Cleveland, TN: CPT Press, 2012).

Bauer, Walter, *A Greek-English Lexicon of the New Testament, and Other Early Christian Literature* (trans. and ed. W.F. Arndt and F.W. Gingrich; Chicago: University of Chicago Press, 1957).

Bloch, Abraham P., *The Biblical and Historical Background of the Jewish Holy Days* (New York: Ktav Pub. House, 1978).

Blomberg, Craig, *Matthew* (New American Commentary; Nashville, TN: Broadman Press, 1992).

–*1 Corinthians* (NIV Application Commentary; Grand Rapids, MI: Zondervan, 1994).

Brown, Francis *et al.*, *The New Brown, Driver, Briggs, Gesenius Hebrew and English Lexicon: With an Appendix Containing the Biblical Aramaic* (trans. Edward Robinson; Peabody, MA: Hendrickson, 1979).

Butler, Anthea D., 'Observing the Lives of the Saints: Sanctification as Practice in the Church of God in Christ', in Laurie F. Maffly-Kipp, Leigh Eric Schmidt and Mark R. Valeri (eds.), *Practicing Protestants: Histories of Christian Life in America, 1630-1965* (Lived Religions; Baltimore, MD: Johns Hopkins University Press, 2006), pp. 159-76.

Castelo, Daniel, 'Tarrying on the Lord: Affections, Virtues and Theological Ethics in Pentecostal Perspective', *Journal of Pentecostal Theology* 13.1 (2004), pp. 31-56.

Chan, Simon, *Liturgical Theology: The Church as Worshiping Community* (Downers Grove, IL: IVP Academic, 2006).

Clines, David J.A (ed.), *The Concise Dictionary of Classical Hebrew* (Sheffield, UK: Sheffield Phoenix Press, 2009).

Culpepper, R. Alan, *Mark* (The Smyth & Helwys Bible Commentary; Macon, GA: Smyth & Helwys, 2007).

de Kock, Wynand J., 'The Church as a Redeemed, Un-Redeemed, and Redeeming Community', in John Christopher Thomas (ed.) *Toward a Pentecostal Ecclesiology: The Church and the Fivefold Gospel* (Cleveland, TN: CPT Press, 2010), pp. 47-68.

Edwards, Jonathan *et al.*, *The Works of Jonathan Edwards* (2 vols.; London: William Ball, 1839).

Fee, Gordon D., *The First Epistle to the Corinthians* (The New International Commentary on the New Testament; Grand Rapids, MI: Eerdmans, 1987).

Finney, Charles G., *Power from on High* (Salem, OH: Schmul Pub. Co., 2001).

Goldingay, John, *Daniel* (Word Biblical Commentary; Dallas, TX: Word Books, 1989).

–*Psalms* (Baker Commentary on the Old Testament Wisdom and Psalms; 3 vols.; Grand Rapids, MI: Baker Academic, 2006).

Green, C.E.W., *Toward a Pentecostal Theology of the Lord's Supper: Foretasting the Kingdom* (Cleveland, TN: CPT Press, 2012).

Hill, Andrew E., 'Daniel', in T. Longman and D.E. Garland (eds.), *The Expositor's Bible Commentary* (Grand Rapids, MI: Zondervan, 2008), pp. 19-212.

Hollenweger, W.J., *The Pentecostals* (Peabody, MA: Hendrickson, 1988).

Horton, Wade H., *Pentecost Yesterday and Today* (Cleveland, TN: Pathway Press, 1964).
Johnson, Luke Timothy, *The Acts of the Apostles* (Sacra Pagina Series; Collegeville, MN: Liturgical Press, 1992).
Kärkkäinen, Veli-Matti, 'Spirit, Reconciliation and Healing in the Community: Missiological Insights from Pentecostals', *International Review of Missions* 94.372 (2005), pp. 43-50.
Köhler, Ludwig, and Walter Baumgartner, *The Hebrew and Aramaic Lexicon of the Old Testament* (2 vols.; Leiden: Brill, Study edn, 2001).
Land, Steven Jack, *Pentecostal Spirituality: A Passion for the Kingdom* (Cleveland, TN: CPT Press, 2010).
Lennox, Stephen J., *Psalms: A Bible Commentary in the Wesleyan Tradition* (Indianapolis, IN: Wesleyan Pub. House, 1999).
Louw, J.P., and Eugene Albert Nida, *Greek-English Lexicon of the New Testament: Based on Semantic Domains* (2 vols.; New York: United Bible Societies, 2nd edn, 1989).
López Rodríguez, Darío Andres, 'The Redeeming Community: The God of Life and the Community of Life', in John Christopher Thomas (ed.) *Toward a Pentecostal Ecclesiology: The Church and the Fivefold Gospel* (Cleveland, TN: CPT Press, 2010), pp. 69-86.
Martin, Lee Roy, 'Longing for God: Psalm 63 and Pentecostal Spirituality', *Journal of Pentecostal Theology* 22.1 (2013), pp. 54-76.
Martin, Ralph P., *2 Corinthians* (Word Biblical Commentary; Waco, TX: Word Books, 1986).
Mays, James Luther, *Psalms* (Interpretation; Louisville, KY: John Knox Press, 1994).
McQueen, Larry R., *Joel and the Spirit: The Cry of a Prophetic Hermeneutic* (Cleveland, TN: CPT Press, 2009).
Roberts, Oral, *Expect a Miracle: My Life and Ministry, an Autobiography* (Nashville, TN: Thomas Nelson, 1995).
Robins, R.G., *A.J. Tomlinson: Plainfolk Modernist* (Religion in America Series; New York: Oxford University Press, 2004).
Symeon, *Symeon the New Theologian: The Discourses* (The Classics of Western Spirituality; New York: Paulist Press, 1980).
Taft, Robert F., 'Lent: A Meditation', *Worship* 57.2 (1983), pp. 123-34.
Terrien, Samuel L., *The Psalms: Strophic Structure and Theological Commentary* (Eerdmans Critical Commentary; Grand Rapids, MI: Eerdmans, 2003).
Thomas, John Christopher, '"What the Spirit Is Saying to the Church": The Testimony of a Pentecostal in New Testament Studies', in Kevin L. Spawn and Archie T. Wright (eds.), *Spirit and Scripture: Exploring a Pneumatic Hermeneutic* (New York: T & T Clark, 2012).
Tomberlin, D. *Pentecostal Sacraments: Encountering God at the Altar* (Cleveland, TN: CPLC, Pentecostal Theological Seminary, 2010).
Wacker, Grant, *Heaven Below: Early Pentecostals and American Culture* (Cambridge, MA: Harvard University Press, 1st Harvard Univ. pbk. edn, 2003).
Wesley, John, *The Works of the Rev. John Wesley* (14 vols.; London: Wesleyan-Methodist Book-Room, 1872).

Wesley, John, *The Journal of the Rev. John Wesley* (8 vols.; London: Robert Culley, Charles H. Kelly, 1909-1916).

Wilkinson, Michael, and Peter F. Althouse, *Catch the Fire: Soaking Prayer and Charismatic Renewal* (DeKalb, IL: Northern Illinois University Press, 2014).

Pentecostal Periodicals

The Apostolic Faith (Los Angeles, CA).

The Apostolic Faith (Portland, OR).

The Bridegroom's Messenger (Atlanta, GA).

The Christian Evangel (Findlay, OH).

The Church of God Evangel (Cleveland, TN).

Confidence (Sunderland, England).

The Household of God (Dayton, OH).

The Latter Rain Evangel (Chicago, IL).

The Whole Truth (Argenta, AR).

Word and Witness (Malvern, AR).

Index of Biblical (and Other Ancient) References

Genesis
25.27-34   2

Exodus
2   81
2.23-25   81
3.7-8   81
3.12   89
24.9-11   2
24.18   16
25.15-18   9
34.2   10
34.28-29   9, 10
34.28   16, 79, 100

Leviticus
10.1-29   11
11   3
16.2   11
16.29-34   12
16.29-31   11
16.31   21, 97
23.27-32   12
23.27   166
23.29   13
23.32   6, 11, 166
24.10-23   11

Numbers
6.1-21   3
11.4-6   3
13-14   13
29.7-11   13
29.7   11
30.13-15   14

Deuteronomy
8.2   15, 94
8.3   3, 4, 15, 44, 58, 94, 159
8.5   15, 94
8.9   15, 94
8.10   15

8.18   15
8.19   15, 94
9   16
9.9   79
9.9-11   16
9.9, 18   16
9.18-19   17, 52, 83, 84
28.49-68   46

Judges
20   85
20.26-28   18
20.26   7, 17

1 Samuel
1.7   18, 19, 79, 86
1.11   19, 86
7   82
7.1   20
7.3-6   20
7.6   7, 19
11.1   23
13.17   20
14   97
14.23   20
14.24   20, 21
14.27   21
14.29-30   21
20.34   21
28.5   22
28.20   22
30.12   22
31   54, 88
31.10-13   23
31.13   22, 54

2 Samuel
1.11   23, 88
1.12   23
1.17-27   80
3.1   24
3.31-36   24, 89
3.35   24

12.13   25
12.14   25
12.16-23   24
12.16-18   166
12.16   25, 84, 158
12.20-23   25
12.22   85, 158

1 Kings
11.1-8   26
11.9-13   26
11.37-38   26
13.8-22   26, 79
13.8-9   26
18.40   27
19   85
19.7-8   27, 90
19.8   27
19.12   100
21   73
21.1-29   27
21.4-5   28
21.7   28
21.21-22   28
21.27-29   28

2 Kings
25.25   36

Isaiah
1.10-17   29
25   2
58   32, 83
58.1   29
58.2   30
58.3-4   30, 96
58.3   30, 96
58.3-14   29
58.3, 5   14
58.5   31
58.6-13   96
58.6-7   31
64.6   151

Jeremiah
14	83
14.10-12	32
14.10	32
25.8-14	46
36.6-10	33
36.6-9	33, 87
36.10	96
41.1	36
52.12-14	36

Ezekiel
24.16-17	34

Joel
1-2	34, 108
1.13-14	34, 82
2.12-18	34
2.12	157
2.15	61
2.28-29	135
2.28	35, 157
2.29	152

Jonah
3.4	35
3.5-10	36, 82
3.5	35

Zechariah
7-8	11, 36
7.2-6	36
7.5	91
7.6	37
7.9-10	37
7.13-14	37
8.1-18	37
8.2	37
8.3	37
8.15	38
8.19	38, 166

Psalms
3	80
34.15-16	30
35	84
35.1	38
35.4	38
35.7	38
35.11-14	39
35.13	38, 84, 158
35.16	39
35.20	39
38	80
39.5	151
42	40, 90
42.1-3	40
42.1-2	1
42.3	40, 79
43	40
51	80
63.1-2	1
63.2	154
69.1-2	40
69.3	40, 41
69.4	40
69.9-13	41
69.13	41
69.10	14, 40
86	80
102	86
102.1-4	42
102.4	41
102.9-10	42
102.12	86
102.17	42, 86
102.20	42
107.18	42
109	86
109.2-4	42
109.21, 26	43, 86
109.22-26	43
109.24	42
109.27	43, 86

Job
23.10-12	43
23.12	3

Esther
4.3	44, 87
4.15-16	44
4.15	87
4.16	6, 44
9.30-31	45, 87
9.31	44

Daniel
6.18-22	46
6.18-20	45
9.3-27	100
9.3-6	47
9.3	7, 46, 52, 83
9.4-6	46
9.10	46
9.13	46
9.24	47
10	8, 49
10.1-21	100
10.1-3	48
10.2-3	48, 85
10.2	8
10.12	48

Ezra
1.1-11	49
6.19	49
7.9-10	49
8.21-31	50
8.21-23	49
8.21	14
9-10	50
9.3-6	51, 84
9.19	51
10.1	51
10.6-11	52
10.6	51, 84

Nehemiah
1.4-6	52
1.4	48, 52, 85
1.5	52, 84
1.8	52, 84
6.15	53
8.1	53
8.9-12	53
8.9	53
9.1-3	53, 82
9.1	53

1 Chronicles
10.11-14	54
10.12	54, 88

Index of Biblical (and Other Ancient) References

2 Chronicles
20.2-4   55
20.3   55, 56, 87
20.15   55, 87

Matthew
1.17, 18 57
1.21   57
2.2   57
3.4   49
3.11   57
3.17   57
4.1-4   57, 58, 66
4.2   166
4.3   94
4.11   100
4.17   58
5-7   59
5.6   157
5.20   59
5.23-24   31
5.44   39, 102
6   61, 91
6.1-18   59
6.1   59
6.2-6   59
6.6-18   57
6.16-18   59, 60, 97
7.7   112
9.14-15   57, 62, 63, 92, 98
9.14   49
15.32   63
17.21   57, 63, 64

Mark
2.16   64
2.18-20   63, 92, 98
2.18   49
2.21-22   64
2.23-24   64
2.27   64
8.3   64
9.28-29   64
9.29   64

Luke
2   71, 90
2.22   64, 91
2.36-37   65
2.37, 38 100
2.37   64, 91, 92
4.1-4   66
4.2   7, 66
4.18   66
5.29   67
5.33-35   67, 92, 98
5.33   49
6.13-16   67
14.11   99
18   83
18.9-14   67
18.12   67, 97, 166
21   141
22.15-18 160
22.16, 18 2

John
4.34   44

Acts
2   35
3.19   20
6.4   71
9.9   6
9.17   93
9.35   20
9.6   69
9.7-19   69
9.9-18   68, 100
9.9   68, 166
9.12   69
9.17   69, 157
10.2   69
10.3   100
10.30-32 70
10.30, 31 139
10.30   69, 85, 100
10.44-45 70
11.21   20
13   61, 71, 90, 93
13.1-4   70
13.1   71, 90
13.2   85, 100
13.3   72, 94
14.15   20
14.22   72
14.23   72, 94
15.19   20
19   139
21.21   73
23.12-14 73
23.12   73
26.18, 20 20
27   79, 85
27.9-10   74
27.9   74
27.10   75
27.20-24 74
27.21-25 88, 100
27.29   74
27.33-35 75, 98
28.27   20

Romans
7.25   155
9.26, 27 81
12.1   92

1 Corinthians
7   75
7.3-5   76
7.5   75
12   128

2 Corinthians
3.16   20
6.4-5   76
6.5   76, 77, 92
6.12   99
9.27   99
11.23-28 77
11.27   77, 92

Galatians
5.17   155
5.19   155

Colossians
3.2   160

Philippians
3.3   65
3.19   99
4.12   156

1 Thessalonians
1.9   20

2 Timothy
13.5   149

Hebrews
12   13

James
4.3   167
4.6-10   100
4.8   100, 170
5.19, 20   20

1 Peter
2.25   20
5.3   149
5.5, 6   100

Revelation
7.15   65
19   2

Other Ancient Lit.

Judith
4   56

Tobit
12.8   59

2 Maccabees
13   56

Acts of Peter
2.2.1   101
2.2.5   101
2.6.17-18   101

Acts of Thomas
9.86   101

Clement of Alexandria
Stromata
7.12   101

Didache
1.3   102
7.4   104
8.1   102

Epistle of Barnabas
3.1-5   101

Mishnah
Berakot
6b   102
Sanhedrin
35a   102

Polycarp
Philippians
7   101

Shepherd of Hermas
Vis.
2.2.1   101
3.10.6-7   101
Sim.
5.1-3   101

Index of Authors

Alexander, Kimberly E. 116, 124
Alexander, N.M. 110
Althouse, P.F. 148, 179
Archer, Melissa L. 116
Aquinas, T. 105
Argue, A.H. 133
Augustine 102, 103
Augustine, Daniela C. 4
Baab, Lynne M. 5, 6, 8, 16, 23, 31, 65, 80, 83, 99, 107, 109, 155, 156, 158, 159, 166, 169
Bainbridge, G. 105
Barr, E.S. 141, 142
Basil 103
Batman, G.W. 120, 131, 132, 140
Bauer, W. 5, 7, 61, 65, 71, 100
Bauers, Anna 121, 140, 141
Bell, E.N. 118, 124
Berghuis, K.D. 3, 103, 104, 107, 108, 162
Beyerhaus, Mr. 137
Bloch, A.P. 11
Blomberg, C. 62, 76
Boddy, A.A. 118
Baumgartner, W. 43
Brattston, D.W.T. 101
Brown, F. 43, 144
Buchanan, M. 16, 95
Buckalew, J.W. 127
Bunkley, Mary 133, 135, 136
Butler, Anthea D. 132, 141, 144, 155
Calvin, J. 108
Carter, G. 173
Cashwell, G.B. 118, 121, 138
Castelo, D. 148, 149
Chan, S. 4
Clement of Alexandria 101
Clines, D.J.A. 5
Culpepper, R.A. 64
de Kock, W.J. 151, 152, 153
Derby, J. 13
Divine, Julia M. 121, 139, 140

Duffy, E. 106
Durham, W. 124
Edwards, J. 108
Fee, G.D. 76
Finney, C.G. 108
Fischer, W.F. 25, 107
Fisher, H.L. 120
Flowers, A.M. 119, 128
Foster, R.J. 109
Franklin, J. 6, 35, 50, 56, 58, 59, 61, 66, 69, 70, 108, 109, 149, 151, 152, 153, 154, 157, 159, 160, 163, 164, 165
Frykholm, A.J. 159
Gardner, C.J. 109
Gill, Margaret 121, 143
Goldingay, J. 39, 40, 41, 47, 48
Green, C.E.W. 4, 116
Hall, F. 48, 81, 113, 115, 123, 124, 146, 150, 151, 154, 155, 164
Ham, W.R. Paul 120, 131
Hatcher, R.L. 123, 124
Herron, C.B. 140
Hickey, Marilyn 27, 32, 109, 151, 159
Hill, A.E. 47, 48
Hirsch, E.G. 3, 7, 55, 105, 156
Hollenweger, W.J. 5, 116
Horton, W.H. 153
Johnson, L.T. 74
Juillerat, F.L. 136
Justin Martyr 104
Kärkkäinen, V.-M. 152, 153
Kelly, Anna 137
Kirby, Anna E. 142
Köhler, L. 43
Lambert, D. 14, 19, 25, 29, 31, 32, 80, 123
Land, S.J. 1, 4, 115, 116, 126, 148, 155
Lennox, S.J. 40
Leo the Great 103
Loughlin, S. 105
Louw, J.P. 65, 76

López Rodríguez, D.A. 152, 154
MacDonald, G.J. 7
Martin, L.R. 90
Martin, R.P. 77, 78
Mason, C.H. 118, 120
Mays, J.L. 40, 178
McKnight, Scot 10, 17, 19, 22, 27, 31, 50, 51, 68, 69, 80, 81, 90, 109, 154, 162, 166
McQueen, L.R. 35, 116, 148
Mead, Bro. 138
Mentzer, R.A. 108
Miles, Margaret R. 103, 104, 105
Mitchell, C.C. 91
Montgomery, Carrie Judd 117, 142
Moorhead, M.W. 129
Murphy, C.M. 31, 83, 103, 104, 106, 109, 151, 156
Murphy, Mrs. G.W. 128
Murray, A. 108, 109
Nelson, Cora 121, 129, 136
Nida, E.A 65, 76
Ozman, Agnes 135
Perry, S.C. 123
Piper, J. 1, 4, 58, 61, 65, 109, 119
Polycarp 101
Post, A.H. 35, 134
Prince, D. 72, 150, 157, 159
Rahner, K. 105
Roberts, O. 78
Robins, R.G. 158
Rose, W.W. 132
Ryan, M.L. 125, 150

Ryan, T. 9, 13, 37, 62, 81, 106, 123, 150
Schmemann, A. 38, 57, 104, 107
Scott, R.J. 121, 128, 129
Sellers, M.D. 137
Seymour, W.J. 117, 118, 126, 139
Shepherd, M.H. 101, 110
Sidersky, P. 126
Simmons, V.P. 140
Sisson, Elizabeth 117
Symeon the New Theologian, 101, 150
Taft, R.F. 106
Taylor, Alice 124, 133, 134
Terrien, S.L. 39, 40, 42
Tertullian 103
Thomas, J.C. 148, 152
Tomberlin, D. 5
Tomlinson, A.J. 117, 118, 125, 158
Towns, E. 109
Vian, A.W. 130
Wacker, G. 120, 148, 155
Wallis, A. 13, 18, 29, 37, 48, 49, 59, 61, 62, 76, 147, 148, 154, 155, 157, 159, 161, 162
Wesley, J. 5, 6, 22, 29, 31, 32, 33, 35, 55, 56, 60, 61, 68, 72, 79, 81, 97, 99, 102, 108, 110-114, 115, 117, 123, 128, 148, 150, 152, 153, 155
Wilkinson, M. 148
Willard, D. 109
Williams, J.W. 117, 140
Williams, W.B. 130

www.ingramcontent.com/pod-product-compliance
Lightning Source LLC
LaVergne TN
LVHW020929090426
835512LV00020B/3271